The Human Tradition i

D0978232

CHARLES W. CALHOUN
Series Editor
Department of History, East Carolina University

The nineteenth-century English author Thomas Carlyle once remarked that "the history of the world is but the biography of great men." This approach to the study of the human past had existed for centuries before Carlyle wrote, and it continued to hold sway among many scholars well into the twentieth century. In more recent times, however, historians have recognized and examined the impact of large, seemingly impersonal forces in the evolution of human history—social and economic developments such as industrialization and urbanization as well as political movements such as nationalism, militarism, and socialism. Yet even as modern scholars seek to explain these wider currents, they have come more and more to realize that such phenomena represent the composite result of countless actions and decisions by untold numbers of individual actors. On another occasion, Carlyle said that "history is the essence of innumerable biographies." In this conception of the past, Carlyle came closer to modern notions that see the lives of all kinds of people, high and low, powerful and weak, known and unknown, as part of the mosaic of human history, each contributing in a large or small way to the unfolding of the human tradition.

This latter idea forms the foundation for this series of books on the human tradition in America. Each volume is devoted to a particular period or topic in American history and each consists of minibiographies of persons whose lives shed light on that period or topic. Well-known figures are not altogether absent, but more often the chapters explore a variety of individuals who may be less conspicuous but whose stories, nonetheless, offer us a window on some aspect of the nation's past.

By bringing the study of history down to the level of the individual, these sketches reveal not only the diversity of the American people and the complexity of their interaction but also some of the commonalities of sentiment and experience that Americans have shared in the evolution of their culture. Our hope is that these explorations of the lives of "real people" will give readers a deeper understanding of the human tradition in America.

Volumes in the Human Tradition in America series:

Ian K. Steele and Nancy L. Rhoden, eds., *The Human Tradition in Colonial America* (1999). Cloth ISBN 0-8420-2697-5 Paper ISBN 0-8420-2700-9

Nancy L. Rhoden and Ian K. Steele, eds., *The Human Tradition in the American Revolution* (2000). Cloth ISBN 0-8420-2747-5 Paper ISBN 0-8420-2748-3

Ballard C. Campbell, ed., *The Human Tradition in the Gilded Age and Progressive Era* (2000). Cloth ISBN 0-8420-2734-3 Paper ISBN 0-8420-2735-1

Steven E. Woodworth, ed., *The Human Tradition in the Civil War and Reconstruction* (2000). Cloth ISBN 0-8420-2726-2 Paper ISBN 0-8420-2727-0

David L. Anderson, ed., *The Human Tradition in the Vietnam Era* (2000). Cloth ISBN 0-8420-2762-9 Paper ISBN 0-8420-2763-7

Kriste Lindenmeyer, ed., *Ordinary Women, Extraordinary Lives: Women in American History* (2000). Cloth ISBN 0-8420-2752-1 Paper ISBN 0-8420-2754-8

Michael A. Morrison, ed., *The Human Tradition in Antebellum America* (2000). Cloth ISBN 0-8420-2834-X Paper ISBN 0-8420-2835-8

Malcolm Muir Jr., ed., *The Human Tradition in the World War II Era* (2001). Cloth ISBN 0-8420-2785-8 Paper ISBN 0-8420-2786-6

Ty Cashion and Jesús F. de la Teja, eds., *The Human Tradition in Texas* (2001). Cloth ISBN 0-8420-2905-2 Paper ISBN 0-8420-2906-0

Benson Tong and Regan A. Lutz, eds., *The Human Tradition in the American West* (2002). Cloth ISBN 0-8420-2860-9 Paper ISBN 0-8420-2861-7

Charles W. Calhoun, ed., *The Human Tradition in America from the Colonial Era through Reconstruction* (2002). Cloth ISBN 0-8420-5030-2 Paper ISBN 0-8420-5031-0

Donald W. Whisenhunt, ed., *The Human Tradition in America between the Wars, 1920–1945* (2002). Cloth ISBN 0-8420-5011-6 Paper ISBN 0-8420-5012-4

Roger Biles, ed., *The Human Tradition in Urban America* (2002). Cloth ISBN 0-8420-2992-3 Paper ISBN 0-8420-2993-1

The Human Tradition in AMERICA between the WARS, 1920–1945

THE HUMAN TRADITION IN AMERICA BETWEEN THE WARS, 1920–1945

No. 12
The Human Tradition in America

Edited by
Donald W. Whisenhunt

A Scholarly Resources Inc. Imprint
Wilmington, Delaware

Scholarly Resources Inc.
104 Greenhill Avenue
Wilmington, DE 19805-1897
www.scholarly.com

Library of Congress Cataloging-in-Publication Data

The human tradition in America between the wars, 1920–1945 /
edited by Donald W. Whisenhunt.
    p. cm. — (The human tradition in America ; 12)
    Includes bibliographical references and index.
    ISBN 0-8420-5011-6 (alk. paper) — ISBN 0-8420-5012-4 (pbk. :
alk. paper)
    1. United States—History—1919—Biography. 2. United States—
History—1933–1945—Biography. I. Whisenhunt, Donald W.
II. Series.

E747 .H86 2002
973.91'092—dc21
[B]   2001049898

♾ The paper used in this publication meets the minimum requirements
of the American National Standard for permanence of paper for printed
library materials, Z39.48, 1984.

For

Will, Matthew, and Kira

with love

About the Editor

DONALD W. WHISENHUNT received a Ph.D. in American history from Texas Tech University in 1966. Since 1991 he has been professor of history at Western Washington University, where his academic specialty is twentieth-century U.S. history. His career has included service at several universities in several states in both instructional and administrative positions. He has published widely; his last three books are *Poetry of the People: Poems to the President, 1929–1945* (1996); *Tent Show: Arthur Names and His "Famous" Players* (2000); and *It Seems to Me: Selected Letters of Eleanor Roosevelt* (2001).

Contents

Introduction

Donald W. Whisenhunt

Following World War I the United States entered a period of change and transition that would have a more profound impact on society, politics, and culture than anyone imagined then. Various interpretations exist about this time. Some call it only a lull between wars, merely an armistice between two parts of a much longer conflict. Others suggest that in the 1920s, Americans enjoyed the fruits of the Industrial Revolution for the first time. Prosperity, prohibition, gangsterism, flappers, and social change all mark this decade. Yet, simultaneously, the country was confronted with hardship in the agricultural sector, a problem that the nation had encountered earlier but seemed to have no better solution for now. Some of the commentators and critics of this decade saw it as a conformist and stultifying era in which the banal and mundane were celebrated. They also saw it as a time of boosterism and business domination under Republican presidents. Even so, some significant events marked the transition of America from a rural to an urban society together with major cultural changes in music, art, and literature.

Few would disagree about the importance of the Great Depression when it came in the 1930s and the influence of Franklin D. Roosevelt's New Deal. The Wall Street crash had silenced the Roaring Twenties in 1929. The country was perplexed by the stagnant economy, and its citizens had no concept of how to deal with it. The 1930s bred a generation of despair and hope at the same time. American radicals took the opportunity to make their case to the people and to bring about the long-awaited revolution. Agitation marked the decade, but, in hindsight, it had little impact.

President Roosevelt and his New Deal were praised and damned at the same time, and the controversy has continued to this day. Some conservative critics complain that historians have not admitted that Roosevelt did not end the depression, yet most historians usually give him credit for his optimism and his buoyant spirit that offered encouragement to the country. Nearly all historians agree that World War II was the catalyst that brought the United States out of the depression. Unlimited military spending and the removal of millions of young men and women from the unemployment rolls for service in the armed forces lifted the economy. One wonders what the results to the economy would have been if Roosevelt had been able to spend as much money on domestic problems as he did for the war effort.

This volume presents biographies of fifteen men and women of influence during the period from 1920 to 1945. A few of them are fairly well known, at least to historians; some are known only to specialists, and others are known to only a handful of people. All of them were chosen for inclusion because they reflect something about America in these transitional years. An effort was made to balance the selections among political figures, cultural leaders, activists, and military figures.

The 1920s was a rich cultural period, as the biographies of Zora Neale Hurston, Jimmie Rodgers, and Ma Rainey show. From the Harlem Renaissance to the country music of the South to the blues, America celebrated its diversity. Although not well known, individuals such as William Lewis Paul, Marshall Keeble, Elaine Goodale Eastman, and Dennis Chavez reflect the ways that various minorities coped with the trials they faced by living in a white America.

This period is noted also for the efforts of many people to bring about change—some of it radical. Activists on the left, such as A. J. Muste, Meridel Le Sueur, and Emma Tenayuca, wanted to effect significant reforms. They stand in stark opposition to right-wingers such as Gerald L. K. Smith. Unlike all of them is Frances Perkins, a woman who broke gender barriers and steered a course toward change without having the left-wing or right-wing orientation of the others.

World War II offers a contrast to the decades of the 1920s and 1930s. Henry S. Aurand, Oveta Culp Hobby, and Ernie Pyle, as these essays show, were vital players in their part of the drama of world conflict. Their authors are specialists in some aspect of recent U.S. history, and many of them have studied their subjects in detail. The result is a rich portrait through biography of the period between the wars.

1

A. J. Muste

Portrait of a Twentieth-Century Pacifist

Charles F. Howlett

In the period between World War I and World War II, many Americans were disillusioned by the outcome of the first war and were determined to avoid U.S. participation in another one. A. J. Muste, known as "the Number One U.S. Pacifist," became famous for his antiwar views and activities, but he was much more important than that. A man of strong religious convictions, he moved as a minister through several denominations in search of one that was more compatible with his own theology and that would allow him to speak freely about public events, especially matters of peace. He went from the Dutch Reformed Church to the Congregational Church and finally ended as a Quaker, in the Society of Friends where he was the secretary for the Quaker peace organization, the Fellowship of Reconciliation. A labor leader and union executive, Muste directed a labor college in the 1920s and, with his socialist and Communist affiliations, represents a radical element in the interwar period.

Charles F. Howlett, the author of a book on the Brookwood Labor College, gives us an overview of the life of Muste with a focus on the 1920s and 1930s. Professor Howlett is a specialist on the peace movement in the United States in the twentieth century and is the author of six books on peace activities, including works on Muste and one on John Dewey. He holds a Ph.D. in American history from the State University of New York at Albany, an advanced degree in higher education from Columbia University, and is a former Fulbright scholar to the Netherlands. He teaches advanced placement history at Amityville (New York) Memorial High School and is an adjunct full professor at Adelphi University.

I n 1939, when war clouds over Europe became darker by the hour, *Time* magazine called A. J. Muste "the Number One U.S. Pacifist."[1] The label was appropriate. Muste had already distinguished himself in the struggle against war and in the fight for social justice among the laboring masses. His role as a leading pacifist organizer and activist between the world wars remains a topic of considerable interest among historians of peace movements. In particular, his leadership role in the Fellowship of Reconciliation and later the War Resisters League and

1

Committee for Non-Violent Action during the Cold War, and his numerous writings that filled the pages of the pacifist press, bear ample testimony to a remarkable career in the human tradition. What events shaped Muste's contribution to American history? Which situations early in his career propelled him to become the leading spokesperson in the name of peace and justice? Most important, how have historians analyzed his role regarding the nonviolent civil disobedience tradition that he helped to perpetuate?

First and foremost, the motivating force behind Muste's convictions was embodied in his Christian faith. One close colleague, David McReynolds of the War Resisters League, observed that Muste's "Christianity was so central to him that his life cannot be understood without realizing that he was, even at his most political moments, acting out his religious convictions." Longtime labor radical and writer Sidney Lens commented that "for Muste the term 'religion' and the term 'revolution' were totally synonymous." And one of his closest pacifist friends, John Nevin Sayre, a former editor of *Fellowship* and executive secretary of the Fellowship of Reconciliation, noted with certainty that religion was Muste's "motivating force . . . right up to the end of his life." Although the many causes Muste supported were, on the surface, "purely political," and in some cases sprinkled with Marxist overtones, the "spiritual qualities of his motives" remains the key to his existence.[2]

Muste's spiritual journey began with his birth on January 8, 1885, in the Dutch shipping port of Zierikzee. In search of a better life, his family left Holland for the United States in 1891. They settled with relatives and friends in the Dutch Reformed community of Grand Rapids, Michigan. Here his parents, two sisters, and a brother were absorbed into the "tightly-knit immigrant community" where, "with the rarest of exceptions, every Dutch family belonged to a church, the Reformed or Christian Reformed, to which it had belonged in the old country."[3] During his early years in America, young Abraham John attended public grammar school and played with his English-speaking classmates. But the "truly orthodox kingdom of Calvinism," with the Dutch Reformed Church at its center, defined his upbringing.[4] He was deeply influenced, notes Muste's biographer, Jo Ann O. Robinson, "by the 'religious and pious' home which his parents kept, where he was 'soaked in the Bible and the language of the Bible,' and by the teaching of his native church that 'you live in the sight of God and there is no respecter of persons in Him, and pretension is a low and despicable thing.' "[5]

Muste's primary education was followed by three years of study at Hope Preparatory School and three years of religious training at Hope College, both run by the Dutch Reformed Church in Michigan. His path of education prepared him for a career in the ministry. Upon graduation from Hope in 1905, and at the tender age of twenty, he "took a year off to teach Greek and English in what was then known as Northwestern Classical Academy, in Orange City, Iowa."[6] This one-year reprieve was followed by his first trip to the East Coast where, in 1906, he enrolled at the New Brunswick Theological Seminary of the Dutch Reformed Church in New Jersey. He supplemented his conservative religious training by taking "graduate courses in philosophy . . . first at New York University, and later at Columbia, where I first saw John Dewey (who later became a devoted friend), and occasionally heard William James lecture."[7] In 1909, Muste became an ordained minister in the Dutch Reformed Church. His graduation from the seminary was also marked by two other notable events: his installation as the first minister of the Fort Washington Collegiate Church, on Washington Heights, in New York City, and his marriage to his former Hope classmate, Anna Huizenga.[8] The marriage would produce three children: Anne Dorothy Muste Baker, Constance Muste Hamilton, and John Muste.

During the next four years his outrage over the economic and social ills of urban-industrial America assumed dramatic proportions. At the same time, he earned a master's degree at New York's Union Theological Seminary, where more radical doctrines exposed the contradictions of the conservative theories of his own church. He reached a crisis in his religious life, which he later described as an " 'agonizing reappraisal' of the beliefs in which I had been reared."[9] By the fall of 1914, he reflected, "I could no longer acquiesce in giving the impression that I accepted the literal inspiration of Scripture and the whole corpus of Calvinist dogma, at least as then interpreted. . . . I was inwardly more confident than ever that I could, and must, preach the essentials of the Christian faith and strive to bring myself and others to its practice."[10] Eventually, he resigned his pulpit. He transferred his church membership to a more liberal denomination and assumed the pastorship of Central Congregational Church in Newtonville, Massachusetts.

His liberation from the theological restraints of Calvinism was also greeted by the onset of World War I. His "growing concern over how to apply Christian precepts to political corruption and class conflict in America became compounded in the new struggle over how to come to terms with massive suffering and dying."[11] Muste found himself participating in the emerging Christian pacifist movement. Pacifism was the link he connected to this "great moment to humanity."[12] He quickly joined the American branch of the Fellowship of Reconciliation (FOR), an international peace group founded in Great Britain in 1915, and later became a Quaker.

By 1917, Muste's sermons were decidedly against the war. Indeed, "as the months passed and the bitter and bloody trench fighting developed, it became clear that the United States would go in, despite protestations that it would not. Thus, along with other Christian preachers, I had to face—not academically but existentially, as it were—the question of whether I could reconcile what I had been preaching out of the Gospels, and passages like I Corinthians: 13, from the Epistles, with participation in war."[13] He now counseled his parishioners not to support military involvement. His message was not well received by his congregation. Neighbors began to avoid Muste and his wife, and threatening phone calls followed. On March 31, 1918, he resigned his pulpit to pursue fulltime antiwar activities.

Muste and Anna then moved in with Quakers in Providence, Rhode Island. But in a few months they decided to return to a communal household in Boston. Now in his new role as Quaker minister, Muste, along with other Fellowship pacifists, began counseling conscientious objectors at nearby Fort Devens. This experience served to strengthen his commitment to human justice and tolerance. He also defended opponents of war who were accused of failing to comply with sedition laws, and he talked of "establishing urban and rural cooperatives from which they could carry on the struggle against war and for economic justice and racial equality."[14]

Firmly committed to peace and justice issues, Muste emerged as a leading figure in the FOR office in Boston. When the war ended, he attempted to apply his Christian pacifism to labor organizing. One congregant from the Newtonville church found Muste's new calling too much to bear. He boldly remarked, "Becoming a pacifist and Quaker in wartime was bad enough, but to go around in a blue shirt and parade on picket lines—this is too much!" Yet from Muste's perspective, it was a logical response to the growing developments facing the labor movement. The prewar years in New York had already conditioned him to the laborer's plight. "The Republicanism in which I had been brought up," he wrote, "received rude shocks. . . . These were the years of mushrooming sweatshops, of the terrible Triangle Fire in a garment factory, of the strikes which marked the founding of the garment trades unions, and, in Paterson and more distant places, of the turbulent I.W.W. [Industrial Workers of the World] organizational campaign and strikes."[15] He was bracing himself for the battle ahead.

That battle broke out when he assumed the role of coalition strike leader in the fierce Lawrence, Massachusetts, textile walkout of 1919. It proved to be one of the big turning points in his career. At Lawrence, he literally risked life and limb and won his badge of bruises. The Lawrence strike provided Muste with the opportunity "to translate the ideal of brotherhood into reality. We had also a feeling that nonviolence had to prove itself in actual struggle; otherwise it was a mere abstraction or illusion."[16] During the long and bitterly cold sixteen weeks of the crisis, he emerged as chairman of the strike executive committee. The owners reluctantly recognized "nonviolence as a form of resistance and not of submission [and] changed their attitude toward us."[17] As tempting as it was, Muste had constantly warned the strikers "that to permit ourselves to be provoked into violence would mean defeating ourselves; that our real power was in our solidarity and in our capacity to endure suffering rather than give up the fight for the right to organize; that no one could 'weave wool with machine guns.' "[18] His personal leadership style proved instrumental in achieving a small victory and launched his seventeen-year involvement in the labor movement. Equally important, his advocacy of nonviolent resistance solidified his credentials as a leading pacifist activist in America. In later years this tactic added a new dimension to civil disobedience—one that Muste helped pioneer within the civil rights movement as well as in protests against nuclear weapons.

The partial victory at Lawrence convinced Muste to accept the position as general secretary of the newly created Amalgamated Textile Workers of America (ATWA), which advocated militant industrial unionism "with a socialistic and revolutionary aura." The union's ideological construct seemed to fit nicely into Muste's own developing philosophy of radical political action in the name of social justice. Although the ATWA rejected outright the extreme posture of the IWW's syndicalism, it still "considered political and economic action indispensable to the establishment of economic justice."[19]

Recognizing the challenges lying ahead, Christian social leaders such as Muste moved into the industrial-labor relations field "hoping to establish industrial peace through unionization and economic justice."[20] One of their more unusual endeavors was aligning themselves with the newly developing workers' education movement of the 1920s and 1930s.

It was in this particular area where Muste made his most impressive contributions to social and economic justice between the wars.

While working for the ATWA, Muste became interested in the workers' education movement. He had learned the value of educating workers regarding nonviolent strike strategies at Lawrence. "In the strike committee, we concentrated on raising funds for relief, bringing influential people from Boston and elsewhere to observe the situation for themselves, and holding daily meetings in several languages. These sessions were study classes in labor problems."[21] Given his propensity for applying knowledge to action, it was no wonder that in the fall of 1921 Muste accepted the position as head of the nation's most famous resident workers' college, Brookwood Labor College, in Katonah, New York.

Located forty-two miles from Manhattan, Brookwood was situated in the quiet, suburban village of Katonah in northern Westchester County. Its reputation rested on training union organizers, especially those who later helped form the Congress of Industrial Organizations (CIO). But what separated Brookwood from the more traditional forms of labor education was its attempt to link union organizing with the postwar crusade for world peace. Under Muste's direction, Brookwood taught its student workers, many of them trade unionists, that there was more to societal change than just reforming the labor movement.

Serving as college chairman-dean of faculty, Muste provided the necessary inspiration and leadership. One faculty colleague noted that he was an impressive figure, "tall, round-shouldered, thin, with long legs wound around each other to be out of the way, a lock of soft, brown hair continually falling down over his glasses, a 'slightly cadaverous face and large mouth,' all within the character of a dignified academic appearance."[22] Yet his demeanor belied a powerful burst of energy generating intense activism and personal sacrifice:

> We might go on and suggest other ways in which without any participation in violence one may advance the cause of labor and social justice, and so bring nearer the realization of brotherhood as, for example, support of the movement for labor education. The member of the Fellowship, however, will hardly be satisfied with activities of this kind, which involve no personal risk. . . . When workers are being clubbed on the picket line, he will wish to take his place on that picket line in order that by the application of the policeman's club he may be at one with his brothers struggling in the defense of their rights.[23]

Although noting that Brookwood's "standing ground was that of radical laborism and not religious pacifism," Muste remained convinced that the struggle for social justice was essentially a religious undertaking, and he pictured labor unions as embodiments of salvation. "Am I writing as if the Labor Union of the Future, the developing labor movement were the Messiah for our modern world?" he asked in 1923. "Quite so." He took steady aim at the capitalist system, branding it "unchristian" and war mongering: "In itself, this regime of capitalism, militarism and imperialism is anti-Christ. . . . Capitalism despite all the good that exists under it, and the kindly personal relationships that obtain here and there, is in its essence uneconomic, unjust, inhumane and unchristian."[24]

As the spiritual and intellectual leader on campus, Muste encouraged the creation of unique tools of learning. One of Brookwood's more interesting educational programs was sponsorship of a traveling troupe that performed at labor colleges and various workers' gatherings in New York and some thirty other major cities during spring semesters. In the early 1930s many of the Brookwood dramas had a decidedly antiwar bias. With Dean Muste's full blessing, students wrote and performed in a number of plays critical of the capitalist roots of war. Muste took great pleasure in these performances, for at the heart of his religious tradition was the call for nonviolent sacrifice on the part of labor and radical activists in the struggle against war.

The Brookwood Labor College Players served as Muste's vanguard in heightening the labor movement's consciousness of world peace. In April 1931, for instance, the touring group performed "Peace Is No Job of Ours" before audiences at Cooper Union in New York City and at the Boston Labor College. The crowds applauded as the play pointed out "the greed of munitions makers as they profit from the murder of human beings" and criticized the way that patriotic businessmen glorified American society.[25] In March 1932 the Brookwood Players performed "Coal Digger Mule Goes to War" in front of receptive audiences at the Philadelphia and Baltimore Labor Colleges. The play depicted the "false glamour and folly of war," thus reminding workers of their own plight during the last war.[26] At the conclusion of both performances the players led their responsive audiences in singing John K. Kendrick's satire of the hymn, "Onward, Christian Soldiers."

Significantly, Muste realized that the workers' theater reflected an abiding interest in the importance of popular activity that might affect the decisions of government and through it society. He hoped that these plays would serve as a vehicle for arousing the spirit of social awareness within the ranks of American labor. Disillusionment with war was particularly strong during this period, and Muste recognized the value of this educational endeavor in promoting peace awareness. In his view, the plays demonstrated that a conservative social and economic philosophy, identified by its champions as Americanism, was bent on destroying those forces calling for reform in the name of peace and justice.

While trumpeting the cause of peace represented one dimension of Muste's innovative leadership in the workers' education movement, his 1928 battle with the American Federation of Labor (AFL) demonstrated how fragile was the issue of reform within the ranks of labor's hierarchy. The ensuing conflict between the AFL and Brookwood catapulted the labor college into the national limelight and helped establish Muste's presence as a powerful figure within progressive labor circles.

By the late 1920s, Muste's disenchantment with organized labor's leadership increased as the new AFL president, William Green, abandoned his previous endorsement of industrial unionism. He opted for continuing the policies of his predecessor, Samuel Gompers—a tradition of voluntarism with its emphasis on "strong, red-blooded, rugged independence." No effort was being made to promote "union recognition among the unskilled workers in the mass production industries."[27] Muste publicly sought a broader role for Brookwood within the labor movement—that of overthrowing the traditional skepticism of oldline craft union leaders toward industrial unionism for fear of losing control of the labor movement.

As early as 1922 encouragement for unionization of industrial workers surfaced when Muste joined the editorial board of the socialist periodical, *Labor Age*. His writings appeared regularly, and under his increasing influence the magazine became, by 1926, "an outlet for the public expression of the thought and activities of labor progressives." Under Muste's intellectual guidance, labor progressives gradually abandoned amalgamation in favor of the type of industrial unionism later championed by the CIO. They were quick to accept Muste's argument that it was time "to get under that psychological foundation upon which the American worker at the present time lives, or we will accomplish absolutely nothing for the things in which we are interested."[28]

Thus hoping to break down the AFL's elitist administrative policies, Muste's articles in *Labor Age* championed industrial unionism as a way to force organized labor to abandon its narrow economic interests in favor of broader social issues. Yet Muste and Brookwood's desire to organize the industrial worker clashed with the long-established policy of AFL craft unionism. After a brief but secret investigation in late 1928,

AFL Vice President Matthew Woll reported to the executive council that Brookwood's curriculum was propagandistic and Communistic; the report also implied that Brookwood's teachings, shaped by Muste and his fellow labor progressives, were a threat to the principles of the AFL, primarily in the form of dual unionism.[29] In August 1928, at its convention in New Orleans, the executive council, basing its judgment solely on the Woll report, publicly condemned Brookwood and instructed federation affiliates to withhold financial support.

Although he was dismayed by the executive council's condemnation, Muste's resolve to carry on remained steadfast. "If all honest and progressive elements in the labor movement stand by as they give indications of doing then we shall be able to accomplish even more in the future than we have in the past."[30] In the end, Muste's confidence was bolstered when unions such as the American Federation of Teachers, United Textile Workers, Railway Clerks and Lithographers, the Hosiery Workers, and Amalgamated Clothing Workers, to name a few, continued sending prospective students as well as financial aid. Significantly, Brookwood's popularity, and Muste's stature within progressive labor circles, grew after the attack and, in subsequent years, the school's students made their own mark in the organizing drives in the southern textile mills.

The AFL's entrenched reactionary policies and condemnation of Brookwood forced Muste and his followers to move in a more radical direction. The college responded with the formal establishment of the Conference for Progressive Labor Action (CPLA) in order to bring about "closer union of all the workers of the world."[31] Thus, those who joined CPLA were urged to fight for the organization of the unskilled and semiskilled, the abolition of racial and national discrimination in the unions, recognition of Soviet Russia, encouragement of cooperative enterprises, and opposition to the National Civic Federation.

The CPLA, or Musteites, as members of the organization were called, began promoting "unity among those advocates of industrial unionism who might offer a middle way for the American workers."[32] In dramatic fashion, the CPLA played a major role in the organizing campaigns of southern textile workers in the years from 1929 to 1931. A number of Brookwood graduates, inspired by Muste's teachings, became active organizers. It was in the South where the Brookwood-CPLA connection set in motion the drive for economic and social justice.

Faced with fierce employer resistance, the "stretch-out" system (longer hours and less pay), the worsening effects of the Great Depression, and the deplorable conditions of the southern mill towns themselves, the Musteites continued to support these textile workers with money, clothing, and recruiting organizers in the summer and early winter of 1929–30. In an effort to popularize the cause, Muste instructed Tom Tippett to write a play based on his personal organizing efforts. His play, "Mill Shadows," emphasized the total domination of the workers' lives by the profit-driven mill owner, who controlled home, job, health care, food purchases, and even church membership. The play was performed by students from the college and raised a considerable sum of money for the striking Piedmont workers.[33]

Specifically, the ensuing and prolonged clash between the strikers, state police, and National Guard units in Marion, North Carolina, more than any other previous strike involving the labor college, further radicalized Muste's humanizing instincts. He was angry at the use of force to beat down the workers. "Thirty-six strikers were wounded in the back, twenty-five of them seriously," he bitterly lamented. "Two died at once, four later—all shot in the back," he pressed on. "Not a single deputy or mill official was scratched."[34] The deliberate killing of these strikers by armed agents of the state raised Muste's ire. No longer could or should the workers accept the existing economic system and its accompanying use of violence.

Although geographical and cultural isolationism presented a formidable barrier to the drive for unionization in the South, Muste and his cadre of CPLA organizers were able to lay claim to a modest victory. With Muste at the helm, Brookwooders were more successful in publicizing to the rest of the nation the wretched conditions of the southern mill towns. They also pointed out the disparity between textile wages in the North and in the South and encouraged the AFL leadership to take a closer look at the possibilities of organizing southern textile workers.[35]

Nevertheless, the failure to penetrate the southern workers' psyche regarding the benefits of unionism, coupled with Brookwood's inability to prevail in the coal miners' strike in the Kanawha Valley of West Virginia during the summer of 1931, exacerbated tensions between militants and moderates within the Brookwood community. The continuing effects of the depression and the lack of overall success in the textile and coal-mining communities acted as a catalyst in disturbing the harmony that had previously existed on campus.

From the start, Brookwood and the CPLA worked closely together, the college emphasizing the educational job and the CPLA that of organizing and strike activity. But as the depression deepened, some faculty members questioned whether more time should be spent on raising money for the college rather than on radical activities of the CPLA. Clearly, so long as Muste engaged the CPLA in reformist programs he was able to keep the support of a fairly wide spectrum of laborites. The championing of unemployment insurance, for instance, helped pave the way for later state and national legislation, including the New Deal's Social Security Act. But the CPLA's "attacks upon racketeering in the AF of L," campaigns "to industrialize existing craft unions," and an "increasingly zealous commitment to organizing the unorganized strained the meaning of the 'progressive' label to which Musteites tried to cling."[36]

Perhaps more devastating to Brookwood's political stability, however, was the marked change in Muste's attitude. He had "entered the labor movement a pacifist, grounded in Christian socialism," conducted the Lawrence strike according to principles of nonviolence, and continued "to follow the thread of pacifist doctrine which opposed imperialist war." Yet by the late 1920s, "Muste had begun to weaken his ties with the FOR" and gradually "adopted a stance of qualified defense of labor violence."[37] Seeking to make the CPLA a left-wing political group, Muste now proposed that Brookwood be transformed "into a training base" for "CPLA fighters." As he would later confess, "The Left had the vision, the dream of a classless and warless world. . . . This was a strong factor in making me feel that here, in a sense, was the true church. Here was the fellowship drawn together and drawn forward by the Judeo-Christian prophetic vision of 'a new earth in which righteousness dwelleth.' " It was clear to many on campus that he was preparing the seeds for the CPLA's absorption into Trotskyism.[38]

Alarm bells began to ring throughout the idyllic Westchester campus. One faction of faculty members objected to Brookwood losing its nonpartisanship by coming under the wings of the CPLA. The situation finally deteriorated throughout the fall months of 1932. On October 22, at a hastily called meeting, Muste was asked his own feelings regarding his alleged dual commitment. To the consternation of the moderate faculty members, he responded by insisting that the CPLA's work was more important. Seven days later, on October 29, the faculty majority submitted a letter recommending to the Brookwood board of directors "that some other member of the faculty assume the duties of director" and that "the school should not be tied to any single working-class party, group, or faction."[39]

Not mincing words, Muste challenged his critics not to play it safe and "to take part in the actual living controversies of the labor and revolutionary movement."[40] The board of directors was not moved by his plea and instead responded, "It is our hope that Brookwood may retain the services of A. J. Muste. As a condition of his continuance as Director, however, we regard it as essential that he resign from the chairmanship of the C.P.L.A. and from its Executive Committee and this condition prevail as long as he remains the director of Brookwood."[41]

Muste responded swiftly and without remorse. Committed more to principle than to political compromise, he and his family departed Brookwood on March 7, 1933. He remained convinced that "a labor school should interest itself directly in the actual struggles of the labor movement." Blaming the 1928 AFL condemnation for causing "the college to play safe and not take sides in controversies so as to incur the ill will of elements of the labor movement," Muste was quick to add that economic considerations now seemed more important than a willingness to plunge into the social and political struggles of the day that directly affected the laborer's plight. In a parting shot he proclaimed: "If the institutions had not been pressed for funds, and if conditions were as good as they were two years ago, I dare say this sudden outburst of conservatism would never have been manifest. The purpose of the directors seems to be to play safe and conserve what they have."[42]

The schism proved "terribly painful" for Muste, a man of compassion with deep feelings. Relationships forged in the "intensity of communal living, some for as long as twelve years, were destroyed."[43] His exit from Brookwood signified his abandonment of pacifist principles; it would be a brief hiatus from nonviolence, one characterized by doubt and uncertainty. Thus, between 1934 and July 1936, he espoused a Marxist-Leninist philosophy and was actively affiliated with the Trotskyist Workers Party of the United States. But the intellectual conversion had taken place much earlier.

In 1928 and 1929 he had begun to read more seriously in Marxist-Leninist writings. In his autobiography, "Sketches," Muste points out, "In the late twenties, for the first time I began to read fairly extensively in the literature of Marxism, including Marx himself, Trotsky and Lenin. . . . I turned to these books . . . as I had turned to the mystics and early Quakers a dozen years earlier, not out of academic interest but because I faced conditions and problems about which I felt I had to make decisions. The result of the reading was in each case *acted out* rather than written about."[44]

This observation does much to define Muste the person. For one year and seven months, Muste, his activist tendencies in high gear, worked with Trotskyists in helping to unionize striking workers in the Toledo Auto Lite plants in Ohio. His conversion of the CPLA, devised originally as a half-political agency and half-educational body, into a militant political party somewhere between the Socialist and Communist Parties, provided the Musteites with their largest impact nationally during the depression years. Muste and his American Workers Party (AWP) established the Lucas County Unemployment League to assist the striking workers. In fact, this league was one of many created by Muste and the CPLA to "put pressure on government relief agencies," to provide for "the medical welfare of children," and to establish "Housing and Eviction Committees, not only to forestall the expulsion of doctors [whose unemployed patients were unable to pay] from their homes but also to help the homeless find shelter and to intervene when the gas and electric company suspended service." The league also played an instrumental role in assisting unorganized workers, which eventually resulted in a stunning union victory for the industrial sector of the labor movement. "The Lucas County unemployment league was affiliated with the American Workers Party, a small radical organization led by A. J. Muste, which emphasized mutual support of employed and unemployed workers, and A.W.P. leaders played an important part in the conflict." Labor historians have described this episode as "an important breakthrough in increasing union consciousness among workers in the early New Deal period, and in laying the groundwork for the CIO."[45]

Unfortunately, this period of "alienation from the religious habits and attitudes of a lifetime" was one of considerable trauma for Muste. Bitter factional fights ensued, thus undermining his persistent efforts to create a truly American labor party. Duplicity on the part of Trotskyist colleagues "reduced the leadership position which he theoretically held in the WP-USA" to a sham. "It was not long before I became convinced," Muste somberly reflected, "that Trotsky controlled his followers about as autocratically as Stalin controlled his, though, of course Trotsky did not have at his command the crude disciplinary instruments which Stalin had in abundance." The disillusionment was complete.[46]

This physical and emotional toll on Muste forced him to consider a new direction. On a warm June day in 1936, he and Anna boarded a ship at Hoboken Pier, New Jersey, and set sail for Paris. It was a long-awaited, and needed, European vacation. In Paris, while visiting a Catholic Church, the recently converted radical Marxist was suddenly overcome by a sense of not belonging among secular revolutionaries. He decided at that moment to renounce his labor contacts and retreated to a church

Abraham Johannes Muste, peaceful protester. *Courtesy of the Fellowship of Reconciliation, Nyack, New York*

to tell its Sunday parishioners something of the ethics that he had failed to find in his personal dealings with politics. He had come full circle. Now rejecting his former arguments that labor violence in the face of capitalist provocation was sanctionable, he declared instead the need to evangelize among the working classes on behalf of the "Christian spirit" and the "method of non-violence." He rejected reliance on "armed insurrection, civil war, and terrorism." Far from being able "to destroy exploitative, political, and economic systems," violence perpetuated them and was their foundation. As long as "advocates of a new social order accepted that same foundation as their own," their every effort was doomed to failure.[47]

Muste's remarkable activist career eventually took another twist, one that lasted another thirty-one years. His new expedition led him into uncharted waters involving applications of modern war-resistance and civil disobedience. His return to Christian pacifism culminated in his acceptance of the post as industrial secretary of the FOR for 1936–37, and then as director of New York City's Presbyterian Labor Temple where, until 1940, he continually urged workers to forgo all forms of violence.

With the advent of another world war, Muste rose to the occasion by insisting that acceptance of nonviolence was humanity's only hope for averting conflict and the tragedies following in its wake. During the war he put into practice what he believed—a consistent trademark of this pacifist activist. While serving as executive secretary of the FOR, he led the peace group in support of draft resistance and conscientious objection. Along with his fellow pacifist and FOR leader, John Sayre, moreover, Muste pleaded for U.S. aid to refugees and victims of persecution in Europe.

In later years, during rising Cold War tensions, Muste's "leadership extended to the War Resisters League and the Committee for Non-Violent Action, where he advocated unilateral disarmament, refused to pay income taxes, defied civil defense laws, and practiced other civil disobedience against atomic testing and construction of nuclear weapons."[48] An important adviser to the civil rights struggles of the 1950s and 1960s, he was admired by Martin Luther King Jr., especially, for his application of nonviolent strategies to the integration battles of that period. At the twilight of his career, Muste inspired younger pacifist revolutionaries to create the strongest and most visible antiwar coalition in American history, the mobilization of protestors against the Vietnam War.

Muste's interwar journey from Christian pacifism to militant labor radicalism and then to nonviolent civil disobedience represents a fitting tribute to one dissident's devotion to human compassion and social uplift. His understanding of the human condition was premised on faith in the power of love. Although he would achieve a considerable degree of notoriety in his later years, it was the interwar decades that shaped his activist tenets. It was during this time that he developed a "keen insight into the nature of violence" as well as a "reputation for political activity and non-conformist activism" that centered around this insight. Thus, when it came to the struggle against war and social injustice, Muste invoked the bible of dissent and promoted the right of free expression in a democratic society. Most important, what sustained Muste and defined his character was his faith. "It lent his political predictions the power of prophetic warning, enriched his pragmatic analysis of society with timeless wisdom about the human condition, and transformed bold confrontations with the state into 'holy disobedience.' "[49] In his actions and in his words, Muste was the twentieth century's "Number One U.S. Pacifist."

Notes

1. *Time* (July 10, 1939): 37.

2. Quoted in Jo Ann O. Robinson, "A. J. Muste and Ways to Peace," in Charles Chatfield, ed., *Peace Movements in America* (New York, 1973), 82. See also David McReynolds in "A. J. Muste Memorial Issue," *Win* (February 24, 1967): 9; Sidney Lens, "Humanistic Revolutionary," *Liberation* (September/October 1967): 7; and John Nevin Sayre, "Fighting Reconciler: A. J. Muste as I Knew Him," *Fellowship* (March 1967): 11. The Muste Papers are housed at the Swarthmore College Peace Collection, Swarthmore, Pennsylvania, hereafter cited as SCPC.

3. A. J. Muste, "Sketches for an Autobiography," in Nat Hentoff, ed., *The Essays of A. J. Muste* (New York, 1967), 26–27.

4. Robinson, "A. J. Muste and Ways to Peace," 82.

5. Quoted in Jo Ann O. Robinson, "A. J. Muste: Prophet in the Wilderness of the Modern World," in Charles DeBenedetti, ed., *Peace Heroes in Twentieth-Century America* (Bloomington, IN, 1986), 148–49. Also consult Robinson's excellent scholarly biography, *Abraham Went Out: A Biography of A. J. Muste* (Philadelphia, 1981); and Nat Hentoff, *Peace Agitator: The Story of A. J. Muste* (New York, 1963).

6. Muste, "Sketches," 42.

7. Ibid., 43.

8. Ibid., 43. See also Robinson, "A. J. Muste: Prophet in the Wilderness," 149; Muste, autobiographical lecture given at New Brunswick Theological Seminary in 1944, located in Swarthmore College Peace Collection; Muste, Oral Memoir 589, Oral History Office, Butler Library, Columbia University.

9. Robinson, "A. J. Muste and Ways to Peace," 82–83.

10. Muste, "Sketches," 44.

11. Robinson, "A. J. Muste: Prophet in the Wilderness," 150.

12. Robinson, "A. J. Muste and Ways to Peace," 83.

13. Muste, "Sketches," 45.

14. Ibid., 52–53; Robinson, "A. J. Muste: Prophet in the Wilderness," 151.

15. Muste, "Sketches," 54, 43.

16. Ibid., 57.

17. Ibid., 58.

18. Ibid., 70.

19. Quoted in Charles F. Howlett, *Brookwood Labor College and the Struggle for Peace and Justice in America* (Lewiston, NY, 1993), 107. See also Betty L. Barton, "The Fellowship of Reconciliation: Pacifism, Labor, and Social Welfare, 1915–1960" (Ph.D. diss., Florida State University, 1974), 108–10.

20. Barton, "The Fellowship of Reconciliation," 104; Howlett, *Brookwood Labor College*, 97–106.

21. Muste, "Sketches," 64.

22. Cara Cook, unpublished memoir, Muste Papers, Box 1a, SCPC.

23. A. J. Muste, *Fellowship and Class Struggle* (New York, 1930), 9–10. See also A. J. Muste, Commencement Speech to Graduating Class of 1930, Brookwood Labor College Papers, Tamiment Library, New York University. The full collection of Brookwood Papers is located at the Walter P. Reuther Archives of Urban and Labor Affairs, Wayne State University.

24. Robinson, "A. J. Muste and Ways to Peace," 83–84; Muste, *Fellowship and Class Struggle*, 11.

25. Pamphlet on Brookwood Labor College Plays, Songs, and Chautauquas, 1931–1936, Brookwood Papers, Box 98, Reuther Archives.

26. Ibid., Box 98. Consult also Colette Hyman, *Staging Strikes: Workers' Theatre and the American Labor Movement* (Philadelphia, 1997), 54.

27. Foster Rhea Dulles, *Labor in America: A History* (Northbrook, IL, 1966), 254–55.

28. Muste, Graduation Speech, May 31, 1929, Brookwood Papers, Box 94, Reuther Archives.

29. Statement by A. J. Muste, January 25, 1919, Edmund B. Chafee Papers, George Arendts Library, Syracuse University. Muste's commitment to social justice was also spelled out in the college's journal. For additional information consult *Brookwood Review* 6 (October/November 1928): 2.

30. Statement by Muste, January 25, 1919, Edmund B. Chafee Papers.

31. James O. Morris, *Conflict within the AFL: A Study of Craft versus Industrial Unionism* (Ithaca, NY, 1959), 124–25; Eugene M. Tobin, "Academics and Insurgents: Brookwood Labor College, 1921–1933," Unpublished paper, Organization of American Historians Meetings, 1981; "Statement of Purpose: Conference for Progressive Labor Action," Brookwood Papers, Box 29, Reuther Archives.

32. Muste, "Sketches," 151; Robinson, "Traveler from Zierikzee: The Religious, Political, and Intellectual Development of A. J. Muste"(Ph.D. diss., Johns Hopkins University, 1972), 289–90; A. J. Muste to Elmer Cope, October 9, 1931, Elmer Cope Papers, Box 8, State Historical Society of Ohio. On the plight of the southern mill

worker see Alfred Hoffman, "The Mountaineer in Industry," *Mountain Life and Work* 5 (January 1930): 2–7; Tom Tippett, *When Southern Labor Stirs* (New York, 1931), 10–12; and Irving Bernstein, *The Lean Years: A History of the American Worker, 1921–1933* (Baltimore, 1966), 13–14.

33. Tippett, *When Southern Labor Stirs*, 29; "Mill Shadows," *Brookwood Labor College Plays* (Katonah, NY, 1931), 44.

34 Muste, "Sketches," 144–45.

35. Herbert J. Lahne, *The Cotton Mill Worker* (New York, 1944), 261–63.

36. Robinson, *Abraham Went Out*, 43.

37. Ibid., 45.

38. Muste, "Sketches," 135; "Muste Quits in Rift over CPLA," *Brookwood Review* 9 (May 1933): 1; "Labor Director Refutes Attack," *Brookwood Review* 9 (May 1933): 2.

39. "Statement with Regard to the Brookwood Situation," February 9, 1933, Brookwood Papers, Box 1, Reuther Archives.

40. "Statement Requested by Brookwood Policy Committee," Brookwood Papers, Box 29, Reuther Archives.

41. "Statement of the Brookwood Board of Directors," 1933, Brookwood Papers; Box 1, Reuther Archives.

42. *New York Times* (March 7, 1933): 4.

43. Robinson, *Abraham Went Out*, 47.

44. Muste, "Sketches," 151–52.

45. Daniel J. Leab, " 'United We Eat': The Creation and Organization of the Unemployed Councils in the 1930s," *Labor History* 8 (1967): 300–315; "Report on Unemployed Activities" (March 1933), copy located in Elmer Cope Papers, Box 10; Robinson, *Abraham Went Out*, 50; Jeremy Breecher, *Strike* (Greenwich, CT, 1974), 200–202.

46. Muste, "Sketches," 167; Robinson, "A. J. Muste and Ways to Peace," 84; Constance A. Myers, *The Prophet's Army: Trotskyites in America, 1928–1941* (Westport, CT, 1977), passim; Roy Rosenzweig, "Radicals and the Jobless: The Musteites and the Unemployed Leagues, 1932–1936," *Labor History* 16 (1975): 54–55.

47. A. J. Muste to Kirby Page, September 2, 1936; Page to Muste, September 4, 1936, Kirby Page Papers, Southern California School of Theology, Claremont College; A. J. Muste, "Return to Pacifism," *Christian Century* 53 (December 2, 1936): 1603–1606; Charles Chatfield, *For Peace and Justice: Pacifism in America, 1914–1941* (Knoxville, TN, 1971), 3–4; Muste, Oral Memoir 589, 270; Robinson, *Abraham Went Out*, 65.

48. Jo Ann O. Robinson, "Abraham John Muste (1885–1967)," in Roger S. Powers and William B. Vogele, eds., *Protest, Power, and Change* (New York, 1997), 335–36.

49. Robinson, "A. J. Muste: Prophet in the Wilderness," 753; idem, "A. J. Muste and Ways to Peace," 91.

Suggested Readings

Altenbaugh, Richard J. *Education for Struggle: The American Labor Colleges of the 1920s and 1930s.* Philadelphia, 1990.

Brameld, Theodore, ed. *Workers' Education in the United States.* New York, 1941.

Chatfield, Charles. *For Peace and Justice: Pacifism in America, 1914–1941.* Knoxville, TN, 1971.

DeBenedetti, Charles, ed. *Peace Heroes in Twentieth-Century America.* Bloomington, IN, 1986.

Hentoff, Nat. *Peace Agitator: The Story of A. J. Muste.* New York, 1963.

Howlett, Charles F. *Brookwood Labor College and the Struggle for Peace and Justice in America.* Lewiston, NY, 1993.

Morris, James O. *Conflict within the AFL: A Study of Craft versus Industrial Unionism.* Ithaca, NY, 1959.

Myers, Constance A. *The Prophet's Army: Trotskyites in America, 1928–1941.* Westport, CT, 1977.

Nelson, John K. *The Peace Prophets: American Pacifist Thought, 1919–1941.* Chapel Hill, NC, 1967.

Peters, Ronald J., and Jeanne M. McCarrick. "Roots of Public Support for Labor Education, 1900–1945," *Labor Studies Journal* 1 (Fall 1976).

Robinson, Jo Ann O. *Abraham Went Out: A Biography of A. J. Muste.* Philadelphia, 1981.

Rosenzweig, Roy. "Radicals and the Jobless: The Musteites and the Unemployed Leagues, 1932–1936," *Labor History* 16 (1975).

Tippett, Tom. *When Southern Labor Stirs.* New York, 1931.

2

Zora Neale Hurston
Folklorist and Storyteller

Laurie Champion and Bruce A. Glasrud

During the post-World War I years an outpouring of African-American culture, focused in New York, was known as the "Harlem Renaissance." Harlem had become the center of black literature, music, and art in a relatively short period as African Americans migrated from the South to northern cities. Among the leaders of this new cultural phenomenon was a black woman, Zora Neale Hurston, who fought her way to a position of prominence among the many men who were active at that time. Some of the fiction that she wrote is considered today among the best African-American literature produced in this century. Yet, in the Great Depression and subsequent years, she faded from sight and eventually died in 1960 in obscurity and poverty. Only in the 1970s did Alice Walker find her unmarked grave and return Hurston to the consciousness of the literary world.

Laurie Champion is assistant professor of English at San Diego State University, Imperial Valley. She has written several books; in 2000 she edited three, two with Glasrud and one alone, *American Women Writers, 1900–1945*. Bruce Glasrud has a Ph.D. in history from Texas Tech University and is dean of Arts and Sciences at Sul Ross State University in Alpine, Texas. In addition to his collaborative work with Champion, he is the author of several other books on ethnic and regional history, with a particular emphasis on African Americans in the American West.

> The truth is that nobody, not even the closest blood relatives, ever really knows anybody else. The greatest human travail has been in the attempt at self-revelation, but never, since the world began, has any one individual completely succeeded. There is an old saying to the effect that: "He is a man, so nobody knows him but God."[1]

During the 1920s an energetic, youthful, and talented group of black writers and artists converged on the Harlem district of New York City. They soon created and participated in the first significant movement of African-American writers and intellectuals in U.S. history. Coined the "New Negro Movement" by Alain Locke in 1925, it called

21

for a vision of African Americans that moves beyond stereotypical views and sees them with fresh perspectives. Locke also stated that African Americans celebrate their historical achievements and current community growth by entering a New Age. In all its cultural ramifications, this new spirit and coming of age became known as the Harlem Renaissance and served as the seedbed for blossoming individual careers as well as a showcase for the "New Negro" efforts to inspire African-American culture in the United States.[2]

Broadly defined, the New Negro movement consisted of demands for rights and privileges, attacks on stereotypes, and massive outpourings of literary and artistic works. The movement also involved political action led by men such as W. E. B. Du Bois and the National Association for the Advancement of Colored People (NAACP), Marcus Garvey and the United Negro Improvement Association (UNIA), and A. Phillip Randolph and the Brotherhood of Sleeping Car Porters, which took place broadly between the years 1917 to 1935. Although the New Negro movement inspired a national black renaissance, it most significantly brought together African Americans in Harlem and led to the Harlem Renaissance. At the spiritual center of this renaissance, or reawakening, gifted writers and artists emphasized black cultural beauty and identity as well as criticized oppression of blacks in a white-dominated society. Among the authors who both contributed to and were influenced by the new movement is Zora Neale Hurston, the most prolific black woman author of the era and one of the most renowned black women writers of the twentieth century.[3]

Hurston's life and career shows the tribulations and, for a few exceptional women, the possibilities for African-American female success in the United States between World War I and World War II. During these years, as a black southern woman in a society dominated by white males, Hurston pursued her career as a student, a researcher, a listener, and a writer. She succeeded in several literary genres—essay, novel, folklore, and short story—but she excelled as a storyteller, an ability central to her life and career. Until the late 1940s, her work and her life were so closely intertwined that they were virtually indistinguishable. After that time, however, her life deteriorated as her work lessened.

Hurston's writing reflects the survival and lifestyles of people, not their confrontation with society, and for that approach she sometimes is criticized. For example, her contemporaries, Alain Locke and Richard Wright, question her depiction of folklore in their reviews of *Their Eyes Were Watching God*, the work now considered Hurston's masterpiece.

Locke praises it as fiction at its best, compliments Hurston's maturity as a writer, and acknowledges her skill in telling a story convincingly, but he criticizes her for not including social commentary—that is, racism— in her writing. Whereas Locke acknowledges the significant contribution that Hurston makes to African-American folklore, Wright deplores her use of the minstrel technique and her emphasis on the quaintness of black society, and so he accuses her of writing not for black but for white audiences.[4]

Wright's review of *Their Eyes Were Watching God* echoes his well-known prescription for black writers. Clearly, Wright and Hurston depict society from two distinct African-American literary traditions.[5] Perhaps June Jordan distinguishes them best by referring to the protest literature of Wright and the writings of Hurston, which she appropriately names black affirmation literature. Jordan says that both protest and black affirmation literature serve purposes and should be revered. She argues, moreover, that the two traditions are not mutually exclusive.[6]

Stung by the harsh critics, Hurston nonetheless continued her research and writing. She emphasized the values of black society within the context of portraying African Americans almost exclusively in her works. About her desire to draw on the experiences of blacks, Hurston recalled, "I was glad when somebody told me, 'You may go and collect Negro folk-lore.' In a way it would not be a new experience for me."[7] As much as she was castigated by her male contemporaries, she is appreciated by today's critics for her depictions of African-American folklore. Since the 1970s, Hurston has been recognized increasingly for having created a specifically feminist black affirmation literature. As a result, her influence on black authors and on the literary tradition of the United States continues to grow.

In her study of black workers in the South, another one of her signal contributions, her influence derived, as Robert Hemenway asserts, from understanding and articulating the ancient black folk song:

> Got one mind for white folks to see,
> 'Nother for what I know is me;
> He don't know, he don't know my mind.[8]

Hurston's strength is in relating the social attitudes and mores of black southerners, especially those of the lower and lower-middle classes. Unlike protest fiction, which represents blacks as victimized and oppressed by an empowered white majority, Hurston's characters have little contact with whites. She shows their customs and beliefs and portrays strong women who overcome obstacles and hardship. During the years between World War I and World War II, Hurston underwent four stages of professional and artistic development: as a student, as a participant in the Harlem Renaissance, as a researcher, and as a mature and acknowledged folklorist and storyteller.

Born on January 7, 1891, in Macon County, Alabama, Zora and her family moved in 1894 to Eatonville, Florida, an African-American community near Orlando. The first all-black town to be incorporated, Eatonville became her home for the next decade and provided her with a wealth of stories and acquaintances. Her father was a Baptist minister and three-term mayor of Eatonville, while her mother encouraged her independence and free spirit, traits that remained with her throughout her life. This all-black community is the setting for most of Hurston's works; moreover, it affords her the philosophy that underlines much of her writing. Unlike the attitude behind certain protest literature, Hurston's artistic vision is influenced by the celebration of blackness expressed in her well-known essay, "How It Feels to Be Colored Me," in which she relates that she only realized she was black when she was thirteen and left Eatonville to attend school in Jacksonville. As she affirms,

> But I am not tragically colored. There is not great sorrow dammed up in my soul, nor lurking behind my eyes. I do not mind at all. I do not belong to the sobbing school of Negrohood who hold that nature somehow has given them a lowdown dirty deal and whose feelings are all hurt about it. Even in the helter-skelter skirmish that is my life, I have seen that the world is to the strong regardless of a little pigmentation more or less. No, I do not weep at the world—I am too busy sharpening my oyster knife.[9]

Focusing on black identity and survival skills, the role of strong black women, and the significance of black community, Hurston's life and career epitomized someone satisfied with her cultural attributes.

Hurston's mother died in 1904. This tragedy split the family and changed the direction of Zora's life. Headstrong, she became estranged from her father (partially because she disliked her new stepmother) and was sent to boarding school near Jacksonville. There she learned that she was a black female in a white man's world. She soon left school and for a few years moved from job to job, chiefly as a domestic worker, and from place to place. In 1915 and 1916 she toured throughout the South with a repertory company. Hurston's wanderings brought her independence, freedom, and, ultimately, an education.[10]

Her work with the repertory company eventually took her to Baltimore, and in September 1917, not long after U.S. entrance into World War I, Hurston enrolled in Morgan Academy. Through diligence and hard work, she completed her high-school education. The following year, after finishing her course work, Hurston moved to Washington, DC, where she matriculated at Howard University, thus beginning her much-loved collegiate career. An intermittent student, supporting herself by working, Hurston attended Howard at both the pre-college and college levels from 1918 to 1924. At Howard she studied with some of the nation's foremost black teachers, such as Alain Locke and Lorenzo Dow Turner. As a result of their guidance and her talent, she published her first short story (it included memories of Eatonville) and wrote poems for Marcus Garvey's *Negro World*. Majoring in English, she graduated with an associate degree from Howard University in 1920, but she did not earn a bachelor's degree from that institution.

In 1924, Locke and Charles S. Johnson, editor of *Opportunity* magazine, urged her to go to New York to participate in the bustling Harlem Renaissance. She undoubtedly also was encouraged because in December 1924 her short story, "Drenched in Light," was published in *Opportunity*. Hurston moved to New York in 1925 and in May attended an award ceremony for *Opportunity* at which she won two writing prizes and met several influential people. She enrolled in classes at Barnard College, where she was the only black student and where she studied anthropology under the guidance of Ruth Benedict, Franz Boas, and Gladys Reichard.

The strongest magnet attracting Hurston to New York in 1925 was the Harlem Renaissance, which gave her the opportunity to continue writing. Her writing career developed in the mid-1920s with the publication of her short stories in *Opportunity* magazine; and in a significant achievement, Locke selected one of her stories, "Spunk," for inclusion in his respected anthology, *The New Negro*. Hurston published essays and stories drawn from Eatonville in the *Messenger* in 1926, and the same year a short tale in *Forum*. In 1927 she published an account of eighteenth-century blacks in Georgia in the *Journal of Negro History*. She also worked with Wallace Thurman and others and edited the short-lived radical journal, *Fire!*, in which her short story "Sweat" and her play *Color Struck* appeared.

The short stories indicate why she was soon considered one of the talented members of the Harlem Renaissance. In "Spunk," the protagonist parades with Lena, Joe's wife, but refers to her as his own wife. Challenged by Joe, Spunk kills him. Spunk is acquitted but later falls on a saw, and just before his death mumbles that Joe has murdered him. The story ends with women wondering who will be Lena's next lover and men speculating about Joe and Spunk while guzzling whiskey. If "Spunk" is powerful and dramatic, "Sweat" is even more so. In "Sweat," Sykes harasses his wife, Delia. Eventually, Sykes attempts to kill Delia by placing a poisonous snake among her clothes in a basket. The snake escapes from the basket, remains in the house, and kills Sykes after Delia decides not to warn him. These stories, written before Hurston began her research trips to the South, are based on recollections of stories that she heard from others and challenge sexism and racism. During the 1920s, Hurston also collaborated with Langston Hughes to write *Mule Bone*, but due to a split with Hughes, the play was neither performed nor published during her lifetime. (It was finally printed in 1991.)

An exceedingly private person, Hurston kept some of herself from others. When she arrived in New York in January 1925 she was thirty-four years old, but she encouraged her acquaintances to believe that she was ten years younger. In her autobiography she gave her date of birth as 1901, not 1891. Witty, articulate, and a consummate storyteller, Hurston was much in demand at social gatherings in Harlem. However, forsaking the glamour of the Harlem Renaissance for the life of a social scientist, Hurston headed to the South in 1927 to collect data for her anthropology degree from Barnard. For six years she traveled throughout Florida, Alabama, and Louisiana, hunting stories and documenting southern black contributions to American culture. Many of Hurston's character traits sparkled during those years—independence, optimism, adventure, individualism, scholarly aptitude, and love of folk culture. One negative outcome of her efforts was a separation early in 1928 from her husband, Herbert Sheen, whom she had married in 1927 (they divorced in 1931); again, in 1939, a short-lived marriage, to Albert Price III, ended in divorce. A significant portion of her Louisiana research was published as "Hoodoo in America" in the *Journal of American Folklore* in 1931.

In 1935, Hurston published the results of her years of scholarly anthropological research when *Mules and Men* burst on the literary scene. The first book of folklore by an African American, it also was the first serious study of African-American folklore. This culmination of her education and research received considerable critical praise. The book is a collection of folktales that help explain the lives and survival skills of black southerners. At the same time, Hurston indicates the means used by black women to advance their position despite their secondary place in society.

Hurston continued her folklore studies, leading to the 1938 publication of *Tell My Horse*, about voodoo in Haiti. On the one hand, *Tell My Horse* represents, as Elmer Davis notes in his early review of the book, "a curious mixture of remembrances, travelogue, sensationalism, and anthropology."[11] On the other hand, it represents Hurston's effort to uncover the survival of African customs in Haiti. Her research led her into some peculiar incidents, but her experiences enlivened her written accounts. By this stage in her career, Hurston had become a skilled folklorist; she received two Guggenheim fellowships, joined the Federal Writers' Project in Florida, and participated in the Federal Theater Project in New York. Her research was sometimes supported financially by whites: expenses for *Mules and Men* were paid by a white woman in the North, and her autobiography, *Dust Tracks*, was written while she resided with a white woman in California. Her initial research trip to the South, however, began with a grant from the Association for the Study of Negro Life and History. Nevertheless, she generally was financially insecure.

By the mid-1930s, Hurston had become a compelling and mature storyteller as well as a scholar of folklore, as evidenced in one of her short stories. In 1933 she published "The Gilded Six Bits" in *Story* magazine, and it has been reprinted often over the years. A husband and wife love each other; however, the husband comes home early one afternoon to discover his wife in bed with a rich man. Unlike "Sweat," this story basically (with irony) ends happily. The carefully crafted conclusion illustrates Hurston's maturity of style, and the story overall shows a strong woman created, no doubt, from the wealth of material that Hurston collected on her sojourn in the South.

In 1934, Hurston published her first novel, *Jonah's Gourd Vine*, which established her reputation as a novelist. Set in her hometown of Eatonville, where blacks reside and control the political structure, *Jonah's Gourd Vine* received very favorable reviews. Based loosely on the lives of Hurston's parents, the novel portrays a black husband who has affairs with many women and his loving and saintly wife. Despite her husband's infidelity, the wife survives and perseveres. Hurston's second novel, *Their Eyes Were Watching God*, appeared in 1937 and is her most critically acclaimed work. Herein is Hurston's feminist characterization of African-American women, first clearly depicted in her short stories. She also explores in the novel important topics such as the search for a sense of community, romantic and platonic relationships, and the need to find one's own personal and cultural identity. In *Their Eyes Were Watching God*, this sense of belonging to a community provides Janie, the protagonist, with a sense of cultural pride and self-identity. When Janie returns to Eatonville at the beginning of the story, she has the courage to retell her story to Pheoby. Because Pheoby will repeat Janie's story to others, Janie has shared with the entire community the knowledge that she has gained about her heritage.

Hurston's next novel, written during the interwar years, is an allegory entitled *Moses, Man of the Mountain*. For some readers, *Moses* is difficult to understand; for others, it appears unrelated to her previous interests and studies. Hurston presents Moses from the point of view of black Americans. Placing an emphasis on magic, Hurston weaves legend and myth into a fascinating story of liberation and leadership. *Moses* is a powerful and sometimes humorous allegory of American slavery, and some reviewers refer to it as her most imaginative and ambitious work.

In the early 1940s, Hurston wrote and published her autobiography, *Dust Tracks on a Road*, at the behest of her publisher, J. B. Lippincott. Although she initially balked at the idea, arguing that it was too soon for her to write her life story because she was only at the midpoint of her career, she agreed, and for her effort received the prestigious Anisfield-Wolf Book Award in Racial Relations. Hurston was fifty-one in 1942 (although many assumed that she was ten years younger), and she published little after this autobiography—one novel, essays in magazines, and a few short stories. Writing *Dust Tracks* challenged Hurston; she thought it necessary to write it in a style acceptable to white America while at the same time refuting prevalent stereotypes of blacks in the South. Perhaps *Dust Tracks* might best be referred to as a simulated story of Hurston's life—Hurston as she sees herself and as she wishes to be remembered. In a first-rate article, Françoise Lionnet-McCumber coins the word "autoethnography" to explain Hurston's memoir.[12] In another analysis of *Dust Tracks*, Kathleen Hassall notes that the novel "has baffled and dismayed many who admire her and provided an easy target for those disposed to attack."[13] Hassall further argues that we should think of Hurston as an actress who is playing a series of performances with this work.

Dust Tracks on a Road is more than a midcareer statement; it is also (in retrospect) her own view of herself. With the 1942 publication of her autobiography, Hurston's literary career began a downward slide, culminating in a decade of poverty and nonrecognition during the 1950s. From the release of *Dust Tracks* in 1942 until her death in 1960, Hurston led a life of obscurity and published little, especially after her last novel, *Seraph on the Sewanee*, appeared in 1948. During this time, her writings were primarily journalistic; her health faltered, and she seemed to become more conservative. A 1959 stroke sent her to the hospital, and she died unknown and penniless the next year. Her body was buried in an unmarked grave in a segregated cemetery. It was not until 1973 that Alice Walker located her forgotten and neglected grave.

Walker was the first of a long line of writers to search for and resurrect the career, life, and contributions of Zora Neale Hurston. Perhaps, as David Headon points out, a succinct depiction of Hurston's "categories of perception" tells us a great deal about her powers as an observer, storyteller, and folklorist: 1) her recognition and celebration of the quality of black communal life; 2) her emphasis on the poetry and creativity of black English; 3) the significance that she attached to notions of personal identity and self-worth; 4) her emergent feminist aesthetic; 5) her suspicion of Western civilization and its machinery of cultural appropriation; and 6) her realization and articulation of the inadequacies of anthropological methods.[14]

Zora Neale Hurston's life can be best summarized in her own words, in which she describes herself as "a brown bag of miscellany propped against a wall."[15] She left many of her own dust tracks on the road to prominence in her journey as a folklorist and storyteller. Her significant contributions to African-American literature and to the role of black women continue to teach and reach us today. Walker placed on Hurston's gravestone the words, "Genius of the South," in a fitting tribute to this respected and talented twentieth-century writer.

Notes

1. Zora Neale Hurston, *Pittsburgh Courier*, February 28, 1953.

2. Alain Locke, "The New Negro," in *The Norton Anthology of African American Literature*, ed. Henry Louis Gates Jr. and Nellie Y. McKay (New York, 1997), 962–70.

3. Ibid.

4. Alain Locke, "Review of *Their Eyes Were Watching God*," in *Zora Neale Hurston: Critical Perspectives Past and Present*, ed. Henry Louis Gates Jr. and K. A. Appiah (New York, 1993), 17.

5. Richard Wright, "Review of *Their Eyes Were Watching God*," in ibid.

6. June Jordan, "On Richard Wright and Zora Neale Hurston," *Black World* (August 1974): 4–8.

7. Zora Neale Hurston, *Mules and Men* (Philadelphia, 1935), 1.

8. Robert E. Hemenway, *Zora Neale Hurston: A Literary Biography* (Urbana, IL, 1978), xxi.

9. Zora Neale Hurston, "How It Feels to Be Colored Me," in *I Love Myself When I Am Laughing . . . And Then Again When I Am Looking Mean and Impressive: A Zora Neale Hurston Reader*, ed. Alice Walker (Old Westbury, NY, 1979), 153.

10. Details of Hurston's life can be found in several sources. See, for example, Steve Glasman and Kathryn Lee Seidel, eds., *Zora in Florida* (Orlando, FL, 1991); Hemenway, *Zora Neale Hurston: A Literary Biography*; and Lillie P. Howard, *Zora Neale Hurston* (Boston, 1980).

11. Elmer Davis, "Review of *Tell My Horse*," in *Zora Neale Hurston*, ed. Gates and Appiah, 24.

12. Françoise Lionnet-McCumber, "Autoethnography: The An-Archic Style of *Dust Tracks on a Road*," in *Zora Neale Hurston*, ed. Gates and Appiah, 241–66.

13. Kathleen Hassall, "Text and Personality in Disguise and in the Open: Zora Neale Hurston's *Dust Track on a Road*," in *Zora in Florida*, ed. Steve Glassman and Kathryn Lee Seidel (Orlando, FL, 1991), 159.

14. David A. Headon, "Beginning to See Things Really: The Politics of Zora Neale Hurston," in *Zora in Florida*, ed. Steve Glassman and Kathryn Lee Seidel (Orlando, FL: 1991), 30–31.

15. Hurston, "How It Feels to Be Colored Me," in *I Love Myself When I Am Laughing*, ed. Walker, 155.

Suggested Readings

Bambara, Toni Cade, ed. *The Sanctified Church: The Folklore Writings of Zora Neale Hurston*. Berkeley, CA, 1981.

Champion, Laurie, and Bruce A. Glasrud. "Zora Neale Hurston (1891–1960)." *African American Authors, 1745–1945: A Bio-Bibliographical Critical Sourcebook*. Ed. Emmanuel S. Nelson, 259–69. Westport, CT, 2000.

Dance, Daryl C. "Zora Neale Hurston." *American Women Writers: Bibliographical Essays*. Ed. Maurice Duke, Jackson R. Bryer, and M. Thomas Inge, 321–51. Westport, CT, 1983.

Gates, Henry Louis, Jr., and Sieglinde Lemke, eds. *The Complete Stories of Zora Neale Hurston*. New York, 1995.

Glassman, Steve, and Kathryn Lee Seidel, eds. *Zora in Florida*. Orlando, FL, 1991.

Hemenway, Robert E. *Zora Neale Hurston: A Literary Biography*. Urbana, IL, 1978.

Holloway, Karla F. C. *The Character of the Word: The Texts of Zora Neale Hurston*. Westport, CT, 1987.

Howard, Lillie P. *Zora Neale Hurston*. Boston, 1980.

Lowe, John. *Jump at the Sun: Zora Neale Hurston's Cosmic Comedy*. Champaign, IL, 1994.

Plant, Deborah G. *Every Tub Must Sit on Its Own Bottom: The Philosophy and Politics of Zora Neale Hurston.* Urbana, IL, 1995.

Walker, Alice, ed. *I Love Myself When I Am Laughing . . . And Then Again When I Am Looking Mean and Impressive: A Zora Neale Hurston Reader.* Old Westbury, NY, 1979.

Wall, Cheryl. *Zora Neale Hurston: Novels and Stories.* New York, 1995.

3

Jimmie Rodgers
The Singing Brakeman

Archie P. McDonald and Mark Daniel Barringer

American culture went through many changes during the interwar years. Just as styles of literature were evolving among both blacks and whites, popular music changed dramatically at the same time. One significant change was the commercialization of country music, a musical form not known much beyond the mountains, hollers, and cotton fields of the South. Technology made possible the recording of the performances of rural entertainers who had not been heard by crowds larger than a country church's congregation. Radio and records brought their voices to a national audience. Jimmie Rodgers, one of the first of the country singers to be recorded and broadcast regularly on the radio, benefited from the new technology of the post–World War I decade, even at a time when rural America did not share in the nation's overall prosperity and sophisticated lifestyle.

Archie P. McDonald and Mark Daniel Barringer, although not historians of music as such, are cultural historians who can place country music and the life of Rodgers in their proper context. McDonald has published widely on southern and Texas history and has been the director of the East Texas Historical Association for many years. He is Regent's Professor of History at Stephen F. Austin State University in Nacogdoches, Texas. Barringer, a younger colleague of McDonald's, is assistant professor of history at Stephen F. Austin State University. He is scheduled to become the director of the East Texas Historical Association upon McDonald's retirement.

O n a chilly January evening in 1986, leaders of the music industry gathered in New York's Waldorf-Astoria Hotel to induct the inaugural class into the Rock-and-Roll Hall of Fame. The list of inductees included Elvis Presley, of course, and Chuck Berry, Buddy Holly, Jerry Lee Lewis, Fats Domino, and the Everly Brothers. A diverse range of styles was represented, and the presence in the first class of Little Richard, James Brown, Sam Cooke, and Ray Charles demonstrated the broad cultural gleanings that had been swept under and sheltered by the rock-and-roll umbrella.

Earlier in the evening, as a prelude to the induction of these music business icons, another ceremony had established the historic roots of rock-and-roll, perceived by many to be unique to post-World War II America. Five men were introduced as the "forefathers" of rock, and they, not the previously mentioned ten, were the true first inductees into the genre's Hall of Fame. Alan Freed, a disc jockey in Cleveland and New York, had coined the term "Rock-and-Roll." Sam Phillips, who owned Sun Studios in Memphis during the 1950s, had gambled on young, unknown musicians such as Elvis Presley and Jerry Lee Lewis. Robert Johnson, nearly forgotten but rediscovered during the 1980s, was judged the best guitar player ever to emerge from the Mississippi Delta, birthplace of the blues. Two other names on this list of pioneers were more obscure. Jimmy Yancey, a piano player in 1920s and 1930s Chicago, had redefined jazz and influenced many future stars, including Ray Charles, with his innovative left-hand "walking bass," yet was relegated to obscurity after his death in 1951. And Jimmie Rodgers, called by many the "Father of Country Music," laid the foundations for both rock-and-roll and modern country music in his brief career.[1]

Jimmie Rodgers was an innovator and a trailblazer in the music business. Visitors to the Rock-and-Roll Hall of Fame in Cleveland or the Country Music Hall of Fame in Nashville—where he was the first person ever enshrined—can see his likeness on the wall and read about his contributions to these American institutions. They will emerge knowing little about his life, however, which is unfortunate, because Rodgers's life is what made his music. He sang about the rural South in the first decades of the twentieth century, and his songs reflected the values, beliefs, and dreams of that region. To say that someone was "shaped by his childhood" has become a cliché; we are all shaped by our childhoods. But the South that shaped Jimmie Rodgers was mirrored in his music and survives in scratchy recordings that teach subsequent generations about the poverty and hardscrabble lives of southerners in an earlier time. In his brief professional career, Rodgers developed a sound that became one of the defining characteristics of the South in popular American perception.[2]

James Charles Rodgers was born on September 8, 1897, to Aaron and Eliza Bozeman Rodgers, in Meridian, Mississippi. His father worked on the Mobile & Ohio Railroad as foreman of an extra gang, a relief or emergency gang that repairs railroad track, and traveled constantly to wherever they were needed. His mother, determined to maintain a wholesome family life despite the nomadic nature of the work, followed her husband from town to town, often setting up housekeeping in tents or vacant boxcars. James—he did not become "Jimmie" until later in life—

was the youngest of three boys born to the couple. Walter, the oldest, married and left home when James was still young, but Talmage shared many of the hardships of those early years with James. Eliza Rodgers, rarely healthy, died in 1903, likely from tuberculosis contracted in one of the railroad camps in which she had lived. After his mother's death, James stayed with various relatives until his father remarried and reunited James and Talmage in a Meridian home in 1906. Like most families of the time, the Rodgerses lived without much material wealth, and the regular absences of their father left the boys without much supervision. After a few months of fighting with their stepmother over disciplinary matters, James and his brother were sent to live with a maiden aunt, Dora Bozeman, in Pine Springs, Mississippi. For the next five years, James experienced the most stable period of his life. He attended school regularly for the only time and became close to Talmage and Aunt Dora, his surrogate mother. In 1910, Aaron Rodgers again decided that the boys should be with him, so they returned to a rented house located near the railroad shops in Meridian.[3]

Meridian was a bustling town that boasted lumber mills, cotton gins, factories, and seven railroad lines along with the attendant warehouses, shipping facilities, and repair shops. It was also a regular stop for many touring companies of entertainers that traveled throughout the South during the summer months. With his father frequently absent and with his stepmother's failure to supervise him, James spent much of his time on the streets. His one refuge was a barbershop owned by an uncle, Tom Bozeman, and from there he embarked on his first musical venture in the summer of 1910. He ran away to sing in a traveling medicine show for a few weeks before being retrieved by his father.

Wandering in search of a home, a career, a family, and an identity became a pattern in Rodgers's life. Following the death of his stepmother in 1911, he accompanied his father all over the South, following the work on the Mobile & Ohio or the New Orleans & Northeastern (NO&NE) railroads. Somewhere along the way, between 1911 and 1917, he may have contracted tuberculosis, the disease that plagued him for years and eventually ended his life. But in January 1917 the young, itinerant, and comparatively healthy railroader appeared in Durant, Mississippi, as a guest in the home of Tom Conn, a fireman on the Illinois Central. There he met Stella Kelly, Conn's cousin. James and Stella soon wed, and Rodgers resumed his nomadic railroading life, dragging Stella along with him. Although the U.S. entry into the World War that spring created a demand for qualified laborers, Rodgers could not interest himself in permanent work. He preferred to spend his time strumming on some instrument, to spend the little money he made on friends, and to drink, with predictable results. Only six months into the marriage, Stella, pregnant with a daughter who would be born in February 1918 and christened Kathryn, left him. Rodgers was twenty years old, Stella, nineteen.

Rodgers eventually found a job with the NO&NE, working as a baggage man and brakeman on the New Orleans-to-Meridian run for thirty dollars per week. He gained a reputation as a ladies' man and went by "Jimmie" rather than James. And he continued to pursue his dream of becoming an entertainer. In the summer of 1919 he again appeared in the home of an attractive young woman, this time sixteen-year-old Carrie Williamson. Music may have been the initial draw, for the Williamson house was a gathering place in Meridian for young men and women of the First Methodist-Protestant Church, of which the Reverend Mr. Williamson was pastor. Soon, however, it was Carrie who caught his eye. Early in 1920, after the war and Railroad Administration controls had ended, Rodgers was laid off from the NO&NE and again had to travel to find work. This time he ranged as far west as Texas and California before returning to Meridian in April 1920 and marrying Carrie.

The next several years were filled with the now-familiar pattern: occasional work on railroads in the Deep South, regular moves from town to town, and, ominously, frequent occurrences of pneumonia and other chest ailments. The only constant was music. No matter where he went, Jimmie always had a guitar, a banjo, or a mandolin to fill the long hours on the road and entertain friends and acquaintances. In 1923 he joined Billy Terrell's Comedians, one of the traveling tent repertory, or "tent-rep," companies that passed through Meridian. Rodgers coined the term "blue yodeling" to describe his unique style.[4] He performed for about a month with the show before being called back to Meridian upon the death of his infant daughter, June Rebecca, in December. Thus ended Rodgers's first attempt to become a professional entertainer. In the winter of 1923–24, Rodgers resumed the life of an itinerant railroader, leaving his family and traveling through Texas, New Mexico, Arizona, Utah, and Colorado.

The diagnosis of tuberculosis came in September 1924 after Rodgers had returned to Meridian and the NO&NE. He refused to acknowledge the severity of the illness that would dramatically alter his life. Tuberculosis, or TB, had been the leading cause of death in the United

States for years and remained so until the 1950s. Between 1900 and 1925 alone the disease killed more than 3.5 million Americans. Everyone was familiar with the symptoms—a frequent, unproductive cough, pleurisy, blood in the sputum, and, in advanced cases, hemorrhaging. Jimmie probably suspected that he was infected for several years, especially after watching his mother die of TB. But his reaction was the same, whether TB was suspected or diagnosed—he ignored it; but, realizing that his time was short, he hastened his quest to become a professional entertainer. Jimmie Rodgers wanted, more than anything else, to be admired as someone who had "made it."

In one concession to his disease, Rodgers spent less time chasing railroad work and more time pursuing his musical career. Railroad labor was simply too taxing for his damaged lungs, and although he continued to work occasionally on various lines across the South, the diagnosis of his disease marked a turning point in his life. Spurning the conventional treatment of bed rest and relocation to a high, dry climate, Rodgers remained restless. A short stint in Tucson ended when he became too weak to work the rails, and he returned to Meridian to recuperate. In January 1927 he left his wife and daughter there and traveled to Asheville, North Carolina, where the high mountain air and the promise of another railroad job beckoned.

All through the 1920s, Jimmie Rodgers had collected musical recordings. The technology was relatively primitive, but the combination of record players, radios, and new musical influences stimulated by the migration north of African Americans during and after World War I transformed American popular music. Jazz influences crept into a corpus over which Enrico Caruso, the great Italian tenor, had previously ruled unchallenged. Orchestras began to incorporate some of the rhythms born in the South and transplanted to great cities through black migration after the war. There was a definite boundary, however; an uncrossable chasm separated "popular" American music from that known in polite society as "race" music. Country, or "hillbilly," as it was originally termed, did not exist except in the Appalachian valleys, along the dusty dirt roads of cotton country, or on the railroads where men from all across the nation met and swapped folk songs and melodies. The records that Jimmie Rodgers collected were likely different from much of the music that he had heard on the rails or in his travels across the South during the first two decades of the twentieth century.

Rodgers arrived in Asheville in January carrying his guitar and a small valise containing most of his possessions. He was twenty-nine years old and had spent most of his life arriving in or departing from one southern town or another, but Asheville would be the last place where he would arrive broke. When he found out that the rumored railroad work did not exist, Rodgers scrounged odd jobs as a cab driver and errand boy for the local police department, and he performed at local dances and weddings. In February, Asheville's first radio station, WWNC (Wonderful Western North Carolina) debuted, and Rodgers began appearing with other musicians, playing popular standards of the day. Carrie and their daughter Anita joined him and the family rented a small cabin in town. In May, Jimmie took over a coveted Monday and Thursday evening show, playing guitar and singing duets with Asheville native Otis Kuykendall, but the job paid little and Rodgers was intent on making a living with his music. He then located three musicians from Bristol, Tennessee, who called themselves the Tenneva Ramblers and brought them to Asheville for the radio job, rechristening the group the Jimmie Rodgers Entertainers. For the next month this "hillbilly orchestra," as Rodgers referred to them, experimented with a musical style that fit no established pattern. Playing a variety of stringed instruments, including banjos, mandolins, guitars, and ukuleles, they treated Asheville residents to early renditions of such later hits as "Sleep, Baby, Sleep," "A Soldier's Sweetheart," and Rodgers's soon-to-be-signature "T for Texas." The hybrid style drew criticism from those who disliked the blues influences, derivative, they thought, of the so-called nigger blues that defined African-American music. So the Jimmie Rodgers Entertainers were fired in July by a station manager who believed that only two kinds of music were suitable for airing: popular standards, and folk—that is, white folk, or mountain hillbilly.

Rodgers was not discouraged. He and his group cast about for work and landed a job playing nightly at dances for the vacationers at a nearby mountain resort. The pay was better than at WWNC, his disease less troublesome—one of the group's members later insisted that he never knew Rodgers was ill—so the Jimmie Rodgers Entertainers settled in for the summer. At least, the others thought so, but Rodgers had other ideas. He was convinced, as always, that better times lay just around the corner. So in July, at the height of the resort season, when he learned that record auditions would be held in nearby Bristol, he did not hesitate. He persuaded his players to quit the resort job, loaded them in the 1925 Dodge that the group had purchased, picked up his wife and daughter in Asheville, and drove to Bristol.

The summer trip of the Jimmie Rodgers Entertainers to Bristol has been described as fate—it was inevitable, some say, that Rodgers's unique style would be discovered by the recording industry and forever change the face of American music. The truth is much different. Rodgers's style was not, in 1927, unique. As a musician, he was barely adequate. As a vocalist, he remained limited and tended to imitate famous singers. His material largely relied on popular standards or traditional tunes. Fate did not bring him to Bristol to be discovered—his relentless pursuit of fame and fortune, his unwillingness to believe that he was just another tent-rep guitar player, his firm belief that he was destined for greatness despite all of the evidence to the contrary, brought Rodgers to Bristol. It was not destiny but stubbornness in the face of overwhelming odds. Rodgers did not know when to quit. That same quality would hasten his death a few years later.

Ralph Peer, one of the pioneers of the record business, conducted the auditions in Bristol. Peer had grown up in Kansas City and worked in his family's drugstore, which sold Columbia Records. He became an expert on Columbia artists and took a job with the company as a salesman and later national sales manager. After serving in World War I, Peer left Columbia for the General Phonograph Corporation, where he headed its Okeh Records division. A relatively small concern, Okeh lagged far behind such industry giants as the Victor Talking Machine Company and Columbia. Peer, however, found the company a niche in "race" music, as he called it. Under his leadership, Okeh became the acknowledged leader in locating new blues artists, and a market emerged for the music. In 1923, Peer concocted a mobile recording setup that allowed him to travel around the country to record new artists. After his local contact failed to come up with anyone worthy of recording on a trip to Atlanta in a search for black blues singers, Peer agreed to audition Fiddlin' John Carson, a white folk artist. The resulting record sold surprisingly well, and a new category of popular music, called "hillbilly," gained public acceptance. Completely separate, by design, from the blues that Peer had been recording, hillbilly music became a phenomenon in its own right.

Although Peer recorded Fiddlin' John Carson for Okeh Records in 1923, it was a Victor artist, Vernon Dalhart, who touched off the hillbilly music craze the following year with the release of "The Prisoner's Song/Wreck of the Old 97." Peer began seeking hillbilly singers but still concentrated on blues artists. For the next two years, in trips through the South he signed on new talent and built Okeh into the leader in race records. He quit Okeh following a dispute over money and joined the Victor Talking Machine Company as an independent talent scout charged with expanding Victor's catalog of race records as well as the newly popular hillbilly sound. His first foray into the South with Victor's mobile equipment brought him to Bristol, a small town in the mountains on the Tennessee-Virginia border and home to some of the purest forms of American folk music.

The Bristol auditions have become legendary among those who cherish the southern musical past. Jimmie Rodgers and his Entertainers arrived in July and arranged a session with Peer. While waiting to audition in the makeshift studio, however, Rodgers and his band members had a falling out. He wanted the group billed as the Jimmie Rodgers Entertainers, but the other three wanted to revive the Tenneva Ramblers name. Rodgers decided to ask for a solo audition. Thus did Jimmie Rodgers embark on an amazing journey.[5]

Rodgers cut two tracks in Bristol, for which Peer paid him $100. Both were familiar songs, "A Soldier's Sweetheart" and "Sleep, Baby, Sleep," a yodeling number that had been recorded by several other singers. Peer, much more interested in copyrightable material, was reluctant to record these songs, but apparently he heard something in Rodgers that he liked. For his part, Jimmie was sure that he had arrived. He moved Carrie and Anita from a boarding house to Bristol's finest hotel. After a few days the family, now permanently separated from the Entertainers, moved to Washington, DC, where relatives had offered free room and board. Despite Jimmie's optimism about his new career, he and Carrie still had almost no money. As he had during his entire life, Jimmie spent whatever he earned. They arrived in Washington flush but quickly resumed their more familiar roles as hand-to-mouth survivors. Jimmie, now billing himself as a "radio star" and a "Victor recording artist," found occasional work playing at dances or parties while Carrie got a job as a waitress in a café. They waited for word from Peer about future recording sessions.

When it did not come soon enough, Rodgers decided to take matters into his own hands. Perhaps he knew, after a flare-up of his TB in October, that time was running short. He used the last of the money earned from his first recording session to go to New York and press Peer for more studio time. Rodgers thought that he had finally made it at the Bristol session, despite the fact that his first royalty check garnered him a meager $27. He refused to acknowledge that literally hundreds of other would-be artists made similar audition records every week, only a small fraction of whom ever entered a studio again. As usual, he ignored this complication and forged ahead with his plan to become a star. Carrie, always the more grounded of the two, kept her job in Washington and waited to see whether the New York trip would bring a happy surprise or one more disappointment in a life littered with letdowns.

Rodgers arrived in New York in November 1927, just as his first record began to sell. He persuaded Peer to arrange another recording session at the Victor studio in Camden, New Jersey. This time, instead of recording barely reworked versions of other artists' songs, Rodgers led off with "T for Texas," or "Blue Yodel," as it was titled when released. This piece became the prototype Jimmie Rodgers song, imitated both by him and by hundreds of other singers. The yodel itself was not new as a musical accouterment, but Rodgers made it seem so. It was a plaintive and mournful wail that lent a distinctive quality to an otherwise commonplace blues number—or it would have been commonplace had Rodgers been black. But no white performer had managed to sing the traditional African-American musical form in such a fashion before.[6]

"T for Texas" became the blueprint for Rodgers's success and spawned a series of similar recordings. A simple blues broken by Rodgers's distinctive, plaintive yodel, the song resonated with American popular music fans. Over the next few years, Rodgers achieved his goal and became a successful entertainer. He persuaded his sister-in-law, Elsie McWilliams, to join him in Washington to collaborate on new material. Their partnership produced hits for the next four years. He began a weekly radio show on WTFF in Washington. Moreover, he signed up with the Loews Theater chain for a national tour and made a triumphant return to Meridian in October 1928, arriving in style with a hired driver in a fancy automobile to repay old debts and to show the cynics who had doubted that he would amount to anything that he had made it. When the Loews tour moved north in the fall, Rodgers stayed in the South and toured with the Paul English tent-rep company for the winter.

In May 1929, Jimmie and Carrie began building an elaborate estate in Kerrville, Texas, that they called Blue Yodeler's Paradise. The 1920s were roaring away and Rodgers's royalty checks rolled in. Newly elected President Herbert Hoover guaranteed prosperity as a permanent condition, and the Rodgers family enjoyed the good times as much as any. But underneath the glitzy exterior lurked the constant reality of tuberculosis.

Health concerns were probably the reason for Rodgers to abandon a lucrative national company such as Loews for a regional show. A northern winter would undoubtedly present difficulties, for the singer's disease was becoming increasingly evident. In January 1929, Rodgers collapsed during a show in Houston, leading Paul English, the head of the rep company, to recruit Jimmie Rodgers imitators to travel with the show in case his star attraction could not perform. Health was definitely the reason that he and Carrie had selected Kerrville as their home. The town hosted several TB sanitariums and enjoyed a reputation for "good air." At that time, rest was the only treatment for the disease, but rest Rodgers simply could not abide. He alleviated the symptoms with whiskey—prescription booze, with Prohibition in full force—and ever-greater doses of morphine supplied by sympathetic physicians. His health deteriorated rapidly, necessitating long periods of bed rest broken by almost manic periods of touring and recording to keep the money coming in. His marriage, too, weakened under the strain of heavy drinking, bouts of ill health, and frequent trips away from home.

Rodgers compacted a lot of living into a few short years. Some observers interpret his frantic pace of recording, touring, and broadcasting between 1929 and 1933 as an unspoken acknowledgment that his time was short. Others blame Ralph Peer for pushing too hard, relying on Rodgers to ensure his own success and thus hastening the singer's death. But both men knew that the record business was heading for hard times due to competition from radio, where music was free, and that tent-rep was dying out because of the growing availability of talking movies. Rodgers probably decided to make as many records as possible while the market was good and to tour while the audiences would still pay to see him. He was a phenomenon—despite the stock market crash in October 1929 and the widening economic depression that followed, in 1930 his royalties alone earned him more than $100,000. But Rodgers, like many of Kerrville's real estate tycoons, sanitarium owners, bankers, and corporate magnates, seemed immune to hard times. He spent money faster than ever, maintaining hotel suites in several cities, collecting automobiles, and treating friends and casual acquaintances to lavish trips. He became active in Texas politics, supporting the controversial Miriam A. Ferguson for governor—the political equivalent of Rodgers's populist, I'm-for-the-little-guy music—and becoming an honorary Texas Ranger.[7] He also spent much less time in the now-completed Blue Yodeler's Paradise.

Although Rodgers seemed unaffected by the financial crisis, the crash eventually caught up with him as it did with the entire nation. Despite widespread belief, the stock market collapse was not the beginning of the Great Depression. In much of the country and certainly in much of the rural South, economic hardship had existed for decades. After reaping uncommon profits during World War I, American farmers witnessed the more familiar scenario of falling commodity prices, high tariffs, and corporate market control that pushed agricultural regions into severe depression as early as 1921. The stock market crash had a ripple effect, however, that drove the whole country deeper into economic difficulty by 1933.[8]

Rodgers depended on rural people, those who led the lives he sang about in his mournful blues, to buy his records. His appeal, while crossing over into urban and middle-class areas previously untouched by hillbilly musicians, was essentially to rural, and thus poor, citizens. After the crash the depression extended its grip from the cities outward into the countryside where the poor grew even more desperate. Rodgers's record sales slowed and he had to find new ways to generate income. At Peer's urging, he recorded with another popular hillbilly act, the Carter Family, but reaped little financial gain from the awkward pairing. He toured for a time with popular comedian Will Rogers, but the collaboration proved equally disappointing. He even made a movie, a short entitled *The Singing Brakeman*, which received polite approval from critics but did little to increase record sales. Rodgers, as many Americans had been for a decade, was living beyond his means, and in the process he was undermining his fragile health.

The end came quickly and ignominiously. In March 1933, Rodgers was suffering from frequent coughing attacks that sometimes lasted for hours and from greater financial difficulties. He and Carrie separated. Blue Yodeler's Paradise was sold to pay bills. The money was nearly gone. Rodgers telephoned Peer that spring, asking for a recording session to cut ten tracks at $250 each to cover his immediate expenses. By this time, Rodgers was desperately ill but would not admit it. He arrived in New York in May and managed, with the help of a hired nurse and generous amounts of whiskey, to record several numbers despite having to rest after only a few minutes of work. One of these songs, "Women Make a Fool Out of Me," was later released as "Jimmie Rodgers' Last Blue Yodel," the thirteenth in the series. After recording only six tracks, Rodgers could not continue. On the evening of May 26, 1933, in a New York hotel room with his nurse, he suffered a coughing attack that led to hemorrhage, slipped into a coma, and died.

Few noted his passing. The *New York Times* obituary, deep inside the next day's edition, referred to him only as a "hillbilly singer."[9] Other newspapers, even in the South where he was so popular, also treated Rodgers's death casually. It was a curiously unheralded end for someone whose impact on the national culture would be so pronounced. The "blue yodels" of Jimmie Rodgers were the perfect soundtrack for the Great Depression. Sung in a style variously described as mournful, plaintive, wistful, or melancholy, they reflected the mood of the nation. His Singing Brakeman persona fit the rollicking 1920s, even in rural America where times were tough, and then gave way to "America's Blue Yodeler" as the depths of the depression and its anguish spread across the land. Rodgers was immensely popular in his day, but his enshrinement as the "Father of Country Music" and widespread acclaim for his music as something other than regionally significant came later.

Rodgers's records continued to sell well for some years after his death, but by 1941 they had almost disappeared from the RCA/Victor catalog. American popular music had moved on to the sounds of swing, but in the hills of Appalachia, along those dusty cotton-country roads, in rail yards across the southwest, even on stage at Nashville's Grand Ole Opry—the mother church, if you are a true believer—the songs of Jimmie Rodgers could still be heard. Nearly all of the now-legendary country singers, including Ernest Tubb, Gene Autry, and Merle Haggard, owe a debt to Rodgers.[10] Even Hank Williams, the most famous hillbilly artist of them all, would not have enjoyed such acclaim if it were not for Jimmie Rodgers. Tribute albums appeared over the years to pay homage to the path-breaking work of America's Blue Yodeler. But country music was a small part of the American music scene for more than twenty-five years after World War II, with an almost cult-like following mainly in the South, and thus Rodgers's influence was unknown to most popular music fans. Then, in the 1970s, country music found a new audience that extended into all regions of America, and "country" became the most pervasive sound in the nation.

Anyone growing up in late-twentieth-century America knows what country music sounds like, and one can still hear Jimmie Rodgers's influence. Sometimes it is buried deeply, somewhere in the melding of traditional folk instruments with blues bass lines or even today in an occasional plaintive wail reminiscent of the 1930s blue yodel. Once in a while, however, Rodgers emerges fully recognizable in offerings from artists such as the late Steve Goodman or Steve Forbert, both of whom have carried on the tradition of mixing musical styles to create unique sounds, still country but with something extra. Contemporary artists, such as Ricky Skaggs, who tend toward more traditional hillbilly styles, make Rodgers's impact even more apparent. Country music has become the music of America, but, thanks to Jimmie Rodgers and his innovations, it will always sound like the South in the years between the wars.

Notes

1. "The Rock and Roll Hall of Fame Forefathers," *Rolling Stone* (February 13, 1986): 48; Michael Hill, David Fricke, Michael Goldberg, and Tim Holmes, "Rock's Top Ten," *Rolling Stone* (February 13, 1986): 36–46; "Rock and Roll's Hall of Fame," *Newsweek* (February 3, 1986): 73; David Fricke, "Rock Hall of Fame Honors Pioneers," *Rolling Stone* (March 13, 1986): 8.

2. Chris Comber and Mike Paris, "Jimmie Rodgers," in Bill C. Malone and Judith McCulloh, eds., *Stars of Country Music: From Uncle Dave Macon to Johnny Rodriguez* (Urbana, IL, 1975), 121–41.

3. Nolan Porterfield, *Jimmie Rodgers: The Life and Times of America's Blue Yodeler* (Urbana, IL, 1979), is the definitive biography of Rodgers and was the primary source for much of the material in this essay. Other full-length biographical accounts include Carrie Williamson Rodgers, *My Husband, Jimmie Rodgers* (Nashville, TN, 1995), and Mike Paris and Chris Comber, *Jimmie the Kid: The Life of Jimmie Rodgers* (London, 1977).

4. "Blue yodeling" was a term that Rodgers or any number of others who claim to have originated the phrase used to describe a unique mixture of diverse musical sounds. Conventional interpretations assert that it was an amalgamation of "rural black blues with traditional folk and hillbilly music." See "The Rock and Roll Hall of Fame Forefathers," *Rolling Stone* (February 13, 1986): 48. Probably the best description of the musical niche occupied by this style is in Henry Pleasants, *The Great American Popular Singers* (New York, 1974), 111–25. Pleasants ascribes the sound to a blending of traditional white folk melodies, southern black blues, and the chants of black railroad workers.

5. The Bristol recording sessions have become controversial as well as legendary. Carrie Williamson Rodgers, in *My Husband, Jimmie Rodgers*, insists that she was instrumental in organizing the solo sessions. Paris and Comber, *Jimmie the Kid*, restates her version of this story. But Porterfield, with some reservations, places the responsibility squarely on Rodgers himself. See Porterfield, *Jimmie Rodgers*, 113; and Pleasants, *Great American Popular Singers*, 120. Part of the legend comes from the fact that Rodgers was only one of the country music stars that Ralph Peer discovered in the small mountain community of Bristol. Others included the Carter Family, with whom Rodgers would later record, and Earl Scruggs. See Porterfield, *Jimmie Rodgers*, 66; and Bill C. Malone, *Country Music U.S.A.* (Austin, TX, 1985), 65.

6. Pleasants, *Great American Popular Singers*, 120–22.

7. Ascribing political overtones to Rodgers's music helps explain the appeal of his sound in the South. Populists such as Miriam Ferguson, her husband James E. Ferguson, and more familiar figures such as Huey P. Long all used symbolism similar to that in Rodgers's songs to connect with marginalized groups. Pleasants, in *Great American Popular Singers*, 121, says that Rodgers was "not just a man speaking or singing, [but] a whole countryside, and entire people, the American South—exclusive, of course, of

the plantation and mercantile elite." Many of the themes in the music were repeated in political messages long after Rodgers's death. See Richard A. Peterson, *Creating Country Music: Fabricating Authenticity* (Chicago, 1997), for an analysis of how music was a part of identity formation for various groups.

8. Rural America during the 1920s was anything but "roaring." Classic accounts of the decade include William E. Leuchtenburg, *The Perils of Prosperity, 1914–32* (Chicago, 1958), and John D. Hicks, *Republican Ascendancy, 1921–1933* (New York, 1960). For more specific analyses of the South, see George Brown Tindall, *The Emergence of the New South, 1913–1945* (Baton Rouge, LA, 1967), and Donald W. Whisenhunt, *The Depression in Texas: The Hoover Years* (New York, 1983).

9. *New York Times*, May 27, 1933, 13.

10. Ernest Tubb was the most closely identified musical disciple of Rodgers. See Ronnie Pugh, *Ernest Tubb: The Texas Troubadour* (Durham, NC, 1997), 185–90.

Suggested Readings

Hicks, John D. *Republican Ascendancy, 1921–1933.* New York, 1960.
Leuchtenburg, William E. *The Perils of Prosperity, 1914–32.* Chicago, 1958.
Tindall, George Brown. *The Emergence of the New South, 1913–1945.* Baton Rouge, LA, 1967.
Whisenhunt, Donald W. *The Depression in Texas: The Hoover Years.* New York, 1983.

4

Ma Rainey
Mother of the Blues

S. Spencer Davis

Americans have often been accused of contributing little to general culture instead being a society that takes from others, especially from Europe. In blues and jazz, however, they have made new and exciting contributions, most of which have been exported throughout the world.

"Ma" Rainey is often described as the first blues singer and certainly one of the greatest. She represents the enduring popular culture of rural African Americans in the time of the Harlem Renaissance, which was largely an urban movement. Her work was taken by whites, most often without acknowledgment, and at the time of her death she was almost alone and forgotten. Ma Rainey was a complex character—exuberant, lusty, and, in her later years, religious. She lived in a period when the two worlds of blacks and whites were more carefully defined than they are today.

Spencer Davis, a professor of history at Peru State College in Nebraska, is a specialist in African-American intellectual and cultural history. His degrees are from Brown University and the University of Nebraska-Lincoln, with a Ph.D. from the University of Toronto. A member of Phi Beta Kappa and Phi Alpha Theta, he is also a member of the Nebraska Humanities Committee Speakers' Bureau. Professor Davis is the co-founder and coordinator of the Black History Workshop of Zion Baptist Church in Omaha.

Gertrude "Ma" Rainey is remembered today as second only to Bessie Smith among blues vocalists—a judgment that is at once accurate in the minor sense and yet inadequate as a full understanding of Rainey's career. She was the first professional singer to incorporate blues numbers into her act, and as an entertainer she was the greatest crowd-pleaser of the women singing blues. But even these substantial "firsts" are not the full measure of her achievements.

Gertrude Pridgett was born in Columbus, Georgia, in 1886, the second of the five children of Thomas and Ella Pridgett. Columbus was a town of 7,000. With its industry and location on the Chattahoochee River, it had attracted Thomas and Ella to migrate from their native Alabama.[1] No evidence beyond a baptism record describes Gertrude's youth, but undoubtedly she was singing at church and school events. At fourteen she sang in a local group called "The Bunch of Blackberries." Soon afterward, she must have begun to sing professionally. At eighteen she married William "Pa" Rainey, the manager and a performer in the Rabbit Foot Minstrels. They immediately worked together in the show as "Pa" and "Ma" Rainey, with an act combining comedy, singing, and dancing. Since Pa Rainey was substantially older than his eighteen-year-old bride, the match must have been as much professional as romantic.[2]

The situation of black entertainers in the first years of the last century was complex. A life of constant travel brought them into collision with the absurdities and indignities of segregation. Within the black community many religious believers frowned on secular music and looked on entertainers as Satan's assistants. The tangled cultural life of the nation put black entertainers in the dilemma of seeing their culture derided by Anglo-Saxon supremacists while their works were being adopted—or stolen—by white performers.[3]

Charles Dudley Warner, Mark Twain's co-author of *The Gilded Age*, toured the South in 1888 and recorded his impressions in *On Horseback: A Tour in Virginia, North Carolina, and Tennessee*. In Asheville, North Carolina, Warner and a crowd of both races were entertained by Happy John. Once a slave of Wade Hampton, one of the largest and most famous slaveowners, and now appearing in Uncle Sam costume and black-face make-up, Happy John sang and told stories. According to Warner, Happy John received the biggest response, from blacks in the audience as well as from whites, when his jokes were at the expense of his race. Warner, perhaps momentarily troubled by the situation, reached a conclusion that did not entirely disguise his anxiety. "I presume none of them analyzed the nature of his infectious gayety, nor thought of the pathos that lay so close to it, in the fact of his recent slavery, and the distinction of being one of Wade Hampton's [slaves], and the melancholy mirth of this light-hearted race's burlesque of itself."[4] The possibility of double-meaning in this stereotyped humor did not occur to Warner.

Happy John may not have been performing in the minstrel format, but there were similarities. The minstrel show is a strange American creation. White minstrel shows first appeared in the 1840s and created a sensation among white audiences. Most of them focused on plantation life, and many or most of them purported to depict "authentic" slave life. How white Americans could believe that is difficult to understand, given the fact that the actors were white people using burnt cork to blacken their faces. Their exaggerated physical movements helped to establish stereotypes that have persisted to this day.

By the middle of the 1850s black actors began to appear as minstrels, and they became firmly established as a part of the show business tradition by the 1870s. Showmen such as Charles Callender and J. H. Haverly were instrumental in making minstrels an integral part of show business. Black-owned companies also formed in the 1860s. Among the more important ones were the Brooker and Clayton Georgia Minstrels, a group that was very popular in the Northeast. Minstrels succeeded partly because they appealed to an essentially illiterate society, but their popularity was not limited to the unlettered. Prominent people, including Abraham Lincoln, reportedly found them very entertaining.

By the 1870s a separation occurred between black and white minstrels. Because black minstrels had the aura of authenticity, especially with "real Negroes," white shows moved away from portrayals of "realistic" plantation and black life to more lavish productions. They became more professional as well but continued to use African-American culture as a major focus. Black minstrels flourished in the later decades of the nineteenth century and the first few decades of the twentieth.[5]

Thomas L. Riis, in his study of jazz, suggests a plausible explanation for the popularity of minstrels among whites and blacks alike. People have wondered why blacks would participate in and attend minstrel shows when portrayals were racist, degrading, and grotesque. He suggests that the actors and audiences of the day may not have seen them in the way that contemporary society does. In fact, he explains the low educational level of the country at the time and the importance of oral-cultural entertainments. In an oral culture, he believes, exaggeration and grotesque portrayals are necessary and are common in most nonliterate or semi-literate cultures. The exaggerations are needed to deliver the message, and the audience does not see the performances as degrading.[6]

Such was the minstrel tradition that Ma Rainey joined when she became a performer. Whether she was conscious of the subtleties of its historical and cultural significance is a moot point. She was essentially illiterate herself; and, if one accepts Riis's conjecture, she might not have seen it as degrading at all. Perhaps the Rabbit Foot Minstrels had no such figure as Happy John in their cast in 1904 when Ma Rainey joined the troupe, but minstrel shows, though they typically had black casts by that time, retained their stereotypes and the indignity of black-face. In the 1870s black minstrel shows and white minstrel shows had begun to diverge; the black entertainers included spirituals as well as stereotypes.[7] To play within but yet rise above the stereotypes was a difficult feat.

The Rabbit Foot Minstrels played only in the South, traveling in their own railroad car and playing one-nighters in their gigantic tent. The program included acrobats and a contortionist; eventually Ma Rainey was the star of the show. The Rabbit Foot Minstrels usually spent the winter in New Orleans, which gave her the chance to perform with some of the greats of New Orleans music such as Joe Oliver, Louis Armstrong, Sidney Bechet, and Kid Ory. In 1914, 1915, and 1916 she toured with Tolliver's Circus and Musical Extravaganza with the billing of "Rainey and Rainey, Assassinators of the Blues." In 1917 she created her own traveling show, Ma Rainey and Her Georgia Smart Set.

There is a fairly detailed account of that show. Rainey was short and heavy-set; she had diamonds in her hair, gold-capped teeth, and heavy jewelry. In order to lighten the tone of her skin she used a great deal of skin cream and powder. Her humor, warm smile, and open sexuality compensated for her lack of classic features. Rainey played to all-black, segregated, and all-white audiences. If the audience was segregated, whites were seated on one side of the tent and blacks on the other side. Her show began with a band number followed by several numbers by male and female dancers. Next came two skits of ethnic humor, the first portraying a Japanese character and the second a black man stealing chickens. A fast number featuring the soubrette and the dancers was followed by another comedy routine. Then Ma Rainey came on stage, began with some comedy, sang half a dozen numbers including "Memphis Blues" and "Jelly Roll Blues," and ended with her specialty, "See See Rider Blues." The show closed with all the cast on stage for the finale.[8]

By this time, Rainey had been singing blues in her performances for a decade and was the preeminent female blues artist. She claimed that while she was working a tent show in Missouri in 1902, she overheard a young woman singing a strange lament about the man who left her. Taken by the unique sound, she learned the song and put it in her act. When asked what kind of song it was, she replied "the blues" and thus named the genre. It is unlikely that Rainey was in Missouri before 1904 and, therefore, equally unlikely that, in a moment of inspiration, she invented the label. But as an explanation of how Rainey became the first professional singer to put blues in a minstrel show, the story is more credible.[9]

The first sheet music with "blues" in the title was published in 1914 by a white band leader from Oklahoma, but the blues genre began almost certainly in the 1890s, almost certainly in the Mississippi Delta, and quite certainly among rural blacks. Defining the blues is more difficult. Blues began in the 1890s (or perhaps a little earlier) in the Delta—the heart of share-cropping, cotton-producing, rural Mississippi. The typical blues artist was a man singing and playing the guitar. The typical blues form was a twelve-bar, three-line stanza with the second line repeating the first (AAB) and the third line ending with the rhyme word. Blues singers drew on familiar lines from earlier songs, added their own, and used filler words or moans to complete lines. Blues numbers could change from one rendition to the next as lines were changed, or formulas from other numbers were added, or new stanzas were improvised. Blues lyrics focused on personal problems such as unfaithful lovers, whiskey, debts, and trouble with the law. The leading study of these original down-home blues finds surprisingly little social protest in them.[10]

Down-home blues were sung at picnics, on the porch, at the depot, and outside the barbershop. But to fit into the structure of the minstrel and tent shows, changes had to be made. Instrumental soloists could improvise, but too much improvising by vocalists would upset the band.[11] Rainey had to standardize the lyrics, but accompaniments had to be worked out for the band or small group.

In the late 1910s, Rainey's act changed. Pa Rainey, always a dim figure, dropped out of the picture. Ma Rainey was then a singles act. She may have spent a year in Mexico, but that is not confirmed. Within a year, however, she was back, entertaining southern black audiences. In 1922 and 1923 she worked with a pianist, usually Troy Snapp, accompanying her.[12] By this time the first recorded blues, Mamie Smith's "Crazy Blues," had appeared, and no doubt Rainey changed to keep up with the popularity of recorded blues—keep up, but never totally imitate. She remained closer to down-home blues than any of the other women recording classic (or vaudeville) blues in the 1920s.

On her own, Ma Rainey performed with many others, but she also befriended and assisted struggling entertainers. One of the most famous was Bessie Smith, who would overshadow Rainey in fame and popularity. In the beginning, however, Rainey gave her a start in the business. Their relationship may have been more than that. Smith later was well known for her bisexuality, and Rainey may have been bisexual as well. *Completely Queer* indicates that Rainey was a lesbian and that she introduced Bessie Smith to lesbian love. "Rainey was one of a number of legendary women singers associated with the Harlem Renaissance who were known to prefer women over men." This reference work also indicates that her nickname, Ma, referred to "the affection and nurturing she lavished on those around her."[13] Whatever her personal affairs may have been, her career flourished in the 1920s.

In 1920, Mamie Smith recorded "Crazy Blues" for Okeh Records. Its success persuaded record companies that there were profits to be made in "race" records. Other vaudeville singers who had the clear tone and distinct pronunciation of Mamie Smith were rushed into studios to record blues. In 1921 about fifty race records were released; by 1927 the number had soared to five hundred.[14] These blues—classic or vaudeville blues—were neither the down-home kind nor the blues of tent show veterans such as Ma Rainey and Bessie Smith. But, in 1923, both Smith and Rainey were recorded.

The phenomenal growth of radio in the 1920s created a crisis for the music industry. Record sales continued to decline throughout the decade. Since music could now be disseminated even to the most rural and unsophisticated audiences, record companies began to look for other entertainers who performed less well-known "folk" music. Company scouts fanned out across the country, especially the South, to find singers who would sound good on wax and whose talents could be promoted. One of the pioneers in this development was Ralph Peer, the man who first recorded Mamie Smith in 1920, but he became better known because he soon focused on recording country singers, including Jimmie Rodgers.

Mamie Smith's records for Okeh were successful and offered a potential new market for black singers—African Americans themselves who preferred to hear people of their own race perform music from their own culture.[15] Several recording companies created separate listings for songs designed for other races—meaning, almost always, African Americans. These became known as "race records." The term "race" in the 1920s was a badge of pride in the black community. "Although race records included spirituals, instrumentals, comedy, sermons, and even occasional classical arias, the biggest money was in the blues."[16] Okeh, Columbia, and Paramount set the pace for race records in the 1920s. Paramount had a black talent scout and recording director, J. Mayo Williams, who aggressively recruited black entertainers.[17]

In December 1923, at age thirty-seven, Rainey went to Chicago to record eight songs at Paramount Records. Despite its array of talent, Paramount was limited when compared to Columbia Records. Paramount recorded Rainey acoustically, "a crude process in which she sang into an enormous horn," and the results were primitive and disappointing.[18] That first session produced one hit, "Moonshine Blues." Rainey did most of her recording for Paramount in Chicago, where she kept an apartment, but in 1924 she had two Paramount recording sessions in New York. The back-up musicians were among the stars of the jazz world: Fletcher Henderson, a leading New York band leader, on piano; Charlie Green on trombone; and, for the second session, Louis Armstrong on cornet. Of these six tracks, "See See Rider Blues" was the most important.[19]

With recording success came the opportunity to move from tent shows to the stages of the Theater Owners' Booking Agency (TOBA), the black vaudeville circuit. TOBA had been around since about 1907, but it really came into its own in the 1920s. The shows were targeted to black audiences, but on Thursday nights a separate performance was given for whites. The "Midnight Ramble" was a standard—a late show featuring the blues—unlike the regular performances that were more like white vaudeville in that various types of entertainment were provided. The typical TOBA show might include "comedy, circus acts, dramatic scenes, and pure vaudeville hokum as well as singing and dancing."[20] While TOBA stood for Theater Owners' Booking Agency, the performers often referred to it as "Tough on Black Artists," or, in more crude moments, "Tough on Black Asses." Even so, and despite low pay, hard work, and poor working conditions, TOBA offered regular employment for hundreds of black entertainers who would have had a difficult time arranging bookings for themselves.[21]

For her TOBA act, Rainey worked with Tommy Dorsey, a prominent musician in years to come, as pianist and music director. He put together and rehearsed a five-piece group, the Wildcats Jazz Band.[22] Evidently "jazz," like "blues," was an elastic and even indefinite term. The publicity photo of Rainey, Dorsey, and the rest of the Wildcats put them in awkward poses that nevertheless captured some of Rainey's energy.

Dorsey defined the connection between jazz and blues in several ways that help place Ma Rainey's music. He described jazz as music played at the better clubs; blues was played in Chicago in the back of saloons, at rent parties, and at buffet flats (unlicensed clubs set up in apartments and patronized by working-class people). Jazz was blues speeded up, a faster and flashier music; blues maintained a slower tempo to fit its sad mood.[23] Dorsey also described slowing down or dragging out popular tunes of the day to suit the taste of couples who wanted to "slow drag" or "shimmy" late at night.[24] Rainey's power over the audience is given in Dorsey's words:

> When she started singing, the gold in her teeth would sparkle. She was in the spotlight. She possessed her listeners; they swayed, they rocked, they moaned and groaned, as they felt the blues with her. A woman swooned who had lost her man. Men groaned who had given their week's pay to some woman who promised to be nice, but slipped away and couldn't be found at the appointed time. By this time she was just about at the end of her song. She was "in her sins" as she bellowed out. The bass drum rolled like thunder and the stage lights flickered like forked lightning. . . . As the song ends, she feels an understanding with her audience. Their applause is a rich reward. She is in her glory. The house is hot. . . . By this time everybody is excited and enthusiastic. The applause thunders for one more number. Some woman screams out with a shrill cry of agony as the blues recalls sorrow because some man trifled with her and wounded her to the bone. [Ma Rainey] is ready now to take the encore as her closing song. Here she is, tired, sweaty, swaying from side to side, fatigued, but happy.[25]

Rainey's record sales and TOBA bookings were very successful through 1928, but at the end of that year conditions changed abruptly. Paramount decided not to renew her recording contract. The competition from sound movies, introduced in 1927, had sent the TOBA theaters into a steep decline, and in May 1929, Rainey quit the circuit with wages owed her. Thereafter came a series of desperate moves to keep her career going, but the depression took its toll on her career as it had on many other black performers. Still she persevered, taking whatever engagements she could find. She toured with some of the tent repertory companies, but the Great Depression was destroying more prestigious careers than hers. Paramount Records went bankrupt in the early 1930s, black vaudeville died, and Ma Rainey quit the business.

In 1935 she returned to Georgia to her hometown of Columbus after the death of her sister Malissa; her mother died during the same year. Rainey purchased two theaters in Rome. During this time, she joined the Friendship Baptist Church where her brother, Thomas Pridgett, was a deacon. Her life in Georgia is not well known today, but clearly she dropped out of entertainment except for owning the theaters, and she essentially was forgotten in blues circles.

Rainey died on December 22, 1939, and was buried in Porterdale Cemetery in Columbus. She was only fifty-three years old; the cause of death was reported to be heart disease—not unexpected considering her lifestyle and weight. Her death went entirely unnoticed by the black press or by any other news medium. It seems especially ironic that her death certificate listed her occupation as housekeeping. One wonders if her neighbors were aware of her career in entertainment.[26]

~

Ma Rainey was a black woman and a professional entertainer. She played minstrel shows, tent shows, circuses, carnivals, clubs, theaters, and even a Texas cattle show. Wherever engagements were offered, she took them until, in the Great Depression, there were none. When wealthy white folks in Jackson, Mississippi, hired her, she serenaded at their homes. When black sharecroppers in Alabama were flooded out, she organized a fund-raising concert. She sang blues, popular tunes, and comedy numbers; she danced; she told jokes, often at her own expense and often ribald; she worked with partners in comedy routines. At times, she managed her road shows. She composed about one-third of the numbers she recorded, or more accurately, she was listed on the copyright forms as composer or co-composer.[27] She paid her musicians on time, treated them well, and never missed an engagement.

For all her versatility, Ma Rainey was most successful singing traditional blues—that is, songs employing many of the formulas and the loose organization of down-home blues but performed by a vocalist and small group as were vaudeville blues. In his poem celebrating the power of Ma Rainey over her audience, Sterling A. Brown tells how her rendition of "Backwater Blues" so perfectly expressed the tribulations of the audience that heads bowed and tears flowed.[28] Brown explained her appeal: "Ma Rainey was a tremendous figure. She wouldn't have to sing any words; she would moan, and the audience would moan with her." She dominated the stage. "She had them in the palm of her hand. I heard Bessie Smith also, but Ma Rainey was the greatest mistress of an audience."[29]

Her commanding presence was also reported by Jack Dupree: "She was really an ugly woman, but when she opened her mouth—that was it! You forgot everything. She knew how to sing those blues, and she got right into your heart. What a personality she had. One of the greatest of all singers."[30] Almost everyone who saw her perform agreed that she was a "blues queen" who, like so many others, acted the part. Strong, unpredictable, and "volcanic," she spoke her mind. She was "soft-hearted and generous; but she was a tigress when roused."[31]

In her recorded blues, Rainey touched upon all the causes of heartache and anguish—unfaithful lovers, violent men, poverty, debt, jail time, alcoholism—of women abandoned, betrayed, or overpowered by life's problems. But in some of her numbers she portrayed aggressive, violent, lustful women—those sinning rather than those sinned against. Thus, in "Bared Home Blues," written by Louie Austin, Rainey's "Mama" matches "Papa," vice for unblushing vice.[32] In "Black Dust Blues," she is a woman who has stolen another one's man but pays the price through the effect of the voodoo potion placed in her house.[33]

In his path-breaking analysis of French folk tales, Robert Darnton discovered a world of constant poverty, death, hunger, starvation, injustice, and cruelty. The poor survived only by tricking others; in such a world the eradication of personal and social problems was inconceivable.[34] Reading the lyrics to Ma Rainey's blues can create the same sense of global despair. But when we turn from the lyrics on the printed page to the recordings, the power of her voice and the gusto in her delivery come into play. The sadness and hurt do not disappear but undergo a transformation. The sheer waste and inwardness of suffering are overcome; artistry gives meaning to the pain of a world we must take as we find it. For Ralph Ellison this was the outrageous, inexplicable truth of African-American culture.[35] Many artists represent Ellison's insight as well as Ma Rainey, but none represents it better.

Notes

1. Hattie Jones, *Big Star Fallin' Mama*, rev. ed. (New York, 1995), 19–21.

2. Sandra Lieb, *Mother of the Blues* (Amherst, MA, 1981), 4–5.

3. W. C. Handy, *Father of the Blues* (New York, 1969). Chapters 1–4 describe the conflict between religion and secular music.

4. Quoted in Alton Hornsby Jr., ed., *In the Cage: Eyewitness Accounts of the Freed Negro in Southern Society, 1877–1929* (Chicago, 1971), 140–42; quote on 142.

5. Lieb, *Mother of the Blues*, 4–7; Thomas L. Riis, *Just before Jazz: Black Musical Theater in New York, 1890–1915* (Washington, DC, 1989), 4–5.

6. Riis, *Just before Jazz*, 5–7.

7. Lieb, *Mother of the Blues*, xiii, 5.

8. Ibid., 10–13.

9. Ibid., 3–5.

10. Jeff Todd Titon, *Early Downhome Blues*, rev. ed. (Chapel Hill, NC, 1994).

11. For the problems created by an improvising soloist in Mahara's Minstrel Show see Handy, *Father of the Blues*, 40–41.

12. Lieb, *Mother of the Blues*, 18–25.

13. Steve Hogan and Lee Hudson, *Completely Queer: The Gay and Lesbian Encyclopedia* (New York, 1998), 471.

14. Titon, *Early Downhome Blues*, 200.

15. Bill C. Malone, *Country Music U.S.A.*, rev. ed. (Austin, TX, 1985), 34–35.

16. Lieb, *Mother of the Blues*, 21.

17. Ibid.

18. Ibid., 22.

19. Ibid., 10, 26, 178.

20. Ibid., 27.

21. Ibid., 26–27.

22. Paramount Records talent man J. Mayo "Ink" Williams paired Dorsey with Rainey. Lieb, *Mother of the Blues*, 29; Michael W. Harris, *The Rise of Gospel Blues* (New York, 1992), 86–87.

23. Harris, *Rise of Gospel Blues*, 53.

24. Ibid., 59.

25. Ibid., 89–90.

26. Darlene Clark Hine, ed., *Black Women in America: An Historical Encyclopedia*, 2 vols. (Brooklyn, NY, 1993), 960; John A. Garraty and Mark C. Carnes, eds., *American National Biography* 18 (New York, 1999), 80.

27. More accurately, she was listed on the copyright as composer or co-composer of these numbers.

28. Sterling A. Brown, "Ma Rainey," in *The Collected Poems of Sterling A. Brown*, ed. Michael S. Harper (Evanston, IL, 1980), 62–63.

29. Quoted in Derrick Stewart-Baxter, *Ma Rainey and the Classic Blues Singers* (New York, 1970), 42.

30. Ibid.

31. Ibid.

32. Angela Y. Davis, *Blue Legacies and Black Feminism* (New York, 1998), 200–201. Davis provides the words to all the songs of Rainey and Bessie Smith, a tremendous aid to scholars, but the interpretive section of her book is another matter.

33. Ibid., 203.

34. Robert Darnton, *The Great Cat Massacre* (New York, 1984), chap. 1.

35. Ralph Elllison, in *Collected Essays*, ed. John Callahan (New York, 1995).

Suggested Readings

Albertson, Charles. *Bessie*. New York, 1982.

Armstrong, Louis. *Satchmo*. New York, 1986.

Cohn, Lawrence, et al. *Nothing But the Blues*. New York, 1993.

Davis, Angela Y. *Blues Legacies and Black Feminism*. New York, 1998.

Floyd, Samuel A., Jr. *The Power of Black Music*. New York, 1995.

Handy, W. C. *Father of the Blues*. New York, 1969.

Lieb, Sandra. *Mother of the Blues*. Amherst, MA, 1981.

Malone, Bill C. *Country Music U.S.A.* Rev. ed. Austin, TX, 1985.

Morgan, Thomas L., and William Barlow. *From Cakewalks to Concert Halls*. Washington, DC, 1992.

Oliver, Paul. *The Story of the Blues*. Boston, 1997.
Oliver, Paul, et al. *The New Grove: Gospel Blues and Jazz*. New York, 1986.
Riis, Thomas L. *Just before Jazz*. Washington, DC, 1989.
Southern, Eileen. *The Music of Black Americans*. 3d. ed. New York, 1997.
Stewart-Baxter, Derrick. *Ma Rainey and the Classic Blues Singers*. New York, 1970.
Titon, Jeff Todd. *Early Downhome Blues*. Rev. ed. Chapel Hill, NC, 1994.

5

William Lewis Paul
Tlingit Advocate

Stephen Haycox

The history of Native Americans has been studied rather extensively from different angles, but much of the emphasis has been on those Indians in the lower forty-eight states. Alaska Natives have not always received the attention that they deserve. Professor Stephen Haycox corrects that oversight here.

William Lewis Paul was a Tlingit leader in Alaska in the first half of the twentieth century. While he was the first Native American attorney in Alaska and the first to serve in the territorial legislature, his organization of the Alaska Native Brotherhood is probably his greatest achievement. He fought for voting rights, and he forced integration of some urban schools in the territory. At the height of his power, he was disbarred, partly because of a campaign by his enemies and partly because of some of his questionable activities. Yet, he continued to work, and he was eventually reinstated by the bar in later life. His contribution to the well-being of Alaska Natives cannot be denied.

Stephen Haycox is a professor of history at the University of Alaska, Anchorage, where he has taught since earning his Ph.D. from the University of Oregon in 1970. He has published widely on Alaska history; his anthology of scholarly articles (edited with Professor Mary Mangusso of the University of Alaska, Fairbanks), *An Alaska Anthology: Interpreting the Past* (1996), has been reprinted several times. His new history of Alaska will be published next year.

Not many Americans have ever heard of the Sealaska Corporation. By the standards of the global conglomerates that generate today's economic news, the southeast Alaska economic development corporation is a small player. But by the economic conditions of many Native Americans today, Sealaska Corporation is big news. It is a profit-making business with more than 16,500 stockholders. Its combined total assets in the year 2000 were more than $355 million, not including its landholdings in Alaska's panhandle. From net earnings of more than $10 million, the corporation paid in excess of $8 million in dividends, including a special December "Christmas" bonus of $2.08 per share.[1]

Any corporate stockholder in America would welcome a Christmas bonus from one of the companies in his investment portfolio. But this distribution is of special interest, for all of Sealaska Corporation's shareholders are Tlingit and Haida Indians. In its mission statement, the corporation acknowledges that all its assets are derived "from the aboriginal assets of the Tlingit and Haida Indians, . . . preserved through the efforts of the Alaska Native Brotherhood and Alaska Native Sisterhood," and passage of the Alaska Native Claims Settlement Act of 1971 (ANCSA). The Alaska Native Brotherhood (ANB) is a Tlingit and Haida self-help and advocacy group founded in 1912. The man most responsible for molding the ANB into an effective organization was William Lewis Paul (1885–1977), who also did more than anyone else to commit the ANB to the pursuit of equal rights for Alaska Natives.

A Tlingit Indian, Paul was the first Native to become a member of the Alaska bar and the first to be elected to the territorial legislature. His leadership in advocacy of Alaska Native rights and his insistence on equity significantly advanced the cause of Native justice in Alaska and left a permanent legacy of Indian dignity and capability. Following in a strong tradition of Tlingit leadership, and aided significantly by his brother, Louis, William Paul passed on that legacy to able people who today direct the fortunes of Alaska's Tlingit and Haida Indians. He also helped to initiate a successful and novel land claim upon which rests today's Sealaska assets.

William Lewis Paul was born in 1885, the second son of Matilda "Tillie" (Tlingit name: Kah-ti-yudt) Kinnon, the adopted daughter of a high-caste Stikeen Indian (the Stikeen were and are a people living on the Stikine River, a major Canadian river that empties into the Pacific Ocean at the present-day Alaska city of Wrangell). Raised from age thirteen in Christian mission girls' homes, she learned Western ideas and manners and became well acculturated, and a star student and translator. In 1882, Tillie Kinnon married Louis Paul Pyreau, son of a French-Canadian fur trader and an Indian woman. Louis also was a Christian and mission-educated. When they were married, Louis dropped his surname. The couple's first son was born in Wrangell, and William was born in Tongass village on May 7, 1885. A third son, Louis Francis, was born in 1887, just three days after Tillie received word that her husband had been lost on a canoe trip while traveling to establish a new mission station.[2]

The family moved to the Presbyterian Sitka Indian Industrial Training School, where Tillie Paul raised her three sons in the most acculturating environment in Alaska. As historian Donald Mitchell has written, the boys "were taught to speak, dress and think white," a program their mother wholly supported.[3] Living their childhood years at the Sitka school, they fully adopted Western modes of thought; they grew up internalizing integration into white society as an ideal. Their aspiration was to move into American middle-class life as equal participants in its civic and economic opportunity.

As the boys came of age, each in turn attended Richard Pratt's Carlisle Indian School in Pennsylvania for acculturating secondary education for Native Americans. Pratt emphasized two precepts at his "civilizing academy": the elimination of contact with aboriginal culture in any form, and the conviction that Indians are equal human beings and equal U.S. citizens, an idea the Pauls embraced. All three left Carlisle fully persuaded that the Fourteenth Amendment guarantee of equality before the law applied as much to them as to any other Americans. When eventually they returned to Alaska, both William and Louis built this notion into a political program directed at perfecting Native rights.[4]

William graduated from Carlisle in 1902 at age seventeen. Later, at Whitworth College in Tacoma, Washington, he thrived, excelling in his studies and playing on the football, basketball, and baseball teams. He was an editor on the school paper, acted in the senior class play, and helped start a literary society and the debating team. He earned money as a bookkeeper for the college. Completing his studies in 1911, he married Frances Lackey, his college sweetheart. The couple lived in Portland, Oregon, and San Francisco where William worked as a bank clerk, insurance company cashier, and insurance agent. Paul earned a law degree by correspondence from La Salle University during this time. A singer of unusual talent, he sang in the foremost church quartets and choruses in Portland. The couple had four children, three boys and a girl.

In 1920, William and his family returned to Alaska, hoping to make their fortune in the lucrative salmon fishery industry. But corporate salmon packers had depleted the resource using elaborate, efficient fish traps, and soon the Pauls found themselves marooned with no money and few prospects. William exercised one of these few prospects and changed his life forever. In October 1920 he passed the bar exam qualifying him to practice law in Alaska. Highly intelligent, ambitious, richly talented, and committed to a vision of Native equality, William Paul became at age thirty-five the first Native attorney in Alaska's history.

The circumstances of the exam were indicative of Alaska in the 1920s. Written by three attorneys appointed by the district judge, who would query the candidate orally, William's exam took three days. He answered 231 questions, 210 correctly. During a break, as one of the examining attorneys passed through the lobby of the hotel where the test was being administered, a bystander called out, "How are you coming failing that Indian?" "No go," the attorney replied. "The damn son of a bitch knows more law than the judge."[5]

William Paul soon had an opportunity, afforded by his brother Louis, to test his vision of Native equality. Louis had joined the army soon after his graduation from Carlisle. When he was released after the armistice, his experience was similar to that of many Indian soldiers. Having served in integrated units during his tour of duty, back home he encountered the prejudice and discrimination routinely visited on minorities in America. The Native brotherhood, Louis thought, offered him the best avenue for fighting such prejudice. He would do so by working to implement the Carlisle principle of Indian citizenship under the Fourteenth Amendment.

To do so meant changing the ANB. Founded at Juneau in 1912, the organization, and its companion auxiliary, the Alaska Native Sisterhood (ANS), pursued a policy of acculturation, working closely with the mission leadership in the territory and with the U.S. Bureau of Education, which operated Native schools in lieu of the Bureau of Indian Affairs (BIA). Initially, membership in the ANB and ANS was limited to Indians who spoke English, signed a sobriety pledge, and agreed to the suppression of traditional ritual. An annual delegate convention elected officers. The bodies' constitutions emphasized members' responsibilities in modeling acculturated behavior, including Christian stewardship. Citizenship was the ultimate badge of acculturation.

Throughout the territorial period the status of Natives in Alaska was ambiguous. There were no treaties with Alaska Natives, and thus no reservations and no formally recognized tribes, generating confusion on the question of Native citizenship. In 1915 the territorial legislature passed a Native citizenship act requiring applicants to solicit affidavits from white citizens verifying their suitability, leaving the final determination to a federal judge. The ANB supported the bill. Soon after joining the ANB, Louis Paul condemned the act in an address to the 1919 convention. Indians already had all rights of citizens, he said, but aside from proclaiming that position, neither he nor the ANB had a program for acting on it. For that, they would need William.

William joined the ANB soon after passing his bar exam, and the two brothers excited the organization's 1920 convention in Wrangell with their idea of Indian equality. The convention elected Louis grand president and William grand secretary; William was also named the ANB's attorney. To signify and clarify their revolution, the Pauls called upon the convention to adopt an official statement articulating ANB principles and policies. Called the "Platform of the Alaska Native Brotherhood, 1920–21," the opening paragraph declared "that all men are created free and equal." The statement that followed articulated the ANB's new understanding of the meaning of that phrase. "We affirm that all people within the United States should be equal before the law and that it is not only un-American in principle to make laws which create within its confines a favored race, but we also affirm that such laws are in the end injurious to the favored peoples."[6]

In other words, Indian equality was unqualified. The Paul brothers neither expected nor desired any special status for themselves and their people. Although both the ANB and national Indian policy changed positions on this issue in the 1930s, this was the thrust of national thinking on Indians in the 1920s. In 1924, Congress passed the Indian Citizenship Act, making citizens of all Native Americans who were not citizens already. As late as 1931, Secretary of the Interior Lyman Wilbur wrote that his department had "a definite plan for the Indian Service, that it shall work itself out of a job." Guardianship—viewing Indians as wards of the government in need of paternalistic supervision—was a discredited policy. The ANB convention summarized its position on citizenship and other issues with a multipoint proclamation written by William, which became his battle cry:

1) Equality of all Natives before the law;
2) Equal rights and privileges as citizens;
3) Equal schools as other citizens, and NO SEGREGATION;
4) Abolition of fish traps;
5) A Convention to meet in Douglas consisting of all the Natives of Southeastern Alaska so that by association there may be a better understanding among our people and a more rapid change from the ties of harmful customs to the practices of a better civilization;
6) The use of but one language, namely, the American language;
7) We believe in ONE LANGUAGE, ONE COUNTRY, and ONE FLAG.

With this program, the Pauls and the ANB intended to integrate Alaska Natives fully into modern white society. It was a bold, courageous initiative, and over the next ten years William worked assiduously to implement it.

The brothers went to work immediately. In 1921, William traveled to Washington, DC, as a representative of the ANB, to testify before a House subcommittee against the use of fish traps in Alaskan waters. The traps had effectively destroyed traditional fisheries on which Indian families depended both for subsistence and for cash income. William's appearance was the first time that an Alaska Native testified directly to a congressional committee.[7]

In the meantime, William and Louis set out to take the ANB message on Indian equality to the eighteen Tlingit and Haida villages and, in the process, to build up the organization. William devised a clever and insightful method. Few of the villages had community centers, so as new camps were established, he urged village ANB members to undertake building campaigns for an ANB hall. Most did, and in most villages it was the largest building. Many included a basketball court and a rehearsal room for a community brass band, along with meeting rooms and a kitchen. Most important, the halls were open for community use. The buildings were symbolic as well as practical, for they brought together people formerly divided by clan competition. Indian equality, not clan precedence, became the mode for expressing Tlingit identity, and the ANB became the primary instrument. At the annual conventions, both the basketball and band competitions between villages became legendary. By 1922 the ANB was a powerful, visible, and effective force in southeast Alaska and, by default, for all Alaska Natives.[8]

Such visibility did much to proclaim Native capability and dignity. But William Paul thought that the body could do more. In 1922 he decided to take the ANB directly into territorial politics. During the election campaign that year, Paul traveled throughout the southeastern villages urging Indians to vote for candidates whom he recommended. For illiterate voters, Paul designed pieces of cardboard with spaces cut out corresponding to the appropriate boxes on the ballot. While the ethics of the technique were questionable, the legality was not. And it worked. Paul controlled enough votes in close races that he was able to determine the outcome. Overnight, William Paul became a major political force in Alaska.[9]

Predictably, Paul's new political power, and that of the ANB, greatly disturbed many white leaders in Alaska. In the racist America of the 1920s, an Indian powerful enough to effect public policy was unacceptable. Not surprisingly, Paul's enemies began to organize against him. But he was ready for the challenge and, in fact, was the first to throw down the gauntlet. In November 1922 he filed a lawsuit on behalf of an illiterate Indian whose attempt to vote had been rebuffed. Remarkably,

Paul won his case. The jury found that despite the Indian's illiteracy, the fact that he paid municipal taxes, purchased Liberty bonds, and contributed to the Red Cross indicated that he was "civilized."[10] William Paul was ecstatic, as much for the victory for Indian equality as for the practical implications of the case.

The practical implications were significant, for Paul had decided to run for the territorial legislature himself. First, he obtained authorization from the Grand Camp to start an ANB newspaper, the *Alaska Fisherman*, suggesting the common interest of virtually all residents of southeast Alaska. In the paper he argued such common issues as better enforcement of fisheries regulations, but mostly he advanced the ANB agenda and his own candidacy. In April 1924 he won the Republican Party's primary election and began to organize his fall campaign.[11]

Political and journalistic attacks against Paul began almost immediately, and their racist nature is arresting to read today. One opponent's newspaper ad stated that "a plan is on foot to extend to the Indians of Alaska all the privilege of whites, including the right to sit on juries, vote irrespective of mental qualifications, and so send their children to the white schools to mingle, regardless of physical condition, with white children."[12] Another cried hysterically: "Keep Alaska and Its Schools Free of Indian Control!" In fact, the white establishment had acted before Paul's filing. Alarmed lawmakers had tried to rush a voters' literacy act through the 1923 legislative session but failed. Wisely ignoring the racist attacks and baiting, Paul stood above the fray, focusing on issues of commonality. In November he won his election, becoming the first Native elected to the territorial legislature. He was reelected in 1926.[13]

Paul's decision to take the ANB into politics was not universally popular. His critics charged throughout his career that he turned the organization into a personal mouthpiece to advance his own career. Paul's manner and demeanor encouraged their discomfiture. While he could be charming and positive when presenting an argument, he was more inclined to be arrogant, stubborn, and defensive. He had little capacity to compromise or to admit error. With his enemies he was often abusive. Yet, by demonstrating that he could play power politics on the same field and by the same rules as the white political and editorial leadership in Alaska, Paul earned respect for himself, and for Natives generally. As an active, intelligent representative, this respect increased. He brought forward several measures to benefit Natives directly, including authorization of child-support payments for divorced and widowed Native women not receiving support from the federal government, and prohibition of the jailing of

William Lewis Paul, Tlingit advocate for Alaska Native rights, c.1970. *Courtesy of Frances Paul DeGermain*

indigents too poor to pay civil fines. He shepherded through the legislature bills to raise the fish trap tax, increase maintenance payments for schools, construct new schools at Yakutat and Douglas, authorize the construction of public libraries, empower cities to tax property owners for public construction, and give watchmen at fish traps and elsewhere a lien for their wages against damage assessments. All of these were Progressive measures, consistent with the reform politics of the period. The governor vetoed many of them.[14]

Paul also introduced legislation creating the Alaska flag, eight stars of gold in the shape of the Big Dipper and the North Star, on a field of rich dark blue. In 1927 the American Legion in Alaska conducted a contest for the flag design, won by an Eskimo orphan, Benny Benson. The Legion submitted the design to the legislature, and Paul wrote the resolution. Some of its language later became the words to the "Alaska Flag Song," the official state song.

Paul continued to publish and edit the *Alaska Fisherman* during his legislative career and to nurture the Brotherhood. He also represented large numbers of Native Americans in law cases, although many of his clients could not pay the fees he assessed them. Paul probably should have worked at building a law practice that would provide adequately for his family, but, as one of his sons related many years later, William was much more drawn to politics, building up the ANB, and the cause of Native equity. Then he made a colossal mistake, one that ended his political career and that severely curtailed his effectiveness as a Native leader. Running for reelection in 1928, well on his way to victory, on election eve his enemies released information that Paul had accepted money from several salmon canneries to lobby for a bill that would allow them to retain their fish traps. As enacted, the bill probably would not have changed the number or effectiveness of traps in Alaska. But for Paul, who had made his reputation partly as a fish trap opponent, to have anything at all to do with their perpetuation was a disaster. Although he acknowledged his role publicly and tried to explain its innocuous nature, such "splitting of hairs" by a lawyer and politician sounded like casuistry to his constituents, and Paul lost the election dramatically. Although he later ran again for public office, his elective career was finished.[15]

In a demonstration of respect, the 1928 ANB convention elected Paul its grand president. William Paul was a fighter, and he treated the office as a mandate more than an honor. Over the next several years he made several even more significant contributions to Alaska Natives. Tlingit lore taught that the Russians had never properly obtained title to Tlingit lands. If that were true, then Tlingit and Haida Indians must still own southeast Alaska. Former judge and territorial delegate James Wickersham took up the cause and in 1929 met with William Paul, who agreed that there was a case.[16]

The ANB convention in Haines that year is perhaps the most famous in ANB history, for the delegates authorized Wickersham to pursue a Tlingit-Haida land claim. The theory behind the claim was that the Indians had aboriginal title to their lands—that is, they retained title to any land they had ever utilized or occupied, unless the United States had formally extinguished that title. That theory would have to be tested in American courts, provided that Congress would authorize a suit. Wickersham, elected delegate again in 1930, agreed to seek the authorization. Although he did not get it, his successor, Democrat Anthony Dimond, working with William Paul, did.

Indian policy underwent a fundamental change when the American electorate gave control of the government to the Democrats in 1932. New Deal Indian Commissioner John Collier persuaded Congress to pass the Indian Reorganization Act (IRA) in 1934, based on the principle of Indian self-determination. Ultimately, self-determination had the potential to provide American Indians with the access and opportunity they had been denied throughout the nation's history. But, during the New Deal, the implementation of the act was highly paternalistic, with the government reaffirming the wardship of most Native Americans even as it sought to provide for their emancipation.[17]

In Alaska, Native services were transferred to the BIA. The ANB resisted BIA paternalism but found it necessary to work with the agency and the Interior Department on several items of vast importance to the territory's Natives. Alaska was excluded from the IRA because of the absence of recognized tribes, but in 1935 Commissioner Collier called on William Paul, because of his experience, to come to Washington to work with Congress on both a land claims act and amendments for extending the IRA. Working together, Delegate Dimond and Paul wrote both bills and pushed them through Congress—two monumental contributions to Alaska Natives. The first, the Tlingit-Haida Jurisdictional Act, authorized the Tlingit and Haida Indians to sue in the U.S. Court of Claims for all of the land in the Alaska panhandle, more than 17 million acres. An essential aspect of the act provided that should the Indians win the suit, compensation would be paid to a "central council" of the Indians, not to individuals or tribes. Although he had not originally favored this method of providing long-term stability and economy, Paul accepted the idea and helped to construct the act around it.[18]

Much more important was the fact that the suit would move forward on the theory of aboriginal title. In 1941, years before the Tlingit-Haida case was argued, the U.S. Supreme Court accepted the validity of aboriginal title. Many years later, in 1959, the Court of Claims would find for the Alaska Indians in the suit, a landmark decision. Years later still, in 1968, the government would pay compensation for the taking of the land by the United States to the Central Council of Tlingit and Haida Indian Tribes of Alaska. The Central Council became one of the most important Tlingit-Haida institutions, using investment of the compensatory award to provide important social and educational services and opportunities to the Tlingit and Haida people. Winning the suit on the basis of aboriginal title set a highly important precedent, for after statehood, other Alaska Natives used the same theory to claim their land. One of their tutors would be William Paul.

The IRA Alaska amendments, passed in 1936, benefited all the territory's Natives directly. The act committed the government to protecting Native land and helping initiate village governing councils. It also authorized the formation of Indian business corporations, which would be eligible for loans from a revolving credit fund. William Paul thought the ANB might be organized into a regional business corporation that could borrow and administer all the loan fund money available for Alaska. He hoped that such would be the case and that he would be appointed to run the new corporation.[19]

In historical analysis, it is clear that this appointment never could have happened, for Paul had alienated too many people. He had developed over his years of service to the ANB and to his Indian clients a reputation for rapacity and mendacity. That reputation would shortly destroy much of the remainder of William's credibility. Before returning from Washington, Paul signed on as auxiliary counsel to a Senate subcommittee traveling to Alaska to hold hearings on Indian conditions. Paul was able to steer the questioning along lines that helped his people. For example, when U.S. Forest Service personnel reported on the work of the Civilian Conservation Corps, which they administered, Paul arranged for Indians who had been victimized to testify that the camps were not integrated as the law provided they should be; Indians were denied inclusion in the program. He was able to reveal other instances of discrimination and prejudice as well, but as the subcommittee was taking testimony in Ketchikan, Paul was served with a subpoena from the district court; he had been charged with unethical acts as an attorney.

The charges were serious. In addition to selling land that he knew he did not own, collecting wages owed to someone else, and pocketing fees for work not done, the court charged that Paul had kept a $3,000 settlement owed by a cannery to Indian fishermen. There are a number of troubling aspects to these charges against Paul. First, they were brought just as he was positioning himself for a powerful responsibility—director of the IRA loan fund for Alaska. It is not clear that the position would have been created, but Paul hoped that it would, and he had the ear of a number of important senators who might have been able to make it happen. Paul had been impecunious for some time, and, in the most careful reconstruction of his career to date, historian Don Mitchell cited numerous documented instances of Paul's demands for funds and his willingness to change political positions and break political promises for money. A number of leaders in Alaska simply did not consider Paul trustworthy. In addition, a number of Paul's Indian enemies in the ANB joined in the complaint against him. On the other hand, the assistant U.S. attorney in Juneau, George Folta, who filed the petition for Paul's disbarment, was clearly prejudiced against him. He considered Paul, he said, "a worthless Indian."[20]

The charges were investigated on the basis of the evidence, not Folta's prejudice, and the decision was rendered by a special committee of three lawyers that was reviewed by the federal judge. Paul did not defend himself. In July 1937 the judge signed an order for William Paul's disbarment. While waiting for the charges to be reviewed, Paul secured a job with the BIA helping to implement the IRA. The disbarment was not sufficient grounds for Paul to be fired as far as the BIA was concerned. Soon afterward he was accused of soliciting a bribe; when the evidence was presented to the government, Paul lost his job. The man who had lifted the ANB from a subservient role as handmaiden to the Presbyterian mission and the government education bureau in Alaska to a level of unanticipated, even unimagined power, and who had been extraordinarily effective in pursuing and advancing Native equity and rights, was humiliated before all who knew him. Within the ANB an anti-Paul faction coalesced around Cyril Zuboff, his longtime opponent, who was elected grand president. The first open rift in ANB history divided the organization. In 1937 the Pauls and those loyal to them boycotted the ANB convention.

Whatever else he was, William Paul was no quitter. A major challenge before the Tlingit and Haida people after passage of the Tlingit-Haida Jurisdictional Act was the establishment of the Central Council mandated by the act and the naming of attorneys for the claim. By 1937, Paul's two oldest sons, William, Jr., and Fred, were in law school at the University of Washington. Their father decided to continue the fight through them.

First, the Pauls succeeded in taking over the 1939 convention in Sitka; Louis was elected grand president and William Paul Jr., grand secretary. Then they secured the delegates' approval that the ANB would be designated the Central Council, whose executive committee would be authorized to hire the claims attorneys and file the suit. This move was too much for Paul's opponents and enemies, who protested to the BIA. Nor did the government approve the Pauls taking over the land suit. The Interior Department insisted that a "land claims convention" of delegates elected from all Tlingit and Haida villages, regardless of ANB affiliation, gather to constitute formally the Central Council and select the attorneys. The convention was held in Wrangell in April 1941, and while the delegates did create the Central Council, they also hired Paul's sons as the attorneys, but with the stipulation that they work as co-counsel to an experienced Indian claims attorney.[21]

In an important sense this was William Paul's "last hurrah." He tried to orchestrate who the experienced attorney would be, a man he had befriended on his trips to Washington. Both he and several subsequent prospects declined, and eventually the Interior Department selected the attorney. William Paul soon moved to Seattle where he qualified for the bar and practiced law. Although he continued to follow Alaska Native affairs and file lawsuits, his direct influence in the territory essentially was eclipsed.

The U.S. Congress approved Alaska statehood in the summer of 1958, and in that same year, Fred Paul petitioned the Alaska bar to reinstate his father. William Paul was seventy-three. Although unsuccessful in his first attempt, in January, after statehood became official, the bar accepted the petition.[22] At least one member of the certifying board admitted that the move was essentially symbolic, Paul being too old to be effective, but William Paul was not finished. He soon became a regular lecturer on Native land claims theory. Native students from all over the region heard Paul, and when officials of the new state of Alaska began to seek title to lands provided in the statehood bill, some of them protested on the basis of aboriginal title. After the discovery of oil in 1968 at Prudhoe Bay made a settlement of Native land claims necessary for economic development, aboriginal title became the basis of Congress's bill on the matter, the Alaska Native Claims Settlement Act (ANCSA). In that act, Congress conveyed title to 44 million acres of land to the state's Natives and paid $962.5 million in compensation for extinguishment of aboriginal title to the remaining 331 million of Alaska's acres. Native leaders participated fully in the drafting of the claims settlement act; in fact, it was their act. Much of their faith in the validity of the theory of aboriginal title rested on the lessons they had learned from William Paul and the success of the Tlingit-Haida land suit.[23] The Tlingit and Haida share of the ANCSA compensation award became the original capitalization for Sealaska Corporation, the economic engine of Tlingit and Haida Indians today.

William Paul was alive to witness the passage of the claims settlement act, which he considered a theft of Alaska Native land. He continued to advise Native leaders during its implementation, as always generating both gratitude and opposition at each turn. He was still active when he died of a heart attack in Seattle on March 4, 1977, at age ninety-one.

William Paul's legacy to Alaska and its Natives is great. His aggressive and effective pursuit of Native equality, even though his theory of how to achieve it was abandoned in the 1930s, provided a compelling model for Native self-responsibility and forced white Alaskans to concede Native capability. His molding of the Alaska Native Brotherhood into a powerful, effective service and political organization gave focus to directed Native action and gave the government a legitimate body with which to interact. His historic firsts—as Native attorney, as Native legislator, as Native publisher and editor—were important milestones in the development of Alaska. The linkage to the Native past, which he represented in the formation of the modern claims settlement, provided context and continuity for its leaders. Yet for Alaska Natives today, William Paul is only a shadowy name of uncertain meaning, and for non-Native Alaskans, no meaning at all. This state of affairs is not only a function of the lack of interest that the study of history commands in modern culture, but it is also the result of Paul's own divided character. It is more likely that historians in the future will focus on Paul's constructive acts on behalf of Native equity. His contribution to that cause was substantive and permanent.

Notes

1. Website http:\\www.sealaska.com, November 20, 2000.
2. Mary Lee Davis, *We Are Alaskans* (Boston, 1931), 223–81; Frederick Paul, "Then Fight for It," unpub. ms. in author's possession, 19–43; Donald Craig Mitchell, *Sold American: The Story of Alaska Natives and Their Land, 1867–1959* (Hanover, NH,

1997), 198–207 and passim. Mitchell's is the most useful reconstruction of the career of William L. Paul. "Autobiography of William Paul," William Paul Papers, University of Washington Library, is Paul's own account and contains many misstatements of fact.

3. Mitchell, *Sold American,* 201.

4. Francis Paul Prucha, *The Great Father: The United States Government and the American Indian,* 2 vols. (Lincoln, NE, 1984), 2:555 ff.

5. Frances Lackey Paul, "Mother's Memoirs," unpub. ms., University of Alaska Anchorage Archive, 47.

6. Curry-Weissbrodt Papers, Box C3A, file ANB, Sealaska Heritage Foundation, Juneau, Alaska.

7. *Fisheries in Alaska: Hearing on H.R. 2394 before the Subcommittee on Fisheries and Fish Hatcheries of the House Committee on Merchant Marine and Fisheries,* 67th Cong., 2d sess., 1922, pt. 2, Statement of William L. Paul.

8. William Paul to Louis Paul, July 14, 1921, file ANB, William Paul Papers. Some of the reconstruction of Paul's career here is based on the author's numerous interviews with Fred Paul, before his death in 1994, and with Frances Lackey Paul, in Seattle, Washington, and Victoria, British Columbia, 1990–1996.

9. George Folta, "The History of the Exploitation of the Indians of Alaska Is Largely a History of the Pauls," Ernest Gruening Papers, University of Alaska Fairbanks Archives; Stephen Haycox, "William Paul, Sr., and the Alaska Voters' Literacy Act of 1925," *Alaska History* 3 (Fall 1986): 17–37.

10. *United States v. Charley Jones,* District Court for the Territory of Alaska, First Division, Nos. 792 and 793.

11. *Alaska Fisherman,* January, February, 1924; "Official Count: Returns of Republican Primaries by Clerk of Court," *Alaska Fisherman,* June 1924.

12. "Attention Republicans," *Daily Alaska Empire,* May 27, 1924; "The White Man's Way Must Prevail," *Daily Alaska Empire,* May 17, 1924.

13. Official Returns of the Election of Delegate from Alaska, Attorney General, Members of the 7th Territorial Legislature and Road Commissioner, Preferential Vote for Governor Held November 4, 1924, Territory of Alaska, First Division, Alaska State Archives; Official Returns Compiled by Canvassing Board of the Election Held November 2, 1926, for Delegate to Congress and Senator and Representatives in the Eighth Territorial Legislature, Alaska State Archives.

14. *Journal of the Alaska Territorial Legislature, 1925, 1927.*

15. "Paul Betrays Indian Followers," *Daily Alaska Empire,* November 3, 1928.

16. Mitchell, *Sold American,* 230–32. Mitchell stresses that Paul took credit for persuading the ANB of the merits of the land claim over a four-year period prior to 1929, but the plan was Wickersham's. Mitchell also discredits a story that Fred Paul made the cornerstone of his own manuscript, viz., that Peter Simpson, ANB founder and patriarch, had taken aside William Paul in 1925 to tell him to fight for the land if he believed that it belonged to the Tlingit and Haida people.

17. Prucha, *Great Father,* 2:940–68; Kenneth Philp, "The New Deal and Alaska Natives, 1936–45," *Pacific Historical Review* 50 (1981): 309–27.

18. Mitchell, *Sold American,* 261, 268–71; 231–32.

19. William Paul to Louis Paul, September 12, 1936, file IRA, William Paul Papers.

20. *United States ex rel. G. W. Folta v. William L. Paul*, U.S. District Court for the District of Alaska, Division Number One, at Juneau, No. 3918 A, Amended Information, October 16, 1936; Memorandum of Findings and Judgment, July 31, 1937; Folta, "History of the Exploitation of the Indians"; see Mitchell, *Sold American*, 246–49.

21. File Land Claims Convention, Curry-Weissbrodt Papers.

22. Minutes of Meeting of Board of Governors of the Alaska Bar Association, May 28, 1958, January 22, 1959, Alaska Bar Association, Anchorage, Alaska.

23. Charles Edwardsen Jr., to William Paul, January 5, 1966, North Slope Claim File, Alaska State Historical Library, Juneau, Alaska.

Suggested Readings

Arnold, Robert. *Alaska Native Land Claims*. Anchorage, 1978.

Champagne, Duane. *The Native North American Almanac*. Detroit, 1994.

Coates, Peter. *The Trans-Alaska Pipeline Controversy: Technology, Conservation, and the Frontier*. Bethlehem, PA, 1991.

Cohen, Lucy Kramer, ed. *The Legal Conscience: Selected Papers of Felix S. Cohen*. New Haven, CT, 1960, 273–304.

Drucker, Phillip. "The Native Brotherhoods: Modern Intertribal Organizations on the Pacific Coast." *Bureau of American Ethnology Bulletin, No. 168*. Washington, DC, 1958.

Mitchell, Donald Craig. *Sold American: The Story of Alaska Natives and Their Land, 1867–1959*. Hanover, NH, 1997.

Murray, Peter. *The Devil and Mr. Duncan*. Victoria, BC, 1985.

Philp, Kenneth. *John Collier's Crusade for Indian Reform*. Tucson, AZ, 1977.

Prucha, Francis Paul. *The Great Father: The United States Government and the American Indian*. 2 vols. Lincoln, NE, 1984.

6

Marshall Keeble
An African-American
Evangelist Faces Prejudice

David E. Walker

David E. Walker, professor of communication studies at Middle Tennessee State University since 1965, has developed a specialty of researching various religious topics, especially those dealing with the Restoration Movement, which he describes here. Walker introduces us to an unknown— at least to most people—African-American minister who made a difference in the early years of the twentieth century.

Marshall Keeble is unusual in that he was a leader in the Church of Christ, a Protestant church of significant influence, especially in the South. He follows a familiar pattern of African Americans who fought against the role forced upon them in post-Civil War society—a role that became more rigid, more segregated, and more violent in the early years of the twentieth century. Keeble practiced his faith in the face of discrimination that would have stopped lesser men. At the same time, he was able to gain the confidence of many of the white leaders of the Church of Christ. Although Keeble was sometimes called an "Uncle Tom," Professor Walker depicts a complex man whose success in preaching and converting people, both black and white, was remarkable.

Professor Walker received his undergraduate education at David Lipscomb University, and his Ph.D. at the University of Florida in 1969. He has edited communication journals and has written numerous historical articles for *Encyclopedia USA*.

Marshall Keeble was born in a log cabin in Rutherford County, Tennessee, on December 7, 1878. His parents, Robert and Mittie Keeble, sharecropped to make a living. Robert had been the slave of John Bell Keeble, the dean of Vanderbilt University Law School. Marshall was named for his grandfather, a slave and valet of Confederate Major Horace Pinkney.

When Marshall was four years old, Robert and Mittie moved to Nashville, where Robert worked for thirty years at "odd jobs, mostly yard and janitorial work."[1] Marshall attended the BellView and Noles schools. As a youth, he held jobs in a bucket factory and a soap factory. When he was nineteen, he married Minnie, the daughter of S. W. Womack, who was a graduate of Fisk University. Keeble credited Minnie with helping him further his education. The couple had five children, two of whom died in infancy; another, at the age of ten, died from contact with an exposed high-voltage wire. The other two, Beatrice Elnora and Robert, survived until 1935 and 1964.[2]

In Nashville, the preachers for the Jackson Street Church of Christ, of which Keeble was a member, were S. W. Womack and Alexander Campbell.[3] The church encouraged beginning preachers with a training class. Both Womack and Campbell rode circuit and sometimes took Keeble with them. He was impressed with their knowledge of the Bible.[4] He was also influenced by Booker T. Washington, whom Keeble had heard deliver messages to overflow crowds at the Sam Jones Tabernacle (later the Ryman Auditorium and home of the Grand Ole Opry) in Nashville.[5]

Keeble preached his first sermon at the age of eighteen and entered the ministry in 1897. His mother-in-law was not impressed with Keeble's early efforts. She declared that he was "not preaching material and if he's not, there is no use for him to waste his time or the people's time. A preacher has to be a preacher; Marshall's not a preacher."[6] She would later admit that she was wrong.

To support his family, Keeble opened a grocery store and ran a produce wagon to sell fresh vegetables in the summer and coal and wood in the winter. He began preaching full time in 1914. Between 1915 and 1918 he delivered almost 1,200 sermons, traveled 23,000 miles, and baptized 457 persons. Attention was drawn to his work by wealthy and affluent whites. A. M. Burton, who founded Nashville's Life and Casualty Insurance Company, began to support Keebler's efforts after 1920.[7]

During the 1920s and 1930s, Keeble's influence grew as a result of his revivals, which drew large crowds. In 1924 he conducted the first revival ever held by an African-American member of the Church of Christ, in Oakland, California. In 1926 he preached in six states, conducted twenty-one revivals, and converted 163 people. During 1927 he converted 295; by October 1928 conversions numbered 343. In 1931 he was responsible for the conversions of 1,071 African Americans and an unknown number of whites; he took part in fourteen revivals and founded six churches.[8] He would stage revivals in Florida when the weather turned cold.

On December 11, 1932, his wife Minnie died at the age of fifty-three. The eulogy was delivered by S. H. Hall, a prominent white minister in the Church of Christ in Nashville and Atlanta, in Keeble's home. Two years later, he married Laura Johnson of Corinth, Mississippi, in a service performed by B. C. Goodpasture,[9] the future editor of the *Gospel Advocate*, the most influential religious publication among white members of the Churches of Christ at that time, and a strong ally of Keeble's.

In 1942, Keeble was named president of the Nashville Christian Institute. It had opened as a night school for adults in 1942 but became, during the first year of his administration, a fully accredited elementary and high school. Keeble was able to persuade well-known white leaders to give talks at the institute. White lecturers at David Lipscomb College were invited to speak at the Institute while they were nearby. Keeble also began to lecture at white colleges. Although he was criticized by some African-American leaders for his lack of education, he was able to use his influence effectively at these schools. (Keeble would resign as president of the institute in 1958 and become president emeritus.[10])

In the 1940s a new religious journal was announced by the *Gospel Advocate*, the *Christian Counsellor*, with Marshall Keeble as editor. In 1928 he had been an associate editor and staff writer for G. P. Bowser's *Christian Echo*, the most influential religious newspaper among African-American members of the Church of Christ. The *Christian Counsellor* died from a lack of interest, but an occasional feature of the past, the "colored page," was revived by the *Gospel Advocate* in 1950. In one issue, Keeble urged "every preacher of the colored brotherhood" to write short articles and to send in reports. It would "mean much toward the salvation of the colored people of America and the whole world, because this paper goes to almost every country of the world . . . Let us show Brother Goodpasture and the Gospel Advocate Company our appreciation for this great favor by working as never before to put the *Gospel Advocate* in every colored home possible."[11]

Keeble continued to be active in later life. His ministry to the Tennessee State Prison lasted for thirty years. On one occasion five whites and five African Americans were converted, as well as a man on death row whose cell was next door to the electric chair.[12] At the age of seventy-seven, he still delivered 365 sermons each year. By that time, he had preached for fifty-eight years and had participated in thirty religious debates. His baptisms were estimated to total more than 25,000. A book of sermons with a biography of Keeble, transcribed by Goodpasture around 1930, still sold 1,500 copies per year.[13]

Keeble spoke at Michigan Christian College in Rochester during the week of April 14, 1968. On his way back to Nashville, he stopped in Ohio, where he delivered his last sermon on April 17. Three days later, he died. His funeral was held at the Madison, Tennessee, Church of Christ, the largest sanctuary owned by the members of the Churches of Christ at that time. The eulogy was delivered by Goodpasture to more than 3,000 people.[14]

~

Keeble had once commented, "You're going to have to suffer for right. You can't talk this thing through. . . . You got to love your enemies." He recalled, "I have suffered greatly for Christ: was . . . shot at with a pistol."[15] One time, when he was preaching in Ridgeley, Tennessee, a young white man took the end seat on the last row. When Keeble concluded his sermon and extended the invitation for people to accept Christ, the young man came forward and hit him with a pair of brass knuckles, cutting open his forehead. The police wanted Keeble to press charges, but he refused.[16]

He had several encounters with the Ku Klux Klan, the first about 1920 in Jacksonville, Florida: "They walked through our meeting wearing those high hats. They told me I had to leave and I told them I certainly would—just as soon as I finished preaching God's word. I stayed all week." At a later service, Keeble recognized one of the Klansmen by his eyeglasses: "He was sitting in the group praying with us. He told me I was to let him know if I had any more trouble."[17] On another occasion when Keeble was preaching in Milledgeville, Georgia, four members of the Klan came in and took the front seats. After the sermon, one of the four was baptized. Keeble commented, "I was not excited, at least, he didn't know I was."[18]

In February 1926 in Summit, Georgia, large numbers of whites as well as African Americans, as was typical of Keeble's audiences, attended a revival. The Klan declared that no whites would hear Keeble's sermons. Klansmen rushed into the school building where the revival was being held and stormed out to confer among themselves. The leader gave Keeble a note that he ordered him to read: "The Ku Klux Klan stands for white supremacy. Be governed accordingly." In using "white psychology," Keeble replied, "I have always known the white man is superior. They brought us from Africa and have lifted us up." He then addressed the audience, "Now you treat these white folks right and they'll treat you right." One of the converts during that revival was the cook for the Klan's leader, a doctor, who had handed Keeble the note. When Keeble encountered the doctor the next year, he was met with a hearty welcome.

Suffering came often to Keeble. At some of his meetings, the tents in which he preached were pulled down. Once, when he was walking back to a boardinghouse where he was staying during a revival, some young men blocked the sidewalk, drew a pistol, and fired some shots. Hearing them whistle by his head, he walked on and said pleasantly, "Good evening, gentlemen." On another occasion, in Atlanta, about "forty rough looking men with overalls on and no respect showed up when the meeting started." Keeble's preaching was so good that "those fellows came back the next night all dressed up with their collars buttoned and their neck ties on. You wouldn't have known them, and they came back every night." But during that same meeting, anonymous threats were received by the chief of police that Keeble would be killed and Clyde Hale, the white minister who was assisting him, whipped.[19]

Hardship never kept Keeble from his duty. When he received a request from Center Star, a small community in Hickman County, Tennessee, he rode the train to Centerville and then walked the remaining twelve miles. After the revival, he slung his payment for the meeting— usually rabbits, a hen, or a jug of molasses—over his shoulder and walked twelve miles back in the dark to catch a late train.[20] Nor did racial discrimination, which he faced throughout most of his life, faze him. For example, in 1945 the white church in Natchez, Mississippi, sponsored Keeble in a revival. When the local white minister took Keeble's photograph to the newspaper to run an advertisement, the newspaper refused to print it—it did not carry pictures of African Americans. Keeble and some young students subsequently walked all over Natchez distributing handbills to African-American homes.[21]

~

Those who have studied Marshall Keeble's sermons have found four basic characteristics in his speaking abilities. The first dealt with his credibility as a speaker. When Keeble was in town, the church was filled with people who appreciated his sincerity and wit. His sermons were "direct and frank; they were clothed in earnestness. The depth of his sincerity was impressive to those who heard him." Honesty and gentleness were fundamental to Keeble's character, and the quality of gentleness gave "calmness to his magnanimity." Added to these characteristics, as Arthur Lee Smith points out, was a strong sense of justice. Keeble said, "I don't know how to use deceit. I have grown on facts. No man with any sense will deny a stubborn fact." In delivering a sermon, he was at ease in the pulpit. He admitted that he never practiced and decided on his topic at the last moment. His delivery was "intense without being violent," and his debate style was "firm but never rude." Keeble used humor effectively to get his point across. He once explained that humor "kept my enemies from bothering me. I have carried along a lot of humor just to flavor my message. . . . People are so easy to teach if you know how."[22]

The second characteristic of his sermons was that he spoke from authority—in his case, the authority of the Bible. To him, "the Bible is right"; it was the basis for his life, and he believed that it should be the same for others as well. Indeed, he rarely quoted secular sources. The third technique was to relate his sermons to everyday happenings by using parables. When Keeble was asked by Smith to name his greatest asset as a speaker, he replied that it was "knowing how to make parables, and always make my sermons simple." Booker T. Washington's example influenced Keeble's decision to present his message in a plain manner. "If I can't make a parable, I'm lost."[23]

The fourth characteristic concerned the balance of intellect with emotions. One might assume that highly charged stereotypical appeals were common with Keeble, but that was not the case. He rarely appealed to fear, although he believed that "if a man rejects the Bible, he's hell-bound." Overall, he "never like[d] to excite people into Jesus Christ."[24]

~

One of the most intriguing facets of Keeble's career is his stand on racial and social issues. Some critics attempted to label him as an "Uncle Tom" who accommodated his viewpoints to white leaders' needs for social control. This interpretation of Keeble's work is a cruel one. The period from 1920 to 1945, the focus of this book, was a harsh one for African Americans, especially in the South. Their economic situation was already difficult, but if they did not "know their place," they could lose all means of support. They were usually kept from voting. The hotels and restaurants of America were generally not open to them. Many stores readily accepted their money, but then humiliated them by not allowing them access to water fountains and restrooms. The Ku Klux Klan, a powerful organization throughout this time, terrorized them into submission. Even the African Americans who served their country in the military were subjected to segregation.

Nor were African Americans welcome as equals in the house of God. One of the leading white Church of Christ ministers of the early 1940s, Foy E. Wallace, objected to reports that had come to him of "white women, members of the church, becoming so animated over a certain colored preacher as to go up to him after a sermon and shake hands with him holding his hand in both of theirs." Wallace stated that such behavior would "turn the head of most white preachers, and sometimes affect their conduct, and anybody ought to know that it will make fools out of the Negroes." He was alarmed to hear that a young white editor had roomed with, and even slept in the same bed with, an African-American minister in not only a violation of the "Jim Crow law . . . [but also] a violation of Christianity itself, and of all common decency."

Wallace then declared that if he ever heard of Marshall Keeble "doing anything akin to such as this," he would "take back every good thing I have ever said of them. Keeble should teach Negro preachers better than that. . . . Their practices will degrade the Negroes themselves. It is abominable." He concluded by stating his support of "Negro meetings for the Negroes," but he was opposed to "Negro meetings for white people . . . and the general mixing that has become entirely too much of a practice in these Negro meetings." Another writer began by praising Keeble but showed his condescension toward African Americans when he argued that his preaching would result in "better farm hands, better porters, better cooks, better housemaids than ever before."[25] In this atmosphere the country was not ready for a Martin Luther King Jr.

Some writers describe Keeble as simply accommodating the white leaders, but the sources do not support this interpretation. Others see him as not being concerned about segregation, although they are not consistent on this point. For example, one critic argues that Keeble "never talks to the church about social problems rising out of racial differences. On integration he once remarked, 'I would rather get it slow than to get it wrong.' "[26] Moreover, "Keeble accepted the prejudices held against the Negro race. He never once in his life preached about the injustices suffered by his race." This critic adds that Keeble never objected to preaching to segregated audiences, nor did he ever preach a sermon on segregation. Ironically, the same critic uses Keeble's preaching on one occasion from what had been a slave auction block in Tuscumbia, Alabama, as an illustration of his lack of concern. At the same time, however, he cites excerpts from one of Keeble's sermons that used the text from Acts 10:15 in which God tells Peter that he should not call something common that he had cleansed. Keeble explained, "God doesn't want you to call a man unclean because he's black. God created him. Don't you call him common or unclean."[27]

Other authors, in discussing Keeble's beliefs about discrimination and segregation, take a more balanced view. One argues that Keeble "learned to accommodate himself to them, and to be ambitious and effective in spite of them." Furthermore, the topics on which Keeble preached did not include "social problems connected with race." One example shows one of his teaching techniques. In 1963 he made four speeches on behalf of Oklahoma Christian College, a school from which African Americans were excluded. As a result of his efforts, he raised $50,000 and thus forced a change of policy. College officials could not logically take money raised by Keeble and turn away African Americans.

The same author also holds that Keeble's work "helped lead to an imperceptible lessening of segregation and discrimination among Christians." To those who criticized Keeble for not speaking out against discrimination and segregation, he replied that "it is possible that if he had, he would not have been invited to speak to whites and to associate with them, and would not have had the opportunity to break down race barriers by being the courteous gentleman that he was." The author also alludes to the speech that Keeble gave at the 1950 Abilene Christian College lectures, noted later.[28]

Keeble's critics continued to hammer away at him. Paternalism, one of them argues, was the dominant relationship between African-American and white Churches of Christ for many years. He explains, "White benefactors supported preachers like Keeble who clearly knew their place, and white churches made sure that their black brothers and sisters had separate places to meet." On the other hand, the same writer says that African Americans such as G. P. Bowser who were militant in their efforts against racial discrimination found it difficult to survive financially.[29]

According to Douglas Foster, James Maxwell, the vice president of Southwestern Christian College, a predominantly African-American school, charged that Keeble's "accommodation to white racism was eventually respected by many black Christians." Foster further declares that Bowser was respected among African-American Churches of Christ. Bowser's publication, the *Christian Echo*, was described as a "place of expression for black frustration at the discrimination they suffered at the hands of their white sisters and brothers."[30]

One critic argues that Keeble angered some African Americans by "reserving racially segregated seating for white visitors."[31] Another states that Keeble was able to manage the racial prejudices of white preachers while Bowser could not.[32] Others suggested that Keeble's relation with white church leaders amounted to a kind of vassalage. Still others saw him as a means of social control: support Keeble so that he could keep African Americans in hand. Following a 1925 revival in Henderson, Tennessee, Keeble noted with irony that "the white people say the influence of the work is manifest . . . as disorder among the people of my race is of very rare occurrence."[33]

Keeble was more concerned with social problems than some historians have allowed. The key to his ideas may be found in his use of parables as a teaching device. Keeble studied the Bible carefully and was familiar with Jesus' liking for parables. In Matthew 13 the disciples ask Jesus why He speaks in parables. In reply, Jesus points out that those who do not agree with Him will see without seeing and hear without hearing. On the other hand, the disciples will understand—sometimes later in their lives, sometimes immediately. Jesus further explains that the ears of those who do not understand his parables are dull of hearing, and their eyes are closed.

Keeble spoke at Abilene Christian College on February 23, 1950, at a time when it did not admit African Americans. He had postponed a month-long engagement in Los Angeles to appear at the college. Keeble argued for further African-American education; without it, African-American preachers would be defeated by the "intellectual giants that strut up and down the country and challenge the Church of Christ. You are responsible for it. You can either prepare us or you can let them slaughter us. Take your choice. It's up to you. Or you can turn around and by silence and indifference help them to slaughter us. You can— you know how to do that."[34] When asked whether a "mixed" or integrated faculty would work, he replied: "Gentlemen, if it'll work in a sectarian school, it ought to work better in a school where everybody is a Christian." He concluded his address by calling on his audience "to look upon no race as being inferior."[35]

In the 1960s, Keeble took a definite stand against segregation. He favored integration in public places but did not believe that force should be used to bring it about. "Force is wrong. . . . We used to have more integration but we didn't know it had a name. We thought it was just being friendly."[36] The *Christian Chronicle* styled Keeble as the "dean of the Negro cause among our brethren. For years he has been quietly sowing the seeds that will eventually break down the barriers that cause mistrust among Negro and white." The article quoted the newspaper in Marshalltown, Iowa, where Keeble was conducting a revival. The paper stated that Keeble was "typical of those Negro moderates who understand and sympathize with the errors and sins of the whites."[37]

One writer misunderstood Keeble's opinion about African Americans shaking hands with whites or worshipping together. After the article was published, Keeble replied in an apparently submissive manner. In part of the letter he wrote, "I hope I can conduct myself in my last days so that you and none of my friends will have to take back nothing they have said complimentary about my work or regret it." The writer saw this "tortuously convoluted . . . sentence," as ambiguous. He went on to comment that Keeble's relationships with whites were often "profoundly ambiguous, because human motives are always ambiguous."[38]

As noted earlier, Keeble was greatly influenced by S. W. Womack, his father-in-law. As early as 1915, Womack was writing that something should be done to change the moral and religious attitudes of whites and African Americans toward each other: "Only a few of the whites have much or any confidence in the black man, and so many have none; and the blacks seem to stand that way toward the whites."[39]

Keeble's beliefs on discrimination and segregation may also be seen in his students. The *Christian Chronicle* argues that his training of young men at Nashville Christian Institute "involved a complex approach to the realities of racial discrimination in society and church." For example, between 1944 and 1947 young Fred Gray traveled with Keeble. Gray attended Alabama State College and then went to Case Western Reserve University to study law, since the University of Alabama's law school was segregated. Gray remained a minister but also became an important attorney in the civil rights movement. He represented, among others, Rosa Parks, Martin Luther King Jr., and the Southern Christian Leadership Conference. He appeared before the U.S. Supreme Court in 1956, at the age of twenty-five, to argue successfully that Montgomery's practice of segregated seating on its city buses was unconstitutional. As a result of his leadership, in 1974 the African-American Church of Christ and the white Church of Christ in Tuskegee, Alabama, merged.[40]

Keeble made a tremendous impact upon his society. During his preaching career, he was responsible for more than 40,000 conversions and the planting of more than 250 churches. At one time, 65 percent of African-American ministers of the Churches of Christ could trace their conversion to him. Furthermore, speaking in a time when civil rights issues became explosive, he preached in parables; African Americans generally understood them, and whites, upon reflection, were converted by them. He also influenced a number of young men who were instrumental in bringing about social change. In later life, he was characterized as the "best known member of the Church of Christ" and the only African-American preacher to participate in the Restoration Movement on a national basis.[41] Harding University conferred an honorary degree on him, and he was made an honorary chief of a Nigerian tribe. The *Christian Chronicle* named him the Person of the Decade for 1940–1950.[42] A religious conservative, he nevertheless argued, "The Supreme Court didn't take praying out of the public school, God did. God didn't want the Supreme Court messing it up."[43] In looking ahead to the end of his life, Marshall Keeble once said, "When my time is up the Lord will let me know. I've been ready. When I have to go; I'll go. But they're gonna' know I've been here!"[44]

Notes

1. J. E. Choate, *Roll Jordan Roll* (Nashville, TN, 1968), 16; Arthur Lee Smith Jr., "A Rhetorical Analysis of the Speaking of Marshall Keeble" (M.A. thesis, Pepperdine College, 1965), 21.

2. Linda T. Wynn, "Leaders of Afro-American Nashville." http:\\www.tnstate.edu/library/digital/mkeeble.pdf.

3. He should not be confused with the white Alexander Campbell who was a minister in the nineteenth century.

4. Smith, "Rhetorical Analysis," 23.

5. Choate, *Roll Jordan Roll*, 9.

6. Smith, "Rhetorical Analysis," 25.

7. Wynn, "Leaders."

8. Forrest N. Rhoads, "A Study of the Sources of Marshall Keeble's Effectiveness as a Preacher" (Ph.D. diss., Southern Illinois University, 1970), 114–15; "It's not Keeble, but the Bible is right," *Christian Leader* 45 (August 25, 1931): 6. http:\\www.mun.ca/rels/restmov/texts/race/haymes7.html.

9. Earl Irvin West, *The Search for the Ancient Order* (Indianapolis, IN, 1979), 3:237.

10. Smith, "Rhetorical Analysis," 27–31; Wynn, "Leaders."

11. Marshall Keeble, "Among the Colored Brethren," *Gospel Advocate* 92 (December 7, 1950): 793–94.

12. Choate, *Roll Jordan Roll*, xii.

13. Rhoads, "Study of the Sources," 128.

14. Willlie Cato, *His Hand and Heart* (Singapore, 1990), 8; "Leaders."

15. Rhoads, "Study of the Sources," 147.

16. Smith, "Rhetorical Analysis," 42–43.

17. George Barker, "Brother Keeble and the Lord," *Nashville Tennessean Magazine* (March 29, 1964): 6–7, 15.

18. Smith, "Rhetorical Analysis," 43.

19. Choate, *Roll Jordan Roll*, 55–68; 86.

20. Barker, "Brother Keeble," 15.

21. Choate, *Roll Jordan Roll*, 119.

22. Smith, "Rhetorical Analysis," 25, 26, 50, 53, 118; Choate, *Roll Jordan Roll*, 96, 98.

23. Smith, "Rhetorical Analysis," 25, 62, 65, 68, 156; Rhoads, "Study of the Sources," 153; Choate, *Roll Jordan Roll*, 97.

24. Smith, "Rhetorical Analysis," 74, 76, 156; Rhoads, "Study of the Sources," 153.

25. Foy E. Wallace, "Negro Meetings for white People," *Bible Banner* 7 (March 1941). http:\\www.mun.ca/rels/restmov/texts/race/haymes8.html. "It's not Keeble, but the Bible is Right," 6.

26. Choate, *Roll Jordan Roll*, 96.

27. Ibid., 106–7.

28. Rhoads, "Study of the Sources," 29, 92, 144, 151–52.

29. Douglas A. Foster, "An Angry Peace: Racial Attitudes in United States History," *ACU Today*, Spring 2000. http:\\www.acu.edu/acu-today/spring2000/cover02.html.

30. Douglas A. Foster, "An Angry Peace: Race and Christian Education," *ACU Today* (Spring 2000).

31. Wynn, "Leaders."

32. West, *Search for the Ancient Order*, 3:237.

33. Don Haymes, "Introduction to the Text: Brother Keeble: Notes Toward an Understanding." http:\\www.mun.ca/rels/restmov/texts/race/haymes6.html.

34. Marshall Keeble, "The Church among the Colored," February 23, 1950.

35. Ibid.

36. Barker, "Brother Keeble," 15.

37. Don Haymes, "Introduction to the Text: Negro Meetings for white People." http:\\www.mun.ca/rels/restmov/texts/race/haymes8.html.

38. "No Hate in His Path," *Christian Chronicle* 17 (March 29, 1960). http:\\www.mun.ca/rels/restmov/texts/race/haymes17.html.

39. S. W. Womack, "Attitude of the Races," *Gospel Advocate* 59 (December 30, 1915): 1326–27. http:\\www.mun.ca/rels/restmov/texts/race/haymes4.html.

40. Don Haymes, "Reading about Race Relations In and Out of the Churches." http:\\www.mun.ca/rels/restmov/texts/race/RRRMBIB.htm; "*Chronicle* Person of the Decade."

41. Choate, *Roll Jordan Roll*, ix. The Restoration Movement began in the nineteenth century. A number of religious leaders, dissatisfied with their religious environment, sought to reform existing churches. After this effort was unsuccessful, they began a movement to "restore" the first-century church.

42. "*Chronicle* Person of the Decade," *Christian Chronicle* 57 (May 2000). http:\\www.oc.edu/ccarchives/0005/p20_person.htm.

43. Barker, "Brother Keeble," 6.
44. Ibid., 15.

Suggested Readings

Cato, Willie. *His Hand and Heart.* Singapore, 1990.

Choate, J. E. *Roll Jordan Roll.* Nashville, TN, 1968.

"*Chronicle* Person of the Decade," *Christian Chronicle* 57 (May 2000). http:\\www.oc.edu/ccarchives/0005/p20_person.htm.

Foster, Douglas A. "An Angry Peace: Race and Christian Education." *ACU Today* (Spring 2000). http:\\www.acu.edu/acu-today/spring2000/cover02a.html.

_____. "An Angry Peace: Racial Attitudes in United States History." *ACU Today* (Spring 2000). http:\\www.acu.edu/acu-today/spring2000/cover02.html.

Haymes, Don. "Introduction to the Text: Negro Meetings for white People." http:\\www.mun.ca/rels/restmov/texts/race/haymes8.html.

_____. "Introduction to the Text: The 'Colored Page.' " http:\\www.mun.ca/rels/restmov/texts/race/haymes10.html.

_____. "Introduction to the Text: Brother Keeble: Notes Toward an Understanding." http:\\www.mun.ca/rels/restmov/texts/race/haymes6.html.

_____. "Reading about Race Relations In and Out of the Churches." http:\\www.mun.ca/rels/restmov/texts/race/RRRMBIB.htm.

"It's not Keeble, but the Bible is right." *Christian Leader* (August 25, 1931): 6. http:\\www.mun.ca/rels/restmov/texts/race/haymes7.html.

Keeble, Marshall. "Among the Colored Brethren." *Gospel Advocate* (December 7, 1950): 793–94.

_____. "The Church among the Colored." February 23, 1950. http:\\www.mun.ca/rels/restmov/texts/mkeeble/keeble1.html.

"No Hate in His Path." *Christian Chronicle* (March 29, 1960). http:\\www.mun.ca/rels/restmov/texts/race/haymes17.html.

Rhoads, Forrest N. "A Study of the Sources of Marshall Keeble's Effectiveness as a Preacher." Ph.D. dissertation, Southern Illinois University, 1970.

Smith, Arthur Lee, Jr. "A Rhetorical Analysis of the Speaking of Marshall Keeble." M.A. thesis, Pepperdine College, 1965.

Wallace, Foy E. "Negro Meetings for white People." *Bible Banner* 7 (March 1941). http:\\www.mun.ca/rels/restmov/texts/race/haymes8.html.

West, Earl Irvin. *The Search for the Ancient Order.* Indianapolis, IN, 1979.

Womack, S. W. "Attitude of the Races." *Gospel Advocate* (December 30, 1915): 1326–27. http:\\www.mun.ca/rels/restmov/texts/race/haymes4.html.

Wynn, Linda T. "Leaders of Afro-American Nashville." http:\\www.tnstate.edu/library/digital/mkeeble.pdf.

7

Elaine Goodale Eastman
Author and Indian Reformer

Theodore D. Sargent and Raymond Wilson

Elaine Goodale Eastman advocated assimilation of Native Americans into the larger American culture. Unlike many reformers, she had lived on reservations and even married an Indian, Dr. Charles Eastman, a physician who supported acculturation. Their relationship was a stormy one, but they worked together, with Elaine assisting her husband in writing his books. The marriage ended in 1921 after charges of adultery and the fathering of a child by Charles. During the 1930s, Elaine Eastman became an ardent opponent of the Native American programs pushed by John Collier, commissioner of Indian Affairs under Franklin D. Roosevelt. A strong woman, she maintained her advocacy until the end of her life at the age of ninety in 1953.

Theodore Sargent is a professor of biology at the University of Massachusetts, Amherst, who has long had an interest in Elaine Eastman. He received a Ph.D. at the University of Wisconsin in 1963 and has been on the faculty at UMass since that time. He is widely known for his papers on the behavioral adaptations of insects, and his book, *Legion of Night* (1976), on the underwing moths. To provide this account of Eastman, he has collaborated with historian Raymond Wilson, professor of history at Fort Hays State University in Hays, Kansas, where he was named the President's Distinguished Scholar in 1992. Professor Wilson, who received his Ph.D. from the University of New Mexico in 1977, has authored or co-authored several books, including *Ohiyesa, Charles Eastman, Santee Sioux* (1983), *Indian Lives: Essays on Nineteenth- and Twentieth-Century Native American Leaders* (1985), and *Kansas Land* (1993), and many articles and essays, most of which deal with Native American issues. He is currently writing a new Kansas history text for public schools and researching several other topics.

"Were we altogether wrong?" asked Elaine Goodale Eastman in a letter she wrote in 1934 to Matthew K. Sniffen, secretary of the Indian Rights Association, regarding their advocacy of assimilation policies for American Indians. For fifty years, both Eastman and Sniffen had been actively involved in Indian affairs. Now, however, she momentarily questioned "our steady demand for early assimilation" in reaction to Commissioner of Indian Affairs John Collier's Indian

Elaine Goodale in 1878 (from a steel engraving in *Apple-Blossoms*)

Elaine Goodale in 1890, just prior to her marriage (from the collection of James W. and Miriam M. Dayton). *Courtesy of Miriam M. Dayton*

Reorganization Act, which challenged many of the past federal policies of assimilation of Indian people into the dominant white society.[1] Such doubts flickered in Elaine's mind from time to time, but eventually she became an ardent critic of Collier's New Deal programs. She had devoted her life to Indian reform and believed that Indians should abandon many of their traditional ways and accept assimilation in order to survive. Her numerous publications on the subject attest to such beliefs. Yet, unlike most of the reformers of her day, she had actually lived among Indians and did not view their cultures with disdain, as did many of her colleagues. Indeed, she expressed regret, at times, over what she considered pristine aspects of Indian cultures that were being replaced by Native Americans adopting contaminated and immoral ways of white society. A study of this remarkable woman's life will reveal a story of noble ambitions, which led to some successes, but more often to disappointment and failure. Some of these results were probably inevitable, while others were largely self-imposed, but many were consequences of some of the oppressive social attitudes prevalent at the time, including prejudice against both Indians and women.

Elaine Goodale Eastman had always wanted to become a writer. Born on October 9, 1863, at her family home in the Berkshires called Sky Farm, located in Mt. Washington, Massachusetts, she was the first child of Henry Sterling Goodale and Deborah Hill Read. She was named Elaine after Tennyson's heroine.[2] Three other children, two girls and one boy, completed the family. Sky Farm's idyllic setting contributed to Elaine's love of nature and her early education. Both parents were widely read and were published authors. Home schooled by her mother, Elaine could read and write at an early age. Her education, which included reading literary classics by Shakespeare, Dickens, Hawthorne, and others, as well as writing her own essays and verses, prepared Elaine well for her future endeavors as an author and Indian reformer. Indeed, Elaine and her younger sister Dora kept a journal of their prose and poems, and in 1877 six of their poems were published in *St. Nicholas Magazine.* In 1878 their book, *Apple-Blossoms: The Verses of Two Children,* appeared to enthusiastic reviews and sold some 10,000 copies in only two years. The two sisters published several other works, including two more books, *In Berkshire with the Wild Flowers* (1879) and *All Round the Year: Verses from Sky Farm* (1881).

Although Sky Farm provided an atmosphere of educational stimulation, the crops that Elaine's father hoped to grow and profit from failed miserably. Increasing debts and marital problems drove the couple apart,

Elaine Goodale Eastman in Amherst, Massachusetts, c.1910 (from the collection of James W. and Miriam M. Dayton). *Courtesy of Miriam M. Dayton*

Elaine Goodale Eastman in Northampton, Massachusetts, c.1925 (from the collection of Theodore D. Sargent). *Courtesy of Theodore D. Sargent*

resulting in their separation in 1883 and the selling of Sky Farm at auction. Her parents' separation had a profound effect on Elaine. She was extremely close to her father and blamed her mother more for the split. Questioning her mother's wisdom in abandoning her marriage to pursue a literary career, Elaine described her mother as having a short temper and a nervous condition.[3] Ironically, Elaine, who would essentially abandon a literary career for her marriage, also had marital problems and eventually separated from her Native American husband, Dr. Charles A. Eastman (Ohiyesa), after nearly thirty years of marriage. Her views on her own marriage and the causes of the separation, which both she and Charles kept secret from the general public, are discussed below and reveal for the first time in print Elaine's side of the story. (Unfortunately, no sources revealing Charles's views have been discovered.)

Her parents' financial problems and separation were factors that forced Elaine to abandon her plans to pursue a formal education at Harvard Annex (now Radcliffe College). Instead, she accepted a position in 1883 to teach Indian students at Hampton Normal and Agricultural Institute, which General Samuel C. Armstrong, an acquaintance of the Goodale family, had founded in Virginia in 1868 to educate African-American students. The addition of Native American students occurred in 1878.[4] At Hampton, Elaine began her long career as an ardent Indian reformer and applied her writing skills to promote federal policies of assimilation. Moreover, she now had a cause to serve. Like many other nineteenth-century career women, Elaine was driven by the so-called feminist Protestant ethic (or Puritan ethic) that demanded self-sacrifice and service to others. In this context, suffering was seen as natural and good, and Elaine seemed to find satisfaction in sacrificing her own interests to those of others. Thus, she would willingly sacrifice her prospects for a literary career to her marriage, and thereafter almost invariably place the career interests of her husband ahead of her own.[5]

Besides teaching classes at Hampton, Elaine also edited the Indian Department's section of the school's newspaper. She became acquainted with other Indian reformers such as Captain Richard Henry Pratt, head of Carlisle Indian School in Pennsylvania, and Herbert B. Welsh, secretary of the Indian Rights Association. In 1885, Elaine and other reformers visited several Sioux reservations in Dakota Territory, and in 1886 she began to teach at the Indian Day School at White River Camp at Lower Brule Agency, which she helped establish. Although many reformers supported off-reservation boarding schools as the best way to educate Indians, Elaine believed that day schools on reservations could be more effective, by reducing the negative effects of family disruptions and encouraging closer communication between teachers and the Indian community. During the summer of 1889, she spent time with a Sioux hunting party in Nebraska, immersing herself in their culture and even learning the Dakota language. In her journal, Elaine recorded her experiences and included one of the first written accounts of the beginning of the Ghost Dance Movement among the Sioux, which ultimately resulted in the Wounded Knee Massacre in 1890. By the end of the 1880s, Elaine Goodale had established herself as a well-known Indian reformer, publishing articles, reports, and letters on Indian issues and speaking at the Lake Mohonk Conference of Friends of the Indian, a national annual meeting of Indian reformers.[6]

In 1890, Elaine became the first supervisor of Indian Education in the two Dakotas. She visited day schools on the Sioux reservations, held teacher institutes, and recommended educational reforms to suit the needs of the students. On her visit to Pine Ridge Reservation during the fall of 1890, she met her future husband, Dr. Charles A. Eastman (Ohiyesa), who was the government physician at the agency.

A Santee Sioux, Ohiyesa was four years old when he was forced to flee with his relatives to Canada after the Minnesota Uprising of 1862. His grandmother and uncle served as his mentors since Ohiyesa's mother died while giving him birth, and his father, Many Lightnings, was presumed dead as a result of the uprising. For over a decade, Ohiyesa was trained in the traditional ways of a hunter and warrior, but his life dramatically changed with the reappearance of his father, who had been imprisoned instead of killed. During his confinement, he converted to Christianity. Many Lightnings encouraged his son to return with him to his homestead at Flandreau, South Dakota, and persuaded him to attend school and adopt white ways. Ohiyesa took the name Charles Alexander Eastman (the surname from his maternal grandfather, Captain Seth Eastman, the famous painter of Indian life) and began his journey in the white world. He attended many schools, ultimately receiving a Bachelor of Science degree from Dartmouth in 1887 and a medical degree from Boston University's School of Medicine in 1890. Desiring to help his people, Eastman accepted the position of government physician at Pine Ridge in November. Although reformers viewed Eastman as the model assimilated Indian, he was more of an acculturated Indian—that is, one who did not totally abandon his Native beliefs but only adopted the aspects of the dominant culture that served his purposes.[7]

Even before they met, Elaine and Charles had heard about each other's work. They shared a mutual interest in the Sioux, and both were attractive and articulate. They were drawn to each other almost immediately, fell in love, and announced their engagement on December 25, 1890, only six weeks after their initial meeting. Four days later, their happiness was interrupted by the massacre at Wounded Knee.

By 1890 conditions among the Sioux were horrible. For example, their land base was diminished, including the loss of the sacred Black Hills; many of their traditional ways were outlawed or condemned; and their people were starving on reservations. In response to this misery, some Sioux at Pine Ridge and at other reservations had adopted the Ghost Dance Movement in an effort to recapture their past—a past devoid of reservations and white men. The federal government then overreacted and sent troops to stop the Ghost Dance and arrest its leaders. Both Elaine and Charles believed that troops were unnecessary and suggested instead that the suffering Indians be given needed supplies of food, medicine, and blankets. With their pleas falling on deaf ears, Elaine and Charles were appalled by the U.S. Army's attack on and destruction of Chief Big Foot's band at Wounded Knee. Charles rode to the battle site and saw the results of the carnage firsthand. Both he and Elaine played major roles in treating the wounded survivors back at the agency and later condemned the army's vicious attack and wanton bloodletting. The trauma brought the couple even closer together.[8]

Six months afterward, Elaine and Charles headed east and were married at the Church of the Ascension in New York City on June 18, 1891. Many members of Elaine's family, and especially her mother, were shocked by her bold decision to marry an Indian. Dora expressed some of this prejudice when she confided, years later, "Elaine's marriage shocked, shocks, and will shock me as long as I live."[9] However, the wedding was carried off without serious incident, and both her sisters, Dora and Rose, served as bridesmaids. The newlyweds then spent their wedding night at Sky Farm in the very room where Elaine was born. After visiting friends in Boston and in Flandreau, South Dakota, they returned to Pine Ridge to begin their new life together.

Elaine recalled in her memoirs that her marriage was "the gift of myself to a Sioux," and that it entailed "life-long service to my husband's people." Here, then, was the clear commitment to duty and service of the feminist Protestant ethic. She would subordinate her own interests to those of another person (her husband) and to a larger cause (the welfare of the Sioux). And she kept her word, "for many a year every early dream and ambition was wholly subordinated to the business of helping my talented husband express himself and interpret his people."[10]

The early years of the Eastmans's marriage were extremely difficult. Major disagreements between Charles and the Indian agent at Pine Ridge resulted in Charles tendering his resignation in 1893. With their first child, Dora, born in 1892 and named after Elaine's sister, the Eastmans moved first to St. Paul, Minnesota, where Charles attempted unsuccessfully to establish a private practice. Other moves to Washington, DC, Carlisle Indian School, Crow Creek Reservation in South Dakota, and Bald Eagle Lake in Minnesota followed. Financial and other problems continued. In addition, Elaine bore four more children during these years. The couple discovered that finding a paying occupation for an educated American Indian was not easy. From Elaine's perspective, over ten years of marriage had yielded five children, no real home, and virtually no money. Concerned with the proper education of her children, Elaine persuaded Charles to move to Amherst, Massachusetts, ultimately settling into a small stone cottage (Lodestone, which her father and brother had recently built) three miles east of town. In the same year, Charles resigned as physician at Crow Creek Reservation, again because of problems with the Indian agent, and secured employment as head of the revision of the Sioux allotment rolls, a position he held until 1909.[11]

The Amherst years were busy and productive ones for the Eastmans. Elaine helped her husband write ten of his books, while she wrote three of her own. In the 1890s, Charles had begun, with the urging and editorial assistance of Elaine, to record his reminiscences of Indian life, some of which were later published as articles. His first of eleven books, *Indian Boyhood*, appeared in 1902. Forsaking medicine but still having an income from revising the Sioux allotment rolls, Charles now became a writer and subsequently a popular lecturer. As always, Elaine played a key role, handling correspondence, publicity, and scheduling for her husband. In addition, all of their six children, five girls and one boy, now attended public school, and two daughters would later graduate from college. Another daughter, Irene, a favorite of their parents, was becoming a talented concert soprano. Finally, the Eastmans opened a summer camp for girls, later called Camp Oahe, on Granite Lake in Munsonville, New Hampshire, in 1915. The nobility of the outdoors and the broad appeal of the Boy Scout movement in the United States during this era convinced many people of the advantages of outdoor life. Both Elaine and Charles loved the outdoors and hoped to secure additional income from the venture, which had the advantage of having a real Indian instruct the campers. Although the entire family worked at the camp, most of the responsibilities fell on Elaine's shoulders.

The bustle of these Amherst years was not without problems and tensions. Overburdened with the demands of the family and the camp, Elaine resented Charles's frequent trips away from home giving lectures and visiting reservations. Charles, on the other hand, became increasingly resentful of Elaine's domineering personality and her critical editing of his manuscripts. Their somewhat conflicting views regarding Indian assimilation versus acculturation must have also contributed to the tense situation. After 1909, when Charles finished working on the Sioux allotment rolls, the family's income from book royalties, lecture engagements, and fees from campers was far less than their expenses.[12] Indeed, Elaine later recalled that three of her books—*Little Brother o' Dreams* (1910), *Yellow Star: A Story of East and West* (1911), and *Indian Legends Retold* (1919)—were "pot-boilers, for our income was never at all adequate to the family needs, in spite of my husband's varied activities and growing reputation."[13] The loss of their favorite daughter, Irene, during the pandemic of 1918 was another blow.

The final parting of ways in the Eastman marriage came in August 1921 at Camp Oahe. Charles was accused of adultery and of fathering an illegitimate child. Although details of this dramatic event remain obscure, Elaine would shed some light on the incident in her correspondence and later publications, especially in *Hundred Maples* (1935), a novel dealing with these matters. Elaine's world, which she had devoted totally to her husband and family, had collapsed. Husband and wife separated; they agreed to keep the separation a secret for social, personal, and professional reasons, but they never saw each other again. Elaine did not even attend Charles's funeral and burial in Detroit in 1939. Fourteen years later, in 1953, Elaine died and was buried in Florence, Massachusetts, a physical as well as a symbolic reminder of their estrangement.

For decades after Charles's departure, Elaine expressed her pain and bitterness about his betrayal in her correspondence with her sisters Rose and Dora. For example, in 1925, Elaine wrote that "when I hear that a friend's husband has died, I envy her!" In 1930 she declared that her husband's behavior "poisoned all my memories of married life," and in 1941 she admitted that she "should have refused to marry Dr. Eastman";

his "tragic failure of character outweighs for me all the blessings of children and grandchildren." As a final example, in 1942, Elaine lamented, "I believe my life has been largely wasted."[14]

Much of Elaine's hurt seemed to be based on what she saw as Charles's rejection of her offer to keep the marriage together, provided that certain conditions were met. She demanded that he acknowledge his betrayal and take responsibility for his indiscretion. His confession was to be private, only made to her. Then she insisted that some arrangement for the care and financial security of Charles's illegitimate daughter be made since the girl's mother was apparently unable, or unwilling, to raise the child herself. Charles, however, refused to meet these conditions and departed.[15]

The woman in question, known only as "Henrietta," apparently worked at the camp, perhaps as a counselor. The child, a girl who sometimes adopted the name of Bonno Hyessa, was raised by another woman in California. Elaine attempted to stay informed about Bonno and received occasional reports on her activities from a friend in California.[16] As with Elaine and Charles's separation, the affair and illegitimate child remained shrouded in secrecy. "How thankful my girls must be," wrote Elaine, "that the story was never made public! Had the whole truth come out in the papers, sensational as it was in some respects, they would never have recovered from the humiliation."[17] According to Elaine, Charles denied his involvement and fabricated stories to prove his innocence, but a furious Elaine had "ample proof" that Henrietta was "the mother of his little girl."[18]

For the remainder of her life, Elaine lived either alone or with her daughters in Northampton, Massachusetts. She frequently complained about her lack of money and eventually had to sell debt-ridden Camp Oahe in the mid-1920s. Especially upsetting to her was Charles's refusal to share his royalties with her. On several occasions in her personal correspondence with her sisters, Elaine reveals her major role in helping him write and publish his books. "I made a mistake," lamented Elaine in a letter to Rose, "in letting the books be published in his sole name— all but one of them."[19] To be fair, Charles did acknowledge his wife's assistance in some of his books; nevertheless, his failure to share the royalties with her seems unconscionable. Moreover, it should be noted that Charles was never able to publish anything after the separation, even though he was working on several projects.

Despite her financial woes, Elaine remained extremely busy during the remainder of her long life. She wrote four books, *The Luck of Old*

Acres (1928), *The Voice at Eve* (1930), *Pratt: The Red Man's Moses* (1935), and *Hundred Maples* (1935), as well as numerous articles, essays, poems, and letters that appeared in a variety of magazines and newspapers. Finally, she continued to be an advocate of Indian reform and commented on other issues and events of post-World War I America.

Like other writers, Elaine drew on her life experiences in her novels and poems. Her love of nature and family and her devotion and service to others are recurring major themes. Her novels, especially, are strongly autobiographical and often depict characters that are readily identifiable as people she has known. For example, in *The Luck of Old Acres*, Elaine writes of a New England family that turns its farm into a summer camp to earn needed income. The parallels with her own family are obvious. And among an array of recognizable characters are Lorna, a beautiful singer, based on Irene, the daughter who died in 1918, and the husband, Harry Bell, irresponsible and away from home, based on Charles. In the end, this fictional family is reunited, unlike Elaine's. But through her fiction Elaine reveals her belief that her own marriage might have been saved had Irene not died.

In *Hundred Maples*, her most powerful and mature novel, Elaine deals directly with the circumstances that ended her marriage. Here, the character Amy is betrayed by her husband Jim, who refused to take responsibility for his actions. The plot permits Elaine to elaborate on her own feelings when she felt betrayed by Charles. Another character, Ellen, is clearly Elaine herself. And Ellen's relationship with a husband who eventually comes to appreciate and support her efforts to forge her own career permits Elaine to describe her own idea of an ideal marriage. Clearly, Elaine still believed in the institution. The implication that her own marriage lacked a loving, caring, and supportive husband is obvious. Charles, of course, has no say in all of this, and that fact must be noted.

In *The Voice at Eve*, a beautiful collection of poetry, of which only 225 copies were printed, Elaine expresses many of her joys and sorrows. Beginning with an essay presenting an overview of her life, she employs her familiar themes of nature, family, and devotion in over fifty poems. Finally, her biography of Richard Henry Pratt, the head of Carlisle Indian School, is still considered a standard source on Indian education. Unfortunately, the small royalties from these books did little to improve Elaine's financial situation and could not compare to the royalties that Charles received.

Besides being actively engaged as a book author, Elaine continued to stay informed on federal Indian policies and reservation conditions.

The time and energy she expended are revealed in her steady stream of correspondence to other Indian reformers throughout the United States and in the many articles, essays, and book reviews she contributed to newspapers and magazines. Elaine's correspondence to the Indian Rights Association demonstrates her commitment. Some of the issues she addressed were general conditions of Indians throughout the United States, citizenship, education, and peyote use, which she vehemently condemned. However, her main focus during the 1930s and 1940s was her opposition to Commissioner of Indian Affairs John Collier and his Indian New Deal. Although she occasionally expressed sympathy for some of Collier's positions, Elaine is most closely identified with the condemnation of what she considered the rejection of assimilation policies in Collier's programs in favor of ones that encouraged reviving tribal ways.[20]

A prime example of their heated exchanges was one that appeared in *The Christian Century* in 1934. The main issue of debate was Collier's directive on allowing Indian religious freedom, which Elaine viewed as radical and fostering paganism. She cited a number of aspects of Indian rituals that she found appalling, such as self-mutilation and whipping, disposal of all personal property at the death of a loved one, and peyote use. She also disapproved of Indian shamans and medicine men and the way they healed by songs and chants. Finally, she used the term "bastard religion" to condemn the union of Indian beliefs and Christian theology and cited the Ghost Dance Movement of 1890 among the Sioux as an example of such a union.[21]

Collier, a trained sociologist who worked among immigrant groups in urban areas, had also gained a reputation as an Indian reformer. His more moderate approach of acculturation—allowing Indians to retain aspects of their culture while adopting ways of the dominant culture—angered many of Elaine's generation of Indian reformers. And in responding to her article, Collier argued that Indians had the constitutional right of religious freedom and could therefore blend Christian aspects with their own beliefs as the Pueblo Indians had already done. As for the Ghost Dance, he noted that it undoubtedly would have vanished had it not been challenged by U.S. troops, an argument that Elaine herself had advanced in 1890. He also pointed out that peyote was not a habit-forming drug, and he supported the way that peyote users blended Christianity into their beliefs.[22]

Elaine's heated sparring with Collier was certainly not her finest hour. But in fairness, it should be noted that she was now over seventy years old. Moreover, Collier seemed to irritate her; he was a little too sure of himself, a little too condescending. She resented being seen as "old school" or as someone who did not understand. After all, she had spent the better part of her life promoting one Indian's efforts to record and promulgate his heritage.

In addition to her views on Indian affairs, Elaine expressed her opinions on other subjects. For example, she lamented the lack of respect and manners of the younger generation, and she opposed for pacifist reasons America's entry into both world wars. She also worked to promote morality in motion pictures and lobbied against the public dissemination of birth control information. While she was not entirely prudish and approved of an active sex life between husband and wife, she opposed virtually anything that threatened the nuclear family unit. Finally, she doubted whether mankind would benefit from dropping the atomic bombs in 1945.[23]

Elaine Goodale Eastman lived a full, albeit sad and tormented, life. One of her most outstanding characteristics was her endurance in the face of adversity. Her sheltered childhood, lack of formal education, disastrous marriage, loss of three children at relatively early ages, and nearly constant financial woes contributed to her sorrow and bitterness. While she found considerable satisfaction in serving others, she always wondered whether she might have put more effort into her career. Elaine was a woman of principle with deep convictions regarding what was right and what was wrong, although she sometimes seemed intolerant of others. Her many publications, both the purely literary and those on Indian issues, are noteworthy. This complex woman—child prodigy, wife of the most famous Native American living in the United States at the beginning of the twentieth century, author, and Indian reformer—deserves a more prominent place in history.

Notes

1. Elaine Goodale Eastman to Matthew K. Sniffen, March 27, 1934, Indian Rights Association Papers, 1868–1968, Microfilm, Reel 51, Historical Society of Pennsylvania, Philadelphia, Microfilming Corporation of America, hereafter cited as IRA.

2. See Kay Graber, ed., *Sister to the Sioux: The Memoirs of Elaine Goodale Eastman, 1885–91* (Lincoln, NE, 1978), for background information on Eastman.

3. Ibid., 14; Elaine Goodale Eastman, "All the Days of My Life," in *The Voice at Eve* (Chicago, 1930), 18, 20.

4. See Ruth Ann Alexander, "Finding Oneself through a Cause: Elaine Goodale Eastman and Indian Reform in the 1880s," *South Dakota History* 22 (Spring 1992): 1–37 for excellent coverage of this subject.

5. Ruth Ann Alexander, "Elaine Goodale Eastman and the Failure of the Feminist Protestant Ethic," *Great Plains Quarterly* 8 (Spring 1988): 90. See also Theodore D. Sargent, "Elaine Goodale Eastman and 'The Nightingale's Burden' " (unpublished manuscript, 1999), Eastman/Goodale/Dayton Papers, Sophia Smith Collection, Smith College, Northampton, Massachusetts, for a study that compares Eastman's life and writings to more well-known women poets covered in Cheryl Walker's *The Nightingale's Burden: Women Poets and American Culture before 1900* (Bloomington, IN, 1982).

6. Alexander, "Finding Oneself through a Cause," 11–34; Alexander, "Elaine Goodale Eastman and the Failure of the Feminist Protestant Ethic," 91. Two examples of Elaine's publications during this period are "The Future Indian School System," *Chautauquan* 10 (October 1889): 51–55; and "How to Americanize the Indian," *New Englander and Yale Review* 52 (May 1890): 452–55.

7. See Raymond Wilson, *Ohiyesa: Charles Eastman, Santee Sioux* (Urbana, IL, 1983), for Eastman's life as an educated Indian functioning in the dominant culture.

8. Ibid., 52–62.

9. Dora Read Goodale to Rose Goodale Dayton, c. 1930, Eastman/Goodale/Dayton Papers, James W. and Miriam M. Dayton Collection, "Lodestone," Amherst, Massachusetts, hereafter cited as Dayton Collection; Rose Goodale Dayton, Handwritten Journal (1925–1932), December 14, 1931, entry, Dayton Collection. James Dayton was the grandson of Rose Goodale Dayton, Elaine's youngest sister. Co-author Sargent acquired access to the collection that contains Elaine's personal correspondence with Rose. These letters offer valuable information on Elaine and her relationship with Charles, which heretofore have never been published. Miriam Dayton, James's widow, has donated the Eastman/Goodale/Dayton family papers to the Sophia Smith Collection, Smith College, Northampton, Massachusetts.

10. Alexander, "Elaine Goodale Eastman and the Failure of the Feminist Protestant Ethic," 92–93; Graber, ed., *Sister to the Sioux*, 173; Sargent, "Elaine Goodale Eastman and 'The Nightingale's Burden,' " 4–5.

11. See Wilson, *Ohiyesa*, 67–130.

12. Sargent, "Elaine Goodale Eastman and 'The Nightingale's Burden,' " 16–17; Wilson, *Ohiyesa*, 150–52, 163–65.

13. Graber, ed., *Sister to the Sioux*, 174.

14. Elaine Goodale Eastman to Rose Goodale Dayton, May 25, 1925; Elaine Goodale Eastman to Dora Read Goodale, December 26, 1930; Elaine Goodale Eastman to Rose Goodale Dayton, c. 1941; Elaine Goodale Eastman to Rose Goodale Dayton, c. 1942, Dayton Collection.

15. See Elaine Goodale Eastman to Rose Goodale Dayton, November 3, c. 1933; Elaine Goodale Eastman to Rose Goodale Dayton, May 5, c. 1938; Elaine Goodale Eastman to Rose Goodale Dayton, January 26, c. 1941, Dayton Collection.

16. Elaine Goodale Eastman to Rose Goodale Dayton, early 1939, Dayton Collection.

17. Ibid.

18. Elaine Goodale Eastman to Rose Goodale Dayton, February 9, c. 1938, Dayton Collection.

19. Ibid. See also Elaine Goodale Eastman to Rose Goodale Dayton, c. 1924; Elaine Goodale Eastman to Dora Read Goodale, June 5, 1931; Elaine Goodale Eastman to Rose Goodale Dayton, 1936; Elaine Goodale Eastman to Rose Goodale Dayton,

February 3, c. 1937; Elaine Goodale Eastman to Rose Goodale Dayton, October 8, 1940, Dayton Collection.

20. Elaine Goodale Eastman, "Uncle Sam Does an About-Face in His Dealings With Indians," *Boston Evening Transcript*, September 9, 1933. Elaine and the IRA exchanged many letters on these issues and others between 1934 and 1942. See, for example, Elaine Goodale Eastman to Matthew K. Sniffen, June 7, 1934, September 7, 1934, September 21, 1934, October 21, 1934, Reel 52, IRA; Elaine Goodale Eastman to Matthew K. Sniffen, March 5, 1935, November 23, 1935, Reel 53, IRA; Elaine Goodale Eastman to Matthew K. Sniffen, May 21, 1936, Reel 54, IRA; Elaine Goodale Eastman to Matthew K. Sniffen, April 6, 1938, Reel 55, IRA; Elaine Goodale Eastman to Matthew K. Sniffen, September 29, 1939, Reel 57, IRA; Elaine Goodale Eastman to Matthew K. Sniffen, December 5, 1941, October 19, 1942, Reel 58, IRA.

21. Elaine Goodale Eastman, "Does Uncle Sam Foster Paganism?" *The Christian Century* 51 (August 8, 1934): 1016–18.

22. John Collier, "A Reply to Mrs. Eastman," *The Christian Century* 51 (August 8, 1934): 1018–20. For information on Collier see Kenneth R. Philp, *John Collier's Crusade for Indian Reform, 1920–1954* (Tucson, AZ, 1977).

23. See Elaine Goodale Eastman to Rose Goodale Dayton, January 26, 1940; Elaine Goodale Eastman to Rose Goodale Dayton, c. 1940; Elaine Goodale Eastman to Rose Goodale Dayton, September 7, 1945; Elaine Goodale Eastman to Rose Goodale Dayton, August 13, 1945, Dayton Collection.

Suggested Readings

Alexander, Ruth Ann. "Elaine Goodale Eastman and the Failure of the Feminist Protestant Ethic." *Great Plains Quarterly* 8 (Spring 1988): 89–101.

_____. "Finding Oneself through a Cause: Elaine Goodale Eastman and Indian Reform in the 1880s." *South Dakota History* 22 (Spring 1992): 1–37.

Collier, John. "A Reply to Mrs. Eastman." *The Christian Century* 51 (August 8, 1934): 1018–20.

Eastman, Elaine Goodale. "Does Uncle Sam Foster Paganism?" *The Christian Century* 51 (August 8, 1934): 1016–18.

_____. "The Ghost Dance War and Wounded Knee Massacre of 1890–91." *Nebraska History* 26 (January 1945): 26–42.

_____. *Hundred Maples.* Brattleboro, VT, 1935.

_____. *Indian Legends Retold.* Boston, 1919.

_____. *Little Brother o' Dreams.* New York, 1910.

_____. *The Luck of Old Acres.* New York, 1928.

_____. *Pratt: The Red Man's Moses.* Norman, OK, 1935.

_____. *The Voice at Eve.* Chicago, 1930.

_____. *Yellow Star: A Story of East and West.* Boston, 1911.

Goodale, Elaine, and Dora Read Goodale. *All Round the Year: Verses from Sky Farm.* New York, 1881.

_____. *Apple-Blossoms: The Verses of Two Children.* New York, 1878.

_____. *In Berkshire with the Wild Flowers.* New York, 1879.

Graber, Kay, ed. *Sister to the Sioux: The Memoirs of Elaine Goodale Eastman, 1885–91*. Lincoln, NE, 1978.

Philp, Kenneth R. *John Collier's Crusade for Indian Reform, 1920–1954*. Tucson, AZ, 1977.

Walker, Cheryl. *The Nightingale's Burden: Women Poets and American Culture before 1900*. Bloomington, IN, 1982.

Wilson, Raymond. *Ohiyesa: Charles Eastman, Santee Sioux*. Urbana, IL, 1983.

8

Dennis Chavez
The Last of the Patrones

Kevin Allen Leonard

Dennis Chavez was one of the more important political leaders in New Mexico in the first half of the twentieth century, but today he is little known beyond a select group of Democratic leaders in the state. His anonymity results in part because he spent much of his time in the U.S. Senate working behind the scenes for his constituents. He took seriously the advice of Speaker of the House John Nance Garner to be an errand boy for those who had elected him.

For his hard work in Democratic politics in New Mexico in the early years of the century, he was rewarded with a clerkship in Washington, DC. While there, he earned a law degree. Back home, in his quest for the Senate seat, he took on popular maverick Republican Bronson Cutting in his re-election bid. Chavez lost, but when Cutting was killed in an airplane crash, Chavez was appointed to replace him until the next general election. He remained in the Senate until his death in 1962. Chavez was one of the few members of the national Congress who had a Spanish-speaking background. During his years in public office, he faced controversy from time to time, but his overall contribution to the advancement of his state and his people was significant.

Kevin A. Leonard has presented a compelling sketch of Chavez's career. Leonard, assistant professor of history at Western Washington University, earned a Ph.D. at the University of California, Davis. His dissertation on the impact of World War II on race relations in Los Angeles won the W. Turrentine Jackson Award from the Pacific Coast Branch of the American Historical Association. He has published essays in a number of books and is currently expanding his dissertation for publication.

The Spanish-speaking residents of most of the Southwest began to lose their political representation shortly after the United States acquired the region in 1848. Gold seekers from the eastern half of the country streamed into northern California in 1849 and the early 1850s. These adventurers quickly outnumbered the Spanish-speaking *californios*, whom they eyed with suspicion. Most Anglo-Americans refused to believe that Spanish-speaking Roman Catholics could understand and represent the interests of English-speaking Protestants. After 1849 few *californios* were elected or appointed to fill even minor offices. The same result occurred in southern California by the 1880s.[1]

In New Mexico, however, Spanish-speaking citizens, who referred to themselves as *hispanos* or Spanish Americans, retained political representation well into the twentieth century. During the early years of New Mexico's statehood, *hispanos* were elected to many local and state offices. They routinely constituted nearly half of the members of the state house of representatives, although they were not as well represented in the state senate. Ezequiel C. de Baca was elected governor in 1916, and Octaviano A. Larrazolo was elected to that office two years later. The success of Spanish-speaking candidates in the early twentieth century seems to have resulted largely from the relationship between the Republican Party and the majority of *hispanos*. Some scholars have argued that wealthy and powerful Republican *patrones* dispensed favors, such as jobs and assistance in hard times, in exchange for the votes of poorer *hispanos*.[2] The analysis of votes from Hispanic counties, however, suggests that these *patrones* did not exert as much control over elections as has often been assumed.[3] Whether or not *patrones* determined the outcome of elections, most of the successful Hispanic candidates were Republicans. De Baca was a Democrat, but Larrazolo's experience suggests how important the Republican Party was to Hispanic electoral success. Larrazolo unsuccessfully sought election as New Mexico's territorial delegate to Congress three times—in 1900, 1906, and 1908—as a Democrat. After he changed his party affiliation, Larrazolo succeeded in his bid for the governorship and in a 1928 campaign for a U.S. Senate seat.

In the 1930s the number of Hispanic officeholders in New Mexico began to decline—a reflection both of the growth of the state's Anglo-American population and of increasing dissatisfaction with the Republican Party. Both Anglos and *hispanos* abandoned the GOP in the 1930s. As a result, most of the *hispanos* elected to seats in the legislature during the 1930s and 1940s were Democrats. Because many Anglo New Mexicans, like their counterparts in California and Texas, refused to cast their ballots for Spanish-speaking candidates, only a few Hispanics were elected to statewide offices during the decades of Democratic dominance. Dennis Chavez was undoubtedly the most significant of these Hispanic Democrats. Chavez, who had served one term in the state house of representatives in the 1920s, was elected to New Mexico's single seat in the U.S. House of Representatives in 1930. In 1934 he nearly unseated the incumbent, Senator Bronson Cutting. When Cutting died in an airplane crash in 1935, Governor Clyde Tingley appointed Chavez to finish Cutting's term. Chavez was elected to the seat in 1936, was reelected four times, and died in office in 1962. Chavez remained in office by channeling federal funds into his state. He encouraged Hispanic voters to support one of their own; at the same time, he tried to avoid alienating Anglo Democrats. Chavez's remarkable record of election and reelection have led some scholars and observers to refer to him as "the last of the *patrones.*"[4]

Dionisio Chavez was born in Los Chavez, New Mexico (about twenty miles south of Albuquerque), on April 8, 1888, the third of eight children of David and Paz Sanchez Chavez. In 1895 his parents decided to move the family to Albuquerque. They hoped that the move to the city would help them escape from poverty and allow the children to attend school. In Albuquerque seven-year-old Dionisio began his schooling. In the English-language environment of the Presbyterian Mission School, "Dionisio" became "Dennis." Despite Dennis Chavez's parents' expectations, Albuquerque did not bring the family prosperity. Chavez was forced to leave school at the age of thirteen to help support the household. For five years he delivered groceries six days each week. In 1906 he was hired by the engineering department of the City of Albuquerque. He advanced to the positions of surveyor and engineer. By the time he left the city's employment in 1915, he had become an assistant city engineer.

While Chavez worked for the city, he became involved in politics. His father had been a loyal lieutenant of the Republican *patron* Solomon Luna. The young man, however, saw that his father's faithful support had not improved his position in life or the living conditions for most people in the county. In protest against Republican policies and in admiration for Thomas Jefferson, Dennis Chavez registered as a Democrat. Even before he was old enough to vote, he had begun to work for Democratic candidates. In 1908 he gave a speech in Gallup in support of Larrazolo's candidacy for territorial delegate to Congress. In 1911, Chavez served as an interpreter for William G. McDonald, the Democrat who was elected the first governor of the state of New Mexico.

Chavez's efforts on political campaigns attracted the attention of party leaders and nurtured his ambitions. In 1916 he left his job and launched his first bid for public office. In addition to working for his own election as Bernalillo County clerk, he also spoke on behalf of other Democratic candidates throughout the state's historically Hispanic counties. Chavez lost the election, but his tireless work for the Democrats earned him a reward. Governor de Baca appointed him state game warden. The governor, however, died shortly after taking office, and the Republican lieutenant governor, now governor, replaced Chavez. In the summer of 1917, Senator A. A. Jones, one of the candidates for whom Chavez had campaigned the previous year, offered him the opportunity to serve as a clerk for the U.S. Senate. While he was in Washington, Chavez continued his schooling. He passed the entrance examinations and was admitted to the law school at Georgetown University. He worked during the day in the Capitol and attended school in the evenings.

In 1920, Chavez completed his law degree and returned to Albuquerque, where he opened a law practice and resumed his political career. In 1922 he won election to the state house of representatives.[5] Because Chavez was a Democrat, however, service in the state legislature did not satisfy his ambitions. In this era of Republican ascendancy, the legislature mostly served the interests of New Mexico's cattle and sheep raisers, oil barons, and the Santa Fe and Southern Pacific railroads. After one term in the house, Chavez left the legislature. He continued to work for the party, however, and he waited for the Democrats' fortunes to improve. In 1930 he decided to seek office again. Widespread criticism of the Republican response to the Great Depression undoubtedly influenced his decision, but another change in the political climate in New Mexico may also have contributed to it. In the summer of 1930 the Club Político Independiente de Nuevo México (Independent Political Club of New Mexico), an organization of about 3,000 *hispanos*, demanded that Hispanics be elected to several statewide offices.[6] Although Chavez did not mention the club's demands when he announced his decision to run for the state's seat in the U.S. House of Representatives, he may have interpreted them to mean that he would have greater support among Hispanics than most previous Democratic candidates. Chavez had accrued so much political capital in more than twenty years of tireless work for the party that he easily secured the nomination.

Chavez's opponent in the 1930 election was the incumbent, Albert Gallatin Simms. A native of Arkansas, Simms had moved to New Mexico in 1912. He had served on the Albuquerque city council and the Bernalillo County commission and in the state house of representatives before he was elected to Congress in 1928. Simms campaigned on his record, arguing that his efforts had led to the appropriation of federal funds for the construction of roads and public buildings in New Mexico and for flood relief for farmers in the Rio Grande Valley.[7]

In his campaign against Simms, Chavez enjoyed the benefit of facing an opponent whose party seemed not to have done much to address the problems of the depression. As he campaigned throughout New Mexico, he blamed the state's problems on the Republicans and their lackluster response to the economy. A polished campaign speaker, Chavez tailored his speeches to his audiences. In southeastern New Mexico— "Little Texas"—he told the mostly Anglo audiences that Republicans were responsible for the low prices of wheat and cotton, and he promised to protect agriculture.[8] In central and northern New Mexico, Chavez told *hispanos* that Republicans had done little for them. "Don't let the Republicans come around and tell you they are your friends because you are Spanish-American," Chavez said in Santa Fe. "It is you who have kept that party in power for over sixty-five years and they have failed in their duty to provide you with educational facilities. I blame the Republicans for negligence in educating the native people. What have they done for you in an educational way? Nothing. Yet, they say, I love you."[9] In both areas he pledged to support restrictive immigration legislation that would protect American labor. In his final campaign speech, delivered in Albuquerque at the beginning of November, Chavez said that he favored immigration restriction so that "the boys from Barelas [the Albuquerque barrio in which Chavez had lived as a child] can get the jobs instead of the boys from Venezuela or Chihuahua."[10] Chavez's statements suggest that both Anglo and Hispanic New Mexicans feared that immigrants, especially from Mexico, would deprive them of jobs. These statements reflect the anti-Mexican sentiment prevalent throughout the Southwest in the early 1930s, and they underscore the fact that "Spanish-Americans" such as Chavez thought that they had little in common with Mexican immigrants.

When the votes were counted, Chavez had won a decisive victory. He defeated Simms by a margin of more than 18,000 votes out of a total of 117,813 cast. Chavez's election coincided with the beginning of a dramatic shift in politics in New Mexico and across the nation. The Democrats emerged from the 1930 election as the majority party in the state legislature. The Democratic majority increased as a result of elections in 1932 and 1936; the 1937 session of the legislature was overwhelmingly Democratic.[11] On the national level, the hundred-member majority that the Republicans had enjoyed in the House of Representatives became a six-member majority for the Democrats as a result of the election of 1930. The Democratic majority grew in the elections of 1932, 1934, and 1936, so that during the 75th Congress (1937–1939) only eighty-nine Republicans remained in the House.

When Chavez arrived in Washington to take his seat in the House, he later recalled, House Speaker John Nance Garner gave him some sound advice: "The men who are most successful as Congressmen are the ones who don't talk much. Good Congressmen are just errand boys for the people who elect them."[12] Chavez rarely participated in debates on the floor of the House or, later, the Senate. Instead, he devoted most of his energy to serving his constituents behind the scenes. He recognized that by serving them, he could also further his political career. From his positions on the Veterans, Public Buildings and Grounds, Public Lands, Irrigation and Reclamation, and Indian Affairs committees, Chavez worked to funnel assistance to New Mexicans. In early 1932, for example, he attempted to amend a bill to enable the Reconstruction Finance Corporation to lend money to reclamation, drainage, or irrigation projects. Although Chavez's proposed amendment was ruled out of order, it demonstrated his willingness to use the federal government to help those of his constituents whose lives had been devastated by the depression.[13] Later in 1932, Chavez shepherded a bill that affected many New Mexico farmers through the Committee on Irrigation and Reclamation. The House passed the bill, which extended a moratorium on farmers' payments to the federal government for reclamation projects. Chavez sponsored a bill to grant the state of New Mexico an additional 76,667 acres of public land for the benefit of Eastern New Mexico College in Portales. The college had previously received a federal land grant of 30,000 acres, but Chavez argued persuasively that the earlier grant was insufficient to support the college. The House passed the bill on March 23, 1932.[14]

In seeking reelection to the house in 1932, Chavez faced Republican José Armijo. Chavez defeated Armijo by 42,000 votes (94,764 to 52,905) and garnered more votes than any other Democratic nominee, including presidential candidate Franklin D. Roosevelt. In his second term, Chavez faithfully supported New Deal legislation sponsored by President Roosevelt and his administration. Chavez saw that this legislation offered hope to New Mexicans who had been hit hard by the depression, and he also saw that New Deal programs offered him a chance to reward his political supporters. Chavez's ability to dispense patronage increased in November 1933 when he was named to the Democratic National Committee.[15]

During his second term in the House, Chavez decided that in 1934 he would challenge Senator Cutting. An enigmatic but powerful figure in New Mexico politics for twenty years, Cutting held only one elected office. He was appointed to the Senate in 1927, when Senator Jones died in office, and won election to the seat in 1928. Cutting attracted the attention of journalists nationwide in the early 1930s, and he has garnered a substantial amount of attention from scholars since his death in 1935. Many of these journalists and scholars considered Cutting the epitome of the *patrón*. In a 1934 article in the *American Mercury*, "Feudalism and Senator Cutting," journalist Jan Spiess referred to Cutting as "the chief of all the *dons*" and "a brilliant young liberal leader in the Senate."

Cutting was born into a wealthy New York family in 1888. After he completed his education at Harvard University, he went to New Mexico in 1912 to recover his health. He purchased a newspaper, the Santa Fe *New Mexican*, and attempted to participate in Republican Party politics. Initially, however, he found himself excluded by well-established party leaders who were suspicious of outsiders. As he plotted his path into politics, he began to cultivate relationships with influential *hispanos*. "Word got about that a Mexican major domo could borrow from him a few dollars to tide him over until he sold his sheep or cattle or harvested his crops," Spiess wrote.[16] After Cutting died in 1935, probate proceedings revealed that he had made 500 "personal loans" for a total of more than $500,000 during the previous twenty years. Nearly one-third of these loans dated from the last five years of Cutting's life, when he was trying to wrest control of Republican county organizations from the "Old Guard" faction of his party. Most of these loans were for $350 to $500, but one was for $36,000. Most of them had not been repaid, and there is no evidence that Cutting ever tried to collect them. He extended loans to at least eleven newspaper publishers. Thus, some of Cutting's opponents charged that he had purchased the state's newspapers as well as many of the state's Hispanic voters.[17]

Scholars have long questioned why Chavez tried to unseat the powerful Cutting. They point out that he would have found it easier to defeat Carl Hatch, New Mexico's other U.S. senator, who had been appointed to fill a vacancy. Chavez, however, certainly was aware of the risks involved in trying to unseat a member of his own party. As a loyal

Democrat who had helped to build the party, he knew that a rift could cost it electoral success. Some scholars have suggested that envy motivated Chavez's challenge of Cutting. William H. Pickens writes that "Dennis Chavez had risen to the top of the State Democratic Party, but practical and shrewd as ever, he realized that the enigmatic Bronson Cutting still held sway over the popular imagination. All the contributions from federal coffers which Chavez could muster could not match the electrifying appeal of New Mexico's lone national hero, or so it seemed to many."[18] Although Chavez may have coveted Cutting's power, it seems unlikely that he wanted to match Bronson's electrifying appeal.

Chavez's actions in the House, and his later performance in the Senate, indicate that he was content to be seen as a quiet representative who worked hard to serve his constituents. He seems to have had little desire to establish a reputation as a "brilliant leader in the Senate." Although Chavez never said exactly why he decided to challenge Cutting, it seems likely that he was motivated both by his ambition to gain greater power and by his belief that he could defeat Cutting. After all, Cutting was a Republican in a state that had become increasingly Democratic. A "Progressive" Republican, Cutting had also waged a protracted struggle with the Old Guard for control of the party in New Mexico. Many Republican leaders made it clear that they would support Cutting's opponent. Chavez's success in two statewide elections may have led him to think that he could oust Cutting.

Chavez found, however, that Cutting was a more formidable opponent than Simms or Armijo. Unlike doctrinaire Republicans, Cutting had suggested bold remedies for the social maladies of the depression—public ownership of utilities and the nationalization of banks, for example.[19] His reputation as a Progressive and his feud with the Old Guard allowed him to draw support from some traditionally Democratic groups. The New Mexico State Federation of Labor—although not the Albuquerque Central Labor Union—and American Federation of Labor President William Green endorsed Cutting rather than Chavez.[20]

This "battle of the *patrones*" attracted some national attention. Liberal and "Progressive" observers generally supported Cutting and declared that Chavez was "hardly of senatorial stature" and that he would be an "administration yes-man."[21] Cutting campaigned as the friend of the people. Drawing attention to the fact that many Old Guard Republicans were supporting Chavez, Cutting declared at one Albuquerque rally that "for the first time in its history, New Mexico has a clean cut political issue, the welfare of the people on one side, and every selfish interest on the other." Chavez also claimed that he was the friend of the people and suggested that Cutting wanted to be a dictator. He told one audience that "the legislation I shall sponsor and strive to get enacted, if I am elected to the U.S. Senate, shall be the legislation the majority of the citizens want sponsored and enacted. I shall never assume the attitude that I know what is best for the people, and that I am so much wiser than they are that my opinion is unquestionable and the only correct one. I shall never strive to be or pose as a political dictator in any sense of the word."[22] Although many New Mexicans, both Democrats and Republicans, may have agreed with Chavez about Cutting's ambitions, ultimately Chavez's campaign was unsuccessful. Cutting's coalition of traditionally Republican *hispanos*, some union members, and some disaffected Democrats allowed him to retain his seat in the Senate. Chavez nearly unseated him, however. Cutting's margin of victory was 2,284 vote out of a total of 152,172 cast.

After the election, both Chavez and the anti-Cutting Republicans accused Cutting of fraud. They argued that he had spent excessive amounts of money in the campaign and that the vote totals from San Miguel County (where the vote was 6,852 for Cutting to 4,006 for Chavez) were fraudulent. Chavez appealed to the state supreme court, and the state legislature appointed a committee to investigate his allegations. Chavez also petitioned the U.S. Senate. The Senate Committee on Privileges and Elections decided that Cutting's campaign expenditures were not excessive, but the committee had not reached a decision on the other charge when Cutting died in a plane crash near Kirkland, Missouri, on May 6, 1935.[23] Governor Clyde Tingley appointed Chavez to fill Cutting's seat until the next general election. In announcing the appointment, Tingley said that Chavez "was undoubtedly the second choice of the people of New Mexico" and that it was "natural" for him to occupy the Senate seat. Once he was appointed, Chavez stated that he would abandon his efforts to have himself declared the winner.[24]

Chavez's charges of election fraud had not endeared him to some of his colleagues in the Senate. When he was sworn in, five "Progressive" senators—Hiram Johnson of California, Robert M. La Follette, Jr., of Wisconsin, George W. Norris of Nebraska, Gerald Nye of North Dakota, and Henrik Shipstead of Minnesota—walked out of the Senate chamber. "I left the chamber because it was the only way, in my helplessness, that I could show my condemnation of the disgraceful and unwarranted fight made to drive Senator Cutting out of public office,"

Norris told the *New York Times*. "Our affection for Senator Cutting was such that our resentment against the contest filed—so utterly without merit—was so great that we simply did not want to see his successor, the author of that contest, sworn in," Johnson said.[25] Chavez, then, was not destined to be regarded as a "Progressive." Instead, following the pattern he had established in the House, he tended to be a dependable supporter of President Roosevelt. Unlike many western Democratic senators, who led the opposition to Roosevelt's "Court-packing" scheme, Chavez offered the proposal lukewarm support.[26]

Chavez did not always back the administration's policies. He emerged as a consistent critic of John Collier and the Bureau of Indian Affairs (BIA). In a 1936 clash, Collier, the commissioner of Indian Affairs, accused Chavez of delaying action on proposed legislation to expand the boundaries of the Navajo reservation. According to Collier, Chavez was responding to the demands of "a handful of wealthy livestock operators who are factors in New Mexico politics" and ignoring the needs of the Indians, who faced "extermination" if the reservation was not enlarged. Chavez argued that not only "wealthy livestock operators" but also state officials opposed the legislation, and he insisted that the Navajos were not unanimous in their support for it.[27] Later the same year, Chavez tried to punish Collier and the BIA by proposing budget cuts. During the budget debate, Chavez complained that "there are getting to be more Indian agents and employees of the Indian office in my state . . . than there are Indians. I do not object to providing money for the Indian Bureau . . . but the difficulty has been that we have had too much Bureau and not enough Indian."[28]

Chavez's sometimes rancorous confrontations with Collier apparently did not hinder the senator's effort to parlay his support for most of Roosevelt's program into federal funds to reward his supporters in New Mexico. In his first few years in the Senate, Chavez worked closely with Governor Tingley to build a strong Democratic machine in the state. Chavez and Tingley conferred about the appointments made by the governor, and Chavez consulted Tingley when the senator was asked to approve appointments to federal positions in New Mexico. Chavez worked to make certain that the heads of New Deal agencies in the state were loyal to him and to Tingley and would only hire others who had supported them.

Although Chavez may have resembled earlier *patrones* in his exchanging of favors for political support, there was a critical difference between him and his Republican predecessors. Unlike wealthy Republicans, including Cutting, who could reward important backers with jobs and loans, Chavez and other Democrats usually had no personal fortunes upon which they could draw to thank them. As early as 1930, when the Democrats began to dominate New Mexico politics, the party had rewarded loyal members with jobs. In return, the party expected these loyal members to hand over a percentage of their pay. This system expanded as the New Deal made the federal government and some state agencies important employers in the state.[29]

All of the scholars who have examined Chavez's career as a senator have agreed that he wanted to control federal patronage in New Mexico in order to remain in office. Some, perhaps uncharitably, have suggested that he was obsessed with controlling federal patronage. One scholar has argued that Chavez's feud with Collier resulted from the fact that Chavez was not consulted before positions within the Interior Department were filled.[30] Chavez did not, however, devote all of his time and energy to the establishment and maintenance of a political machine. He responded promptly to his constituents' requests, and most of them seem to have been satisfied with his actions on their behalf.[31]

Chavez's obvious efforts to construct a political machine, however, erupted into scandal in the late 1930s. In 1937, Chavez's longtime ally, Governor Tingley, proposed an amendment to the state constitution that would allow the governor to serve more than two consecutive terms. Many New Mexicans, including some state officials, opposed the amendment. Chavez, fearing the power that it might give Tingley, did not support the governor's proposal. Voters rejected the amendment in September 1937. Tingley felt betrayed by Chavez and attempted to punish the senator.[32] In September 1938, Harry Hopkins, the head of the Works Progress Administration (WPA), fired Fred Healy, the WPA administrator for New Mexico, for permitting "local political interference with the WPA program."[33] In the next month seventy-three people were indicted on a variety of charges. Among those accused of misusing WPA funds and of illegally forcing WPA workers to take part in political activities were four of Chavez's relatives—a sister, his son-in-law, a nephew, and a cousin. His secretary was also indicted.[34] Chavez's sister, nephew, and cousin were acquitted, but the jury could not agree if the secretary was innocent or guilty.[35]

Although the scandal did not drive Chavez from office, charges of political corruption continued to dog him. He eked out a narrow victory in the 1940 primary election—the first primary in New Mexico's history. His opponent, Representative John J. Dempsey, insisted that voters had "been intimidated." Dempsey told reporters that FBI agents would be dispatched to Santa Fe to investigate the corruption, and he compared Chavez's machine to "the Pendergast gang in Kansas City."[36] Chavez's Republican opponent in the 1940 general election apparently did not claim that the senator's reelection resulted from fraud. In the 1946 primary, Dempsey again challenged Chavez, and again charges of fraud surfaced.[37] In the 1946 general election Chavez defeated Republican Patrick J. Hurley by about 5,000 votes. Hurley, who had served as secretary of war in Herbert Hoover's cabinet and as American ambassador to China, suggested that the Senate Campaign Investigating Committee should look into the election. Apparently, however, he did not press the issue.[38]

Hurley thought that he could win a rematch with Chavez in 1952. He and other Republicans were heartened by a rift that had opened in 1949 in the Democratic Party between the Chavez faction and the faction headed by Governor Thomas J. Mabry. Chavez accused the governor of keeping "political leeches and barnacles" on the state payroll. Mabry countered by pointing out that Chavez had "relatives and close friends on the payroll and is always asking me to give his friends and relatives jobs."[39] Despite the divisions within the party, Chavez won the election by about 5,000 votes. This time, however, Hurley did not readily accept defeat. Even before all of the votes had been counted, he had asked for ballot boxes in four counties to be impounded.[40] Hurley claimed that Chavez had violated both federal and state election laws, and he petitioned the Senate to refuse to seat Chavez.[41] With assistance from the Republican majority in the Senate, Hurley pursued his case for nearly two years. The efforts of Hurley and some Republican senators to reverse the outcome of the election cast national attention on voting practices in New Mexico. Former governor A. T. Hannett, Chavez's counsel during the investigation, admitted that some requirements of the state's election laws "were customarily and widely disregarded."[42]

The Senate Subcommittee on Privileges and Elections oversaw a recount of votes from some counties and absolved Chavez of fraud charges. In December 1953 the two Republican members of the three-member subcommittee recommended that 30,000 votes be thrown out for "lack of secrecy." Such a move would have given Hurley a victory.[43] In March 1954 the Senate Rules Committee by a 5-to-4 vote recommended that Chavez should lose his seat.[44] Later that month the full Senate rejected the recommendation: fifty-three senators voted that Chavez should retain his seat; thirty-six voted that he should lose it.[45]

Hurley responded to the Senate's decision by declaring that "unless the situation is changed, the election this fall in New Mexico will be about as free and as secret as one in East Germany or North Korea under Communist control."[46] Two weeks after the Senate confirmed Chavez's right to a seat in that body, a federal grand jury in New Mexico began an investigation, which concluded in September 1954. The grand jury declared Hurley's charges unfounded and "irresponsible."[47] The protracted struggle over the 1952 election reveals that Chavez's consistent support for the New Deal and the Fair Deal had alienated him from his Republican colleagues. His final election campaign, in 1958, did not generate any controversy.

Opponents such as Hurley may have been especially angered by the hold that Chavez had over Hispanic voters. In his campaigns for reelection, Chavez reminded Hispanics that they would lose their most powerful representative in a statewide office if they abandoned him for a Republican candidate.[48] Hispanic support for Chavez may have remained strong, too, as a result of his stand against employment discrimination. In 1945 and 1946 he defended the President's Committee on Fair Employment Practices from segregationist senators and sponsored legislation to outlaw discrimination in employment. Chavez's support for fair employment practices undoubtedly resonated among Hispanic Americans who felt increasingly marginalized as more Anglos moved into the state.

After the struggle over the 1952 election, Chavez's name rarely appeared in national news headlines. Chavez continued to work quietly for his constituents. From his positions on the Subcommittee on Defense Appropriations and the Committee on Public Works, he made certain that federal money and jobs would continue to flow into New Mexico. Scholars have given him credit for establishing the military and research installations in New Mexico that became the backbone of the state's economy after World War II.[49] As early as 1950, rumors surfaced that Chavez's health was declining. Although he was reelected in 1952 and 1958, his health deteriorated throughout his final decade, and he underwent a number of operations and hospitalizations. He died on November 18, 1962, after an eighteen-month battle with cancer.

Notes

1. See Leonard Pitt, *The Decline of the Californios: A Social History of the Spanish-Speaking Californians, 1846–1890* (Berkeley, CA, 1966); and Albert Camarillo, *Chicanos*

in a Changing Society: From Mexican Pueblos to American Barrios in Santa Barbara and Southern California, 1848–1930 (Cambridge, MA, 1979).

2. See, for example, E. B. Fincher, *Spanish-Americans as a Political Factor in New Mexico, 1912–1950* (New York, 1974), 130–61.

3. See Jack E. Holmes, *Politics in New Mexico* (Albuquerque, NM, 1967), 21–29.

4. Fincher, *Spanish-Americans*, 161.

5. The details of Chavez's childhood and early adulthood are described in Roy Lujan, "Dennis Chavez and the Roosevelt Era, 1933–1945" (Ph.D. diss., University of New Mexico, 1987), 5–11; Maurilio E. Vigil, *Los Patrones: Profiles of Hispanic Political Leaders in New Mexico History* (Lanham, MD, 1980), 149–50; and *Current Biography 1946*, 109. Little has been written about Chavez's personal life. In 1911 he married Imelda Espinosa of Albuquerque. The couple had two children, Dennis Jr. and Imelda.

6. Lujan, "Dennis Chavez," 34.

7. Ibid., 49–50.

8. Ibid., 42.

9. Quoted in ibid., 46.

10. Quoted in ibid., 53.

11. See John C. Russell, "Racial Groups in the New Mexico Legislature," *Annals of the American Academy of Political and Social Science* 195 (January 1938): 65; and Fincher, *Spanish-Americans*, 256.

12. Quoted in Lujan, "Dennis Chavez," 61.

13. Lujan, "Dennis Chavez," 66.

14. Ibid., 67–71.

15. William H. Pickens, "Bronson Cutting vs. Dennis Chavez: Battle of the *Patrones* in New Mexico, 1934," *New Mexico Historical Review* 46 (January 1971): 19.

16. Jan Spiess, "Feudalism and Senator Cutting," *American Mercury* (November 1934): 373.

17. Holmes, *Politics in New Mexico*, 163.

18. Pickens, "Bronson Cutting vs. Dennis Chavez," 20.

19. Ibid., 20.

20. Ibid., 22.

21. Fleta Springer, "Through the Looking Glass," *New Republic* (November 7, 1934): 358.

22. Quoted in Pickens, "Bronson Cutting vs. Dennis Chavez," 5.

23. Fincher, *Spanish-Americans*, 152.

24. "Chavez Is Named to Cutting's Seat," *New York Times*, May 12, 1935.

25. "Progressives 'Cut' Chavez in Senate," *New York Times*, May 21, 1935.

26. See Barry A. Crouch, "Dennis Chavez and Roosevelt's 'Court-Packing' Plan," *New Mexico Historical Review* 42 (October 1967): 261–80.

27. "Says Navajos Face Death in Landgrab," *New York Times*, June 6, 1936.

28. Quoted in Lujan, "Dennis Chavez," 393. See also Suzanne Forrest, *The Preservation of the Village: New Mexico's Hispanics and the New Deal* (Albuquerque, NM, 1989), 129–50.

29. For a more complete description of this arrangement, see Holmes, *Politics in New Mexico*, 209–14.

30. Donald Parman, *The Navajos and the New Deal* (New Haven, CT, 1976), 142–48.

31. See Lujan, "Dennis Chavez"; and Forrest, *Preservation of the Village*.

32. Lujan, "Dennis Chavez," 219–23.

33. "Head of New Mexico WPA Removed by Hopkins on Charge of Politics," *New York Times*, September 25, 1938.

34. "73 Leaders in New Mexico Politics Are Indicted for WPA Violations," *New York Times*, October 21, 1938.

35. "Chavez Relatives Freed in WPA Case," *New York Times*, February 11, 1939.

36. "Chavez Victor in Primary; Rival Says FBI Is Acting," *New York Times*, September 17, 1940.

37. "New Mexico Orders Inquiry," *New York Times*, June 5, 1946.

38. "Read to Hear Hurley: Senate Campaign Group Asks Affidavits on New Mexico Vote," *New York Times*, November 17, 1946.

39. "GOP in New Mexico Optimistic Over '50," *New York Times*, October 10, 1949.

40. "New Mexico Contest Brings 4 Impoundings," *New York Times*, November 6, 1952.

41. "Senate Ban Asked on Langer, Chavez," *New York Times*, January 3, 1953.

42. "State Voting Laws on Trial in Inquiry," *New York Times*, May 31, 1953.

43. "Senate Group Shifts Vote Margin of Chavez in New Mexico Inquiry," *New York Times*, December 19, 1953.

44. "Senate Unit Votes to Unseat Chavez," *New York Times*, March 17, 1954.

45. "Chavez Sustained in Senate as All Democrats Back Him," *New York Times*, March 24, 1954.

46. "Hurley Scores Senate," *New York Times*, March 25, 1954.

47. "Chavez Election Is Upheld; Grand Jury Scores Hurley," *New York Times*, September 26, 1954.

48. Fincher, *Spanish-Americans*, 153.

49. See Maurilio Vigil and Roy Lujan, "Parallels in the Career of Two Hispanic U.S. Senators," *Journal of Ethnic Studies* 13 (Winter 1986): 1–20.

Suggested Readings

Crouch, Barry A. "Dennis Chavez and Roosevelt's 'Court-Packing' Plan." *New Mexico Historical Review* 42 (October 1967): 261–80.

Donnelly, Thomas C. *The Government of New Mexico*. Albuquerque, NM, 1947.

_____. "New Mexico: An Area of Conflicting Cultures." In *Rocky Mountain Politics*, ed. Thomas C. Donnelly. Albuquerque, NM, 1940.

Fincher, E.B. *Spanish-Americans as a Political Factor in New Mexico, 1912–1950*. New York, 1974.

Forrest, Suzanne. *The Preservation of the Village: New Mexico's Hispanics and the New Deal*. Albuquerque, NM, 1989.

Holmes, Jack E. *Politics in New Mexico*. Albuquerque, NM, 1967.

Lowitt, Richard. *The New Deal and the West*. Bloomington, IN, 1984.

Lujan, Roy. "Dennis Chavez and the Roosevelt Era, 1933–1945." Ph.D. diss., University of New Mexico, 1987.

Pickens, William H. "Bronson Cutting vs. Dennis Chavez: Battle of the *Patrones* in New Mexico, 1934." *New Mexico Historical Review* 46 (January 1971): 5–36.

Russell, John C. "Racial Groups in the New Mexico Legislature." *Annals of the American Academy of Political and Social Science* 195 (January 1938): 62–71.

Seligmann, G. L. "The Purge that Fails: The 1934 Senatorial Election in New Mexico, Yet Another View." *New Mexico Historical Review* 47 (October 1972): 361–81.

Spiess, Jan. "Feudalism and Senator Cutting." *American Mercury*, November 1934, 371–74.

Vigil, Maurilio E. *Hispanics in Congress: A Historical and Political Survey.* Lanham, MD, 1996.

———. *Los Patrones: Profiles of Hispanic Political Leaders in New Mexico History.* Lanham, MD, 1980.

Vigil, Maurilio, and Roy Lujan. "Parallels in the Careers of Two Hispanic U.S. Senators." *Journal of Ethnic Studies* 13 (Winter 1986): 1–20.

Walter, Paul, Jr. "The Spanish-Speaking Community in New Mexico." *Sociology and Social Research* 24 (November 10, 1938): 150–57.

9

Frances Perkins
Always Working for Labor

Lisa L. Ossian

Frances Perkins, the first woman appointed to a presidential cabinet, is usually mentioned in history textbooks for that signal event in her life. But most people know very little about her. Perkins broke tradition from almost the beginning of her career. As a social worker she proved to be both tough and caring. She made her mark working for Governor Alfred Smith of New York and then for his successor, Franklin Roosevelt. When Roosevelt moved to the White House in 1933, he took Perkins with him as secretary of labor.

Her appointment was not popular at first among union members, who felt betrayed that the new labor secretary had not been named from their own ranks. Given the cultural environment of the time, labor leaders must have been appalled that a "mere woman" had been chosen as their spokesman and champion. Any reservations were soon dispelled by her forceful actions on behalf of working men and women. She held her cabinet post throughout the New Deal and for a few months into the Truman administration—the second longest cabinet service in the nation's history.

Lisa L. Ossian received her Ph.D. in agricultural history from Iowa State University in 1998. Her dissertation was "The Home Fronts of Iowa, 1940–1945." She teaches English at Southwestern Community College, Creston, Iowa.

Which men would he choose? Cabinet speculation began in the winter of 1933 before Franklin D. Roosevelt's first term as president of the United States. Newspapers reported that the Democratic Party, now back in power after twelve years of Republican rule, would put forward several qualified men. However, President-elect Roosevelt's choice for the Department of Labor—a position newly created in 1913 and traditional stronghold of labor unions—instead was a woman with no ties to labor. Who was this woman, dressed in black with a tricorn hat? Frances Perkins had assisted both New York governors, Alfred E. Smith and Roosevelt, after many years in social investigative work. Roosevelt believed that she was uniquely qualified and, because she was free from union pressures, had no ax to grind.

Frances Perkins served as the first woman in a presidential cabinet as Roosevelt's secretary of labor from 1933 to 1945, the second longest cabinet term ever. Her service was so great that it should not be forgotten. Her biographer, George Martin, was correct when he said, "Consider for roughly twenty years, from 1925 to 1945, on social legislation hers was the knowledgeable, dominant voice at the ear of the leader of the Democratic party." In assessing her impact, Martin considered her one of the most important women of her generation: "Even today, because of her work on minimum wage and on accident, unemployment and old age insurance, she has a hand in our daily lives."[1]

Fannie Caroline Perkins was born in Boston in 1880. Her parents soon moved to Maine, where Fannie grew up in a New England small town and a middle-class Victorian setting. Her father ran a stationery store; he read Greek for pleasure and taught his eight-year-old daughter to do so. Fannie attended a private high school and from there went to Mount Holyoke, a women's college, where she majored in chemistry and physics, the "exact sciences." Perkins's labor education began in her senior year when Professor Annah May Soule, believing her students innocent of the industrial process, took them to observe several paper mills and textile factories. Perkins was both astonished and fascinated.

After Fannie received her degree in 1902, both parents expected her to begin teaching, but she had other ideas. Initially, she wanted a position at the Charity Organizations Society in New York City. Fannie went straight to the organization's leader, a Mr. Devine, but he realized after several direct questions that Perkins was too young and inexperienced for social work. He recommended that she teach while studying the problems of poverty, and he urged her to read Jacob Riis's *How the Other Half Lives*. For the rest of her life, Perkins cited the book that had opened her eyes to the consequences of an inhuman and unjust industrial urban setting.

Perkins found a position at Ferry Hall, Lake Forrest, near Chicago, but never developed a desire to continue teaching. The work felt confining but provided an escape from her parents' home. Later, a friend's aunt introduced her to Hull House, and Frances (who had changed her first name) spent her free days at Jane Addams's settlement house. Perkins found that many immigrant women were earning pennies, not a living, through sweatshop work, and she discovered through urban organizer Gertrude Barnum's emotional speeches the necessity for union organizing. She was exposed to life's cruelties when she went on house calls with the nurses and witnessed scenes of families spun out of control by illness, injury, alcoholism, and extreme poverty.

One of her responsibilities was advocacy, collecting workers' wages from unethical employers, and by threatening to inform the employers' landlords she succeeded. Yet, despite difficult and sometimes gruesome experiences, she recognized that the experience of poverty was very different from her parents' definition. Like many Victorians, they believed that poverty was the result of alcoholism. Rather, poverty was shaped by harsh, intolerable working conditions—conditions that could only change with legislation and unionism. An individual's hard work was not enough. Perkins's devotion to social progress started at this point. Later, in *People at Work* (1934), Perkins paid tribute to Addams, the mother of social work, for she "taught us to take all elements of the community into conference for the solution of any human problem."[2]

Frances wanted direct involvement in social work. She wrote to many charities until she found an opening as executive secretary in a newly formed organization, the Philadelphia Research and Protective Association. She was to gather facts concerning the exploitation of newly arrived immigrant girls who were deceived into staying at commercial roominghouses or brothels. Southern black girls were also held at these "bawdy houses."

In Philadelphia, Perkins witnessed conditions that would have amazed her naive parents. She met girls who lived on $4 per week, eating only bread and bananas. Perkins learned to face difficult, even dangerous situations, especially with obstreperous men. And she also learned to work with socially minded, well-to-do women. Her professional success relied on gathering facts and speaking concisely—to say something meaningful in a few minutes.

Fact gathering required more education, and Frances decided in 1909 to earn her Master's degree in social economics at Columbia University in New York City. Perkins later stated for an interview that she "discovered her mind in graduate school. I never knew before that I had a mind. I learned easily, but I never knew that I had a mind that starts, operates on its own scheme, inquires, penetrates, goes to the bottom of things, puts two and two together and comes to some logical conclusions that have authority."[3] She devoted her first year to graduate study and in 1910 completed her thesis, a social survey of an impoverished immigrant neighborhood, Hell's Kitchen.

Frances started at the Consumers' League as executive secretary with the famed director Florence Kelley, a vocal workers' advocate. The League's purpose was "to improve the working conditions of laboring men and women by every means known for the prevention of ill health and poverty." Perkins's areas of social investigation were the sanitary conditions of East Side bakeries and fire prevention in factories, and she also lobbied for the League's Fifty-four Hour Bill. Rather than organizing unions, Perkins concentrated her energies on trying to "get a law."

The Fifty-four Hour Bill, which would limit the work week for women by guaranteeing one day of rest, had been formally introduced four years before Perkins started lobbying in Albany. After months of frustration, Perkins finally went to Al Smith, an apparently interested state senator, because the bill had stalled. Upstate canneries had blocked legislation with the canners' amendment, exempting them from overtime because of the seasonal nature of their output. These interests counted on their amendment defeating the bill because the League had initially rejected any alterations to the proposed legislation. At the last minute, however, Perkins agreed to the alteration because the proposed bill, even with its amendment, could still assist 400,000 working women in the state. She decided to continue working for the exempted 50,000 women employed at canneries if she did not lose her much-loved position at the League. Instead, Kelley embraced her for gaining some legal limitation on women's labor. Perkins learned from that incident to take, politically, what she could at the moment and called this delicate art of compromise being "a half-loaf girl"—that is, half a loaf is better than none.

The investigation of factory fire safety and common accidents such as hands mangled and hair "scalped" by machinery were other League interests. A turning point in industrial history was the Triangle Shirtwaist fire, which destroyed a factory on the ninth and tenth floors of a New York City warehouse. The fatal fire was started simply by a cigarette dropped in a basket of fabric and lace cuttings, but the deadly flames spread within minutes. Owners had locked the exits to prevent the entrance of union organizers and any alleged stealing by employees. The fire quickly turned tragic with the horrible sight of women hanging from windowsills where they dropped to their deaths and others jumping in panic with their dresses aflame. Frances happened to be having tea nearby when she heard the fire alarm. According to biographer Bill Severn, "Frances watched the fire with a horror she was never able to forget. The tragedy and the shock of it marked a turning point in the social conscience not only of New York but of the nation. It was, as she wrote years later, 'a torch that lighted up the whole industrial scene.' "[4] One hundred and forty-six women died.

A political investigative group appointed the Factory Commission in 1911 to conduct a four-year study of New York factory towns. Perkins as executive secretary took Senators Al Smith and Robert Wagner to see the realities of factory life. She showed them little children working at dawn in canneries. Although commission members also visited facilities that were well constructed, equipped, and operated, three conditions were common to most factory workers: low pay, long hours, and an extreme fear of the bosses' power.

During this period, life was not all work for Frances in New York City, where she met her husband, Paul C. Wilson. Both were attractive, politically active young adults in their thirties when they married in 1913. Paul was Mayor John P. Mitchel's assistant. One of Frances's friends thought that she would be lost to the social work movement once married, but Frances insisted on keeping her job. She claimed that she had wrestled with the idea of matrimony so much that she finally married "to get it off her mind."[5] She recognized, however, the disadvantage of being a Mrs. rather than Miss. With Mrs., people assumed that the husband's interests came first. Although her college alumnae records, the federal payroll, and her mother continued to style her "Mrs. Paul Wilson," professionally she remained "Miss Perkins."

In 1915, Frances suffered a serious illness at the end of her first pregnancy, and her baby died shortly afterward. Confined at home for several months, she continued her political work by telephone. The next year her daughter Susanna was born—Frances and Paul's only child. Frances worked for a year and a half after the birth of her daughter as the executive director of the Committee for Organizing Maternal Care. In a mother-daughter photo, Frances, dressed in white lace, holds her infant daughter joyfully in the air with both of them locked in a loving gaze.

In the winter of 1919, Frances described her husband as "better" when he left for Washington to undergo a combination of treatments. Paul believed that his illness was due to overwork and that he had neglected his health while serving as the assistant to New York's mayor. He never fully recovered. For the rest of his life he was not able to work and could only socialize on an infrequent basis. Sometimes he was hospitalized; at other times he required an aide at home. Sometimes his moods were elated; at other times he was depressed. Frances kept this matter entirely to herself, only sharing the stress of his constant care and medical bills with one friend, and never with the public or the press. It appears that she never considered leaving her husband.

When Governor Smith took office on January 1, 1919, one of his first appointments was Frances Perkins. The annual salary of $5,600 was critically needed for her family's needs, especially for her husband's medical bills, but many people thought that this was too much money for a woman. The appointment came as a complete surprise to Frances. Although she had campaigned for Smith, she did not consider herself part of his inner circle and supposed that their scheduled meeting concerned proposed child labor legislation. Governor Smith came right to the point—would she consider being a member of the Industrial Board? Perkins replied, "You mean it, Governor? You mean it?"[6]

Years later, Frances remembered walking, speechless, to a large window in his office and hanging onto a blue velvet curtain. Smith wanted to appoint a woman, but not a wife or sister of some male official; such an appointment would be an insult to women's new political aspirations, he thought. He wanted Frances for her knowledge and commitment. When she told her mentor the news over coffee the next morning, Kelley exclaimed with tears that she never thought she would live to see this day.

During Smith's second term as mayor, he insisted on speaking to Frances about her need to register as a Democrat. With rolled-up shirtsleeves and a big cigar, he told her, "Commissioner, you ain't got anything by being independent." Any politician needed a political party, he said, people to stand by you: "A party's a rallying point."[7] Smith won such a rally, gaining the presidential nomination at the 1928 Democratic convention. Although Perkins had attended the 1920 and 1924 conventions, she could not be present in 1928 because of her mother's stroke, her husband's illness, and her young daughter's needs. Although she thought that conventions were usually only "talk, talk, talk," she nevertheless thought them necessary for party strength. By chance, she heard the convention broadcast from Texas one night on her neighbor's radio, marveling over the new technology even as it kept her awake.

Many voters' animosities against the Catholic Smith went very deep. Perkins was one of several Protestant Democratic Anglo-Saxon women sent on a tour of the South to make little speeches about how great a man Smith was. There, Frances learned how deep anti-Catholic prejudice could be, especially in areas where the Ku Klux Klan was operating. In Independence, Missouri, part of a crowd turned on the women and started throwing tomatoes and eggs. Although a tomato hit her skirt when she spoke, Frances kept her composure and did not duck.

Smith lost, and Franklin Roosevelt retired early on election night, believing that he too had lost his first bid for the New York governor-

A typical portrait of Frances Perkins, c.1939. *Courtesy of the Franklin Delano Roosevelt Library, Hyde Park, New York*

ship—a bid he had made on Smith's insistence. Roosevelt had conducted an energetic campaign despite his desire to continue with physical therapy for his polio, but that night he thought that he had been buried in the national Republican landslide. In the morning, however, Roosevelt was awakened with the news that he had won the state by 25,000 votes out of 4.2 million cast. Smith had not even carried his home state of New York.

Only two women—Frances Perkins and Mrs. Sara Roosevelt, FDR's mother—stayed awake at Roosevelt's headquarters that night to hear the election returns along with the telephone operators and the tally men. Frances remembered her "ridiculous theory"—that election results might change if she did not give up her watch. Mrs. Roosevelt, an older woman not initially in favor of woman's suffrage but now deeply interested in politics, thought that she should not desert her boy. By 4 A.M. the tally men agreed that Roosevelt had narrowly won. Frances escorted Mrs. Roosevelt home that dawn in "a private if exhausted jubilation."[8]

Frances had first met Roosevelt years earlier in 1910 at a tea dance in New York City. In her biography, *The Roosevelt I Knew*, she contrasted their lives as young people. "I was studying at Columbia University for a Master's degree and working in a settlement house on a survey of the social conditions in the neighborhood. Roosevelt had just entered politics with a Duchess County campaign, which was not taken too seriously either by Roosevelt himself, his supporters, or his friends."[9] In 1920 he campaigned as the Democratic vice presidential candidate, but the following summer he contracted polio. When he appeared at the 1924 Democratic convention to deliver a nomination speech for Al Smith as the "Happy Warrior," Roosevelt was on crutches, "so pale, so thin, so delicate," but Frances remembered his voice as "strong and true and vigorous." After the speech, Frances realized that he somehow had to get off the dais. She and several other women ran up to congratulate him but also to hide him from the audience with their skirts while he was assisted off stage knowing "how hard it was for him."[10]

Governor Roosevelt wanted to prove that he was more broad-minded than Governor Smith by appointing Perkins to be head of the Industrial Commission rather than a board member. Smith had believed that men would not take direction from a woman but might listen to her advice from the board. Each governor believed that he had made a bold move, but Perkins reminded Roosevelt that Smith had appointed her when no woman had ever been named to any high state post. Roosevelt invited Frances to his family estate, Hyde Park, along the Hudson River. After lunch, he drove her in his hand-operated automobile around the grounds to discuss not only his trees and plantings but also business. Perkins wanted Roosevelt to understand that she expected to do serious reorganizational work with the Factory Act and workmen's compensation, perhaps even uncovering corruption. Although she thought that her previous position on the board was "the perfect job," she realized that she must take this next step even though it would mean more administrative headaches and less time with her family. She wrote, "I had been taught long ago by my grandmother that if anybody opens a door, one should always go through. Opportunity comes that way."[11]

Perkins gained national attention in January 1930 when she disputed President Herbert Hoover's unemployment report. The national figures were misleading, she believed; he was projecting optimism when the nation instead was falling deeper into an industrial depression. The lack of accurate unemployment statistics had been an ongoing concern of hers for years, and so she angrily sent her report to the newspapers. An editorial appeared in the *New York Times*: "Miss Perkins, State Industrial Commissioner, cites data on factory unemployment in New York by way of comment on alleged excessive optimism in Washington."[12] Perkins thought that FDR would criticize her rashness in contradicting the president, but instead Roosevelt admired her courage and her desire for accuracy. When she told him that she had sent the report to the press, he exclaimed, "The hell you have!" She then asked him if he was going to fire her, but he burst out, "I think that was bully!"[13]

After Perkins's challenge to Hoover, she made dozens of speeches around the country about the Great Depression. Governor Roosevelt advised her not to talk politics but to be "an outraged scientist and social worker." Frances was part of the general political buildup for the governor's possible presidential candidacy. By the end of 1931 she knew that Roosevelt would run: "It was one of those things that sort of rose. It was like the way water rises by osmosis."[14]

During the 1932 election year, Perkins campaigned for Roosevelt mostly in New York, but she did speak in several major cities that summer. In Chicago she was introduced as "the lady who disputed Herbert Hoover and turned out to be right," and Boston's mayor described her as "the little lady here from New York." When Roosevelt won the election by a landslide, Perkins was one of several campaign members who made a "bedraggled" 2 A.M. train trip back to the city from Hyde Park. "We were all tired and worn out, but happy as clams."[15]

As rumors started to circulate that winter about cabinet nominees, Perkins decided to "forget manners" and write to Roosevelt directly with her honest opinion that he consider someone from labor's ranks. Roosevelt believed otherwise. Frances Perkins's appointment as secretary of labor was announced on February 12, 1933. Molly Dewson, an influential leader of the Women's Division of the Democratic National

Committee, backed Perkins as a needed female presidential appointment to acknowledge the power and influence of the women's vote. A Boston newspaper viewed this appointment as a precedent—presidential cabinets would no longer be composed solely of men.

Many people thought that Eleanor Roosevelt, the First Lady, was instrumental in influencing her husband's decision, but in her memoirs she wrote, "As a matter of fact, I never even suggested her. She had worked with Franklin in New York State and was his own choice, though I was delighted when he named her and glad that he felt a woman should be recognized."[16] Eleanor considered Frances an old friend and included her in the weekly luncheons for cabinet and senators' wives. The First Lady was appalled at some of the unfair treatment of Frances by the press and even by women's groups over her twelve years. One of the initial slights came that first spring when Perkins was excluded from the annual all-male Gridiron Club dinner of politicians and journalists. Eleanor decided to host an all-female dinner at the White House in protest. The evening was a splendid success until, as *Time* reported, the Roosevelt police dog (the only male present) nipped Senator Hattie Caraway of Arkansas on the arm.[17]

When Perkins first discussed her possible appointment with Roosevelt, she suggested a list of policies, including unemployment insurance, public works, a minimum wage, maximum hours, old age insurance, and abolition of child labor. When the new president agreed with her proposed agenda, she accepted the appointment as secretary of labor. Frances received no invitation from the outgoing secretary, William Doak, although he appeared "nice enough" when she arrived at the Department of Labor. The building, cluttered with papers and books, looked dirty and grimy. Nothing was packed in Doak's office, and the staff was disorganized. When an assistant assembled all the employees for introductions, seven people told the new secretary of labor that they were in charge of immigration. Perkins recalled, "They often talk about a new broom coming in and cleaning house when a new administration comes in. We literally had to clean house in the good old-fashioned meaning of the word housecleaning. We actually had to sweep, clean and get rid of cockroaches before we could do much of any important work."[18]

In her lobbying days Frances had learned to dress and act like a mother because most men respect their mothers. As "carefully as an actress" she wore dark dresses with a white bow and a small tricorn hat. Her mother had thought that the shape balanced her long face, but Frances also liked the revolutionary symbol of the tricorn. The press noted that she even wore her hat through long days at the office. Her poker face proved difficult for most people to read, especially during labor negotiations, and her dark brown eyes were described as unblinking. When asked by the press if being a woman hampered her life, she pointed to her skirt and replied, "Only in climbing trees."[19]

Perkins had the advantages of high energy and good health to help her survive the stressful twelve years in national politics. *Time* reported in May 1933 that Madam Secretary's chauffeur quit after two months because he could not keep up with the seventeen-hour days of her morning-to-midnight schedule, but her next chauffeur did not mind. He told reporters, "Say! You can put this down. She's the sweetest little woman in the world to work for!"[20]

The depression decade, however, was not a time of sweetness and light. Perkins wrote in 1946 about that first year's difficulties: "It is hard today to reconstruct the atmosphere of 1933 and to evoke the terror caused by unrelieved poverty and prolonged unemployment." She continued, "Looking back on those days, I wonder how we ever lived through them. I cannot, even now, evaluate the situation. One thing I do see—it was dynamic. It was as though the community rose from the dead; despair was replaced by hope."[21]

Part of that hope was to unionize workers, who could then demand better hours, higher wages, and better conditions. In 1933 some 2.225 million workers were union members, but by 1945 the number had risen to nearly 14 million. In August 1933 almost 50,000 soft coal miners were on strike in Pennsylvania. The Republican mine operators did not realize that their old, hard-fisted methods of fighting strikes with armed guards would not reopen their mines this time. But did hard-fisted methods require the negotiation of a two-fisted male? William Green, the American Federation of Labor's union representative, declared, "The Secretary of Labor should be representative of labor, one who understands labor, labor's problems, labor's psychology, collective bargaining, industrial relations. . . . Labor can never become reconciled to the selection [Perkins] made."[22] But when Perkins stood up at the National Recovery Administration's steel code hearing in the first test of the union versus nonunion issue, Green was not only reconciled to Perkins's role as mediator but also felt jubilant about her effectiveness.

Perkins was not only considered a tough labor negotiator but could also be described by the press as "a generous, ingenious New England Auntie." When she learned late that summer of 1933 that six million children were starting school undernourished, she called a conference of doctors, dietitians, and educators to tackle this problem with solutions, not with government reports. She stated, "No amount of statistics and no number of bulletins can take the place of a lamb chop and a glass of milk at the right moment."[23]

Her role as a mother and her overall sense of fair play certainly helped her in her approach to the nation's problems, but so did her deep religious faith as an Episcopalian. A Midwestern reporter described her faith as "a central fact in Miss Perkins's life which is too often ignored." He remembered the difficulty of the new and potentially violent workers' tactic of the sit-down strike against General Motors in 1937. In church one Sunday, Perkins agonized over this drawn-out strike and returned to her office to write a letter about the Golden Rule to GM's president Alfred Sloan. Although she did not send the letter, she read it to reporters. Marquis Childs commented, "If Miss Perkins had sent her letter, I should have given a great deal to have a photograph of Mr. Sloan's face as he read it."[24]

Before Roosevelt's first inauguration, he had agreed with his new secretary to explore methods for unemployment and old age insurance in the United States. Much of this legislation could be based on Great Britain's example but primarily on insurance principles and workers' contributions. The president wanted an enduring social security system but not one based on "the dole." Perkins began her educating work in the cabinet and deliberately brought up the subject at the afternoon meeting on every second Friday. Then Congress held hearings with experts invited to testify. Perkins herself made more than one hundred speeches in different parts of the country in 1934, "always stressing social insurance as one of the methods for assisting the unemployed in times of depression and in preventing depressions."[25] The result was the Social Security Act of 1935.

In a radio address in September 1935, Perkins spoke about "The Principles of Social Security." The program, she stated, "does not represent a complete solution of the problems of economic security, but it does represent a substantial, necessary beginning." She concluded, "During the fifteen years I have been advocating such legislation as this I have learned that the American people want such security as the law provides. It will make this great Republic a better and a happier place in which to live—for us, our children, and our children's children."[26]

Despite her success, a whispering campaign began that claimed she was either a Communist or a foreign-born Jew because no record of her birth in 1882 in Boston could be found. Perkins had started listing 1882 as her birth date, giving herself two fewer years as some women did in that era. The rumors of Communist connections led a few disgruntled conservative Congressmen to call for her impeachment by the House of Representatives, but the controversy ended there. In the face of the challenge, she conducted herself with restraint. Perkins always had her detractors, however. In the 1940 presidential campaign, FDR's Republican rival, Wendell Willkie, made a speech before an audience of labor men that Perkins thought was "pretty good" until he declared, "I will appoint a Secretary of Labor directly from the ranks of organized labor." As the cheers died down, Willkie got another hand when he added, "And it will not be a woman either." Following the speech Perkins received more than 500 letters and telegrams of support, mostly from Republican women. Roosevelt was quick to catch his rival's blunder and commented to Perkins, "That was a boner Willkie pulled."[27]

One Sunday afternoon on December 7, 1941, the cabinet members were called back to Washington. When they reached the White House that evening, the president began, "We can't tell you too much news, but the Japanese have attacked us and have made an all-out assault on Pearl Harbor. That is an aggressive act of war." Frances was struck by the president's apparent calm in the midst of disaster. She recalled, "In my own mind I kept turning it over, 'How could there be a surprise attack? How could it be?' "[28]

Perkins described her World War II years as a period of straightening out tangles. She sat on several interdepartmental committees such as the War Labor Board and strengthened the Department of Labor's role and increased its appropriations. It was Perkins who created the Rosie the Riveter image for wartime propaganda. By the end of Roosevelt's third term in 1944, Perkins wanted to resign. She gave the names of several suitable replacements to the president and cleaned out her desk. But after the first cabinet meeting in January 1945 concluded, she wondered why he had not announced her resignation and waited until the others had left to ask him. He said to her in a soft and strained voice, "Frances, you have done awfully well. I know what you have been through. I know what you have accomplished. Thank you." She later wrote how deeply his comment touched her. "He put his hand over mine and gripped it. There were tears in our eyes. It was all the reward that I could ever have asked—to know that he had recognized the storms and trials I had faced in developing our program, to know that he appreciated the program and thought well of it, and that he was grateful."[29] She stayed.

Perkins's biographer, George Martin, described their long professional relationship as one of tenderness and trust. Roosevelt saw her as one of his most loyal friends. And Roosevelt could tease her as well. Once, during an important White House dinner that she had been unable to attend, he joked that if Hitler dropped a bomb on this gathering, the United States would have Frances Perkins as the first woman president.[30]

In the first week of April 1945 the president spoke to her about his planned visit to Great Britain the next month with the First Lady. Frances described the last time she saw him: "Although we were alone in the room, he put his hand to the side of his mouth and whispered, 'The war in Europe will be over by the end of May.' " She concluded his biography: "It comforts me to know that he was so sure, two weeks before his death, that the end of the war was at hand."[31] On April 12, Perkins received a phone call in her office late that afternoon directly from the White House that announced a cabinet meeting for 6 P.M. When she walked into the Oval Office, she saw only Vice President Harry Truman and Fred Vinson, the director of war mobilization and reconversion. When she inquired about the unusual hour, Truman replied, "The President is dead." Frances turned aside to make the sign of the cross. Roosevelt had had a stroke earlier that afternoon in Warm Springs, Georgia, and had died soon afterward. To Perkins, it seemed sad that Roosevelt had died before the creation of the United Nations and the end of the war. She described the cabinet that day as "a dreadfully shattered group of people."[32]

Perkins served only briefly, until that summer, in President Truman's cabinet. Although she admired his work, she had wanted to resign since 1944. The secretary of state, Cordell Hull, had also served on Roosevelt's cabinet for those twelve dramatic years and complimented his only female colleague in his 1948 memoirs: "Miss Frances Perkins, Secretary of Labor, has never received the full credit she deserves for her ability and public services. She was unusually able, very practical, and brought vision and untiring energy to her work."[33] In Deborah Felder's 1996 study, *The 100 Most Influential Women of All Time*, Frances Perkins is ranked twelfth as "the architect and engineer of some of the most profound social changes in U.S. history."[34]

After serving as secretary of labor for twelve years, Perkins now faced new challenges at age sixty-five. She completed her book, *The Roosevelt I Knew*, in 1946 and served on the Civil Service Commission as President Truman's nominee until 1953. She accepted a position in 1957 as visiting professor at Cornell University in the School of Industrial and Labor Relations. Always working for labor, Frances Perkins continued her teaching and public speaking until shortly before her death in 1965 at age eighty-five.

Notes

1. George Martin, *Madam Secretary: Frances Perkins* (Boston, 1976), ix.

2. Frances Perkins, *People at Work* (New York, 1934), 41.

3. Frances Perkins, *The Reminiscences of Frances Perkins* (Glen Rock, NJ, 1977), Book I.

4. Bill Severn, *Frances Perkins: A Member of the Cabinet* (New York, 1976), 39.

5. Perkins, *Reminiscences*, Book I.

6. Ibid.

7. Ibid., Book II.

8. Frances Perkins, *The Roosevelt I Knew* (New York, 1946), 48.

9. Ibid., 9.

10. Perkins, *Reminiscences*, Book II.

11. Ibid., 57.

12. *New York Times*, January 24, 1930.

13. Perkins, *Reminiscences*, Book III.

14. Ibid.

15. Ibid.

16. Eleanor Roosevelt, *This I Remember* (New York, 1949), 5.

17. *Time* (May 8, 1933): 9.

18. Perkins, *Reminiscences*, Book IV.

19. James G. Barber and Frederick S. Voss, *Portraits from the New Deal* (Washington, DC, 1983), 26.

20. *Time* (May 15, 1933): 14; ibid. (June 19, 1933): 41.

21. Perkins, *The Roosevelt I Knew*, 182, 212.

22. *Time* (August 14, 1933): 11.

23. Ibid. (September 25, 1933): 38.

24. Marquis W. Childs, *I Write from Washington* (New York, 1942), 270.

25. Perkins, *The Roosevelt I Knew*, 278.

26. Howard Zinn, ed., *New Deal Thought* (New York, 1966), 279, 281.

27. Perkins, *The Roosevelt I Knew*, 116–117.

28. Perkins, *Reminiscences*, Book VIII.

29. Perkins, *The Roosevelt I Knew*, 396.

30. Roosevelt, *This I Remember*, 249.

31. Perkins, *The Roosevelt I Knew*, 396.

32. Perkins, *Reminiscences*, Book VIII.

33. Cordell Hull, *The Memoirs of Cordell Hull* (New York, 1948), 210.

34. Deborah G. Felder, *The 100 Most Influential Women of All Time: A Ranking Past to Present* (Secaucus, NJ, 1996), 45.

Suggested Reading

Badger, Anthony J. *The New Deal: The Depression Years, 1933–1940.* New York, 1989.

Biles, Roger. *A New Deal for the American People.* DeKalb, IL, 1991.

Bird, Caroline. *The Invisible Scar: The Great Depression and What It Did to American Life, From Then until Now.* New York, 1966.

Brock, William R. *Welfare, Democracy, and the New Deal.* Cambridge, MA, 1988.

Childs, Marquis W. *I Write from Washington.* New York, 1942.

Davis, Kenneth S. *FDR: The New York Years, 1928–1933.* New York, 1994.

Felder, Deborah G. *The 100 Most Influential Women of All Time: A Ranking Past to Present.* Secaucus, NJ, 1996.

Goldston, Robert. *The Great Depression: The United States in the Thirties.* Indianapolis, IN, 1968.

Hull, Cordell. *The Memoirs of Cordell Hull.* New York, 1948.

Hurd, Charles. *When the New Deal was Young and Gay.* New York, 1965.

Josephson, Matthew and Hannah. *Al Smith: Hero of the Cities: A Political Portrait Drawing on the Papers of Frances Perkins.* Boston, 1969.

Kennedy, David M. *Freedom from Fear: The American People in Depression and War, 1929–1945.* New York, 1999.

Leuchtenburg, William E. *Franklin D. Roosevelt and the New Deal, 1932–1940.* New York, 1963.

Martin, George. *Madam Secretary: Frances Perkins.* Boston, 1976.

Mohr, Lillian Holmen. *Frances Perkins: "That Woman in FDR's Cabinet!"* Croton-on-Hudson, NY, 1979.

O'Connor, Richard. *The First Hurrah: A Biography of Alfred E. Smith.* New York, 1970.

Perkins, Frances. *People at Work.* New York, 1934.

_____. *The Reminiscences of Frances Perkins.* Glen Rock, NJ, 1977.

_____. *The Roosevelt I Knew.* New York, 1946.

Roosevelt, Eleanor. *This I Remember.* New York, 1949.

Severn, Bill. *Frances Perkins: A Member of the Cabinet.* New York, 1976.

Smith, Page. *Redeeming the Time: A People's History of the 1920s and the New Deal.* New York, 1987.

Ware, Susan. *Beyond Suffrage: Women in the New Deal.* Cambridge, MA, 1981.

Zinn, Howard, ed. *New Deal Thought.* New York, 1966.

10

Meridel Le Sueur
A Voice for Working-Class Women

Kathleen Kennedy

Meridel Le Sueur was one of a number of women during the period between the wars who was a successful and significant writer. Along with several others, she was a radical and a Communist, but she was not as ideological as one might expect. Her work captured the experiences of working-class women, which was her main purpose. Following World War II she faded into obscurity, partly because of the questions that had been raised about her politics, yet in the 1970s and 1980s she was rediscovered by the women's movement and her works were reprinted. Still alive at the time, she became something of a model for the newer feminists. Her struggles during the interwar years are instructive as to the nature of American society and culture in that transition period.

Kathleen Kennedy is associate professor of history at Western Washington University. She is the author of *Disloyal Mothers and Scurrilous Citizens: Women and Subversion during World War I* (1999).

Meridel Le Sueur was born into a pioneer family in Murry, Iowa, in 1900. Raised by her divorced mother and grandmother, Le Sueur, even as a child, participated in the major social movements of the first half of the twentieth century. At age fifteen she moved to Chicago to study dance and acting at the McFadden Physical Culture School. After graduation, she briefly tried the stage in New York, where she lived with the infamous anarchist Emma Goldman, and then went to Hollywood, where she secured work as a stuntwoman. Depressed and lonely, Le Sueur returned to the Midwest in the late 1920s and became one of the most prolific "proletarian writers" of the 1930s and 1940s. At the height of her career, Le Sueur's work appeared regularly in leftist literary magazines and collections of short stories. As the nation's politics turned increasingly to the right in the 1950s, Le Sueur was blacklisted and able to publish only her books for children. For the next thirty years her work languished in obscurity until it was rediscovered by the women's movements of the 1970s and 1980s. Supported by feminist presses, Le Sueur began a second literary career that continued until her death in 1996.

The significance of her second career notwithstanding, Le Sueur's lasting legacy is her portrayal of midwestern folk during the Great Depression. As one contemporary critic notes, "Through reportage and fiction, Le Sueur became the biographer of ordinary 'anonymous' men and women, especially the destitute."[1] As a social historian, she sought to reconstruct "the voice of the people." She believed that true American culture came from the oppressed and that knowledge about oppression could not be found in abstract theory but rather in the everyday experiences of workers, farmers, and women. Although she was a member of the Communist Party, Le Sueur's critique of exploitation derived less from Marxist theory than from what historians have called a "progressive regionalism," which located the battles against fascism and injustice in the native democratic tradition of the Midwest.[2]

Le Sueur's life and writings offer us insight into a midwestern radical tradition that sought social and economic justice for workers, migrants, farmers, and poor women—individuals whose lives, she argued, were buried in abstract unemployment statistics of the depression. Her stories are unique even among midwestern radicals because she took particular interest in the lives of poor women. Raised by two divorced women and often living among extended families of women, Le Sueur drew inspiration from women's relationships with each other. By telling their stories, her writings broke new literary and historical ground.

Her family history influenced her writings. Raised by pioneers who were active in the social movements of the day, Le Sueur saw herself as part of an indigenous American tradition of resistance against oppression. She viewed her family's own struggles against the worst excesses of monopoly capitalism as her inheritance. Her grandmother, Antoinette Lucy, migrated to Oklahoma to escape an alcoholic and abusive husband. Aware of the irony of her grandmother gaining her freedom from land illegally taken from Native Americans, Le Sueur wrote, "My grandmother sat in her buggy on the line of the Indian Territory of Oklahoma, when the stolen land was opened as a state. With her shotgun over her knees, she made the run and held the land till the claim was filed."[3] Land served as an important metaphor for Le Sueur: it signified freedom and self-ownership to migrants like her grandmother. Her work paid homage to the labor of ordinary folk, like her grandmother, who "wore the country on each foot. They salted it with their sweat, changed it with their labor, and had little more than six feet for their bodies. They kept alive the dignity of dissent and the right to impose upon it change; the cry for justice."[4]

As the experience of Native Americans illustrated, however, corporations, railroads, and the federal government dispossessed many people of their land. The result was growing rural poverty. Lucy was concerned about its effects on women and their children. Because of her middle-class upbringing, Lucy understood poverty as the result of individual moral breakdowns rather than systemic inequalities. Specifically, she blamed alcohol for this growing poverty and joined the Women's Christian Temperance Union (WCTU) to help women control their husbands' drinking.

Lucy defined poverty and violence against women as caused primarily by men's intemperance. She began organizing for the WCTU, often taking young Meridel to temperance rallies. Lucy's efforts on behalf of poor women made a lasting impression on her granddaughter:

> With her peculiar [singular] courage . . . she packed her small bag every week, set out by buckboard, into the miserable mining communities where she met in shacks and white steepled church[es] the harried, devout half-maddened women who saw the miserable pay checks go weekly at the corner saloon, and who attempted to stave off poverty and the disappearance of their husbands by smashing the saloons.[5]

As the irony of Le Sueur's last sentence suggests, she believed that her grandmother's political critique was limited. Because Lucy blamed social problems on the behavior of individual men, she sought legislation that would regulate men's behavior. In contrast to her grandmother, Le Sueur believed that alcohol abuse was a symptom of a more systemic problem. Le Sueur would come to see these efforts to control the behavior of working-class people as ineffective and unjust.

Le Sueur learned to view poverty as a systemic rather than individual problem from her mother and, later, her stepfather. Like her mother, Le Sueur's mother, Marian Wharton Le Sueur, divorced her first husband after he lost the farmland given to them by her father. Living in Texas at the time, Wharton fled to Lucy's home in the middle of the night because under Texas law, she could not divorce her husband and still retain custody of her children. Wharton turned to the women's rights movement both to explain her condition and to find employment.

Wharton made her living lecturing for women's rights and took part in that movement's more controversial actions. For example, she was arrested in Kansas City for giving out birth control information, and in 1918 she chained herself to the White House fence to protest President Woodrow Wilson's opposition to women's suffrage. Le Sueur, who accompanied her mother on her speaking tours, found this political activity thrilling. "It was a daring and wonderful thing," Le Sueur wrote, "to take the road to talk about the rights of women, in the beginning to stand trembling with nervousness, to be the butt of jokes, to see the frightened, asking eyes of the women who packed the opera houses."[6]

Women's rights organizing also provided Wharton with a framework for understanding the poverty that she encountered in the Midwest. Her political activity on behalf of workers and poor women eventually converted her to socialism. Wharton's commitment to socialism led her to the People's College in Ft. Smith, Kansas, founded by Eugene Debs, the best-known socialist of the early twentieth century, to educate workers' children. There, Wharton taught English. She also met Arthur Le Sueur, a logger-turned-lawyer who served a stint as the mayor of Minot, North Dakota. They soon married. In Le Sueur, Wharton found a loving companion who shared her commitment to workers' movements.

The Le Sueurs' relationship seemed to represent the revolutionary new marriage proposed by many socialists in the second decade of the twentieth century. Socialists advocated a type of companionate marriage in which men and women formed relationships from their common commitment to political and social causes. Such relationships were ideally based on affection and a mutual respect. Unlike the middle-class man, who kept his wife confined within the domestic sphere, the revolutionary new man saw his wife as his companion, as an intellectual and political equal. Together, husband and wife worked for economic and political democracy.[7]

Despite this ideal, socialist relationships often suffered from the same social inequalities that shaped middle-class marriages. Many socialist men still subscribed to middle-class assumptions about appropriate gender roles and greeted women's political and economic equality with the same scorn as any anti-feminist male. As Le Sueur observed about her parents' marriage, even when socialist men recognized their wives as their partners, the ideal proved difficult. "Marian found herself back in the cage of marriage she had tried to escape," Le Sueur wrote. "She was no longer Comrade Wharton, head of the English Department, with her own house and life. She was now doubly servant; she went to office at nine after getting her children off, she came back at four, cleaned the house, and got supper; in the evening she ran up and down between the apartment they occupied upstairs and the children's lessons in the front room."[8]

Influenced by her mother's experience, Le Sueur never married. She feared that marriage would cost her her identity and freedom. She also rebelled against the sexual repression that she believed had victimized her grandmother and that continued to characterize middle-class and even socialist relationships. Several of her stories explored women's heterosexuality and the conflicts between sexual pleasure and violence in those relationships. Middle-class ideologies of pure womanhood, Le Sueur argued, taught women sexual denial and shame and only contributed toward the violence that often warped sexual relationships between men and women. Rather than do as her grandmother had done—deny herself any sexual pleasure to avoid sexual exploitation—Le Sueur searched for an alternative model that allowed for women's sexual pleasure. This search proved difficult because Le Sueur had few models of writings by women that examined their sexuality in all of its complexities. Her efforts to explore these complexities distinguished her writings from her more conventional socialist and feminist colleagues.

Still, Le Sueur admired the political legacy left by her parents and grandmother. From them she learned about class exploitation and with them she participated in the major social and political movements of the day. But with the coming of the World War, the social and political movements that had nurtured her childhood came to a crashing halt. Vigilantes attacked her parents for their opposition to the war and burned the People's College to the ground. Moreover, many of her friends, including Emma Goldman, were imprisoned for their opposition to the war. Her stepfather defended those charged with interfering with the American war effort; he continued to defend workers and members of the left against charges of disloyalty until his death in 1950.

The immediate postwar period proved difficult for Le Sueur. Bickering with her mother but unhappy to be apart from her, Le Sueur entered into a period of depression. She could find little solace in the social movements that had generated excitement in her youth. Wartime demands for loyalty fractured left political movements, which kept the left in disarray throughout the 1920s. The two largest left organizations, the Socialist Party and the Industrial Workers of the World, lost many of their leaders because of wartime repression and never recovered their prewar strength. The Bolshevik Revolution and the creation of the Soviet Union further divided the left between those who supported communism and those who aligned with the more moderate socialists. In 1924, Le Sueur took her own side in these debates when she joined the American Communist Party and began writing pieces for its journal, the *Daily Worker*.

By the late 1920s, Le Sueur's life changed. She moved to Minnesota to be with her mother, and they settled in Minneapolis. In 1927, Le Sueur published her first short story, "Persephone," in *The Dial*. That same year, she was arrested for protesting the executions of Nicola Sacco and Bartolomeo Vanzetti, who had been convicted of the murder of a security guard and sentenced to death. Liberals and members of the left disputed their guilt. They argued that anti-immigrant and anti-radical sentiment had denied them a fair trial. While their actual involvement in the crime remains unclear, their cases attracted national attention and became symbols of the class and ethnic biases of the criminal justice system.

While in prison, Le Sueur decided to have a child. Her first daughter, Rachel, was born in 1928; a second daughter was born a year later. She never revealed the name(s) of the fathers. Raising children by herself proved challenging. She went to work during the day and, after putting her daughters to bed, would write. To keep awake, Le Sueur would immerse her head in cold water. She shared with social feminists the belief that women's experiences as mothers gave women a unique vision of the world. Putting a particular working-class spin on social feminism, Le Sueur argued, along with Lenin, that the mother-child bond was one of the few communal relationships left in the world. That relationship, she hoped, could serve as a model for building a new society in which the concerns of communities outweighed those of profit and individual achievement.

Le Sueur also recognized that for poor women, motherhood was often fraught with ambivalence. Her stories told of daughters ripped from their mothers by "dark Pluto-like men" (the Persephone legend) or forced to leave their families because of economic crises.[9] Separated from their mothers, such girls often met tragic ends. She relayed stories of women she had met who, lacking a male provider, were keeping together large, starving families. "The men are gone away from the family; the family is disintegrating," Le Sueur wrote. "The women try to hold it together, because women have the most to do with the vivid life of procreation, food, and shelter."[10] For such women, motherhood centered around the price of milk. As poor mothers focused on staving off death rather than continuing life, Le Sueur contended that monopoly capitalism denied to them their rightful inheritance—the affirming experience of creating new life.

The theme of women left alone to care for disintegrating families was common in Le Sueur's writings. Men, she noted, left when economic circumstances forced them to seek employment elsewhere. Women, on the other hand, had to stay behind and raise their children. Lacking the economic means to do so, women often died quietly and alone. Le Sueur believed that this experience bound women in a common history: "The women were often left alone, the men gone to better fields. The pattern of a migrating, lost, silent, drunk father is a mid-west pattern, and accompanying that picture is the upright fanatical prohibitionist mother, bread earner, strong woman, isolated and alone. My grandmother raised her own children, my mothers hers, and I mine."[11]

Le Sueur's writings addressed the great migration of women from the countryside to midwestern cities such as Minneapolis. There, in January 1930, more than 300 women applied through social services for work, and settlement house staffers could place only seventy. By 1934 an estimated 7,000 unemployed women applied for work. These numbers overwhelmed private and public welfare agencies.[12] Despite these numbers, women were invisible in unemployment statistics and in the labor movement. The Communist Party and the labor movements of the 1930s romanticized the male worker. As one historian argues, the language of the working class "forged a web of symbols which romanticized violence, rooted solidarity in metaphors of struggle, and constructed work and the worker as male."[13] This language represented women as mothers or as mere auxiliaries to the male worker.

Yet conditions in Minnesota also fostered women's participation in radical politics. The labor movement was strong in Minnesota during the 1930s, as was the Farmer-Labor Party. Led by Floyd Olson, the Farmer-Labor Party gained control of the statehouse and governorship. While in office, the Farmer-Labor Party expanded local relief, abolished labor injunctions, passed a moratorium on farm mortgages, and appointed women and leftists, including Le Sueur's stepfather, to public office. Their programs met only limited success. Republicans, who controlled the state senate, limited the Farmer-Labor Party's agenda by withholding funding for its key programs.[14]

Le Sueur found the political climate of the 1930s especially exciting. With the left and workers' movements reinvigorated, she discovered a political home for her writings. In addition to having political movements in which to participate, Le Sueur was surrounded by a community of "proletarian writers." According to Douglas Wixon, "Proletarian literature is identified . . . by its view of society in class terms and its sympathy with the outcast, the unemployed worker, the marginalized people in society." Midwestern literature in general took a pragmatic view of life, revealing an "intimate familiarity with one's surroundings, a sensitivity towards the unyielding limits on small town life and the hardships imposed by change."[15] Le Sueur, like many of the midwestern proletarian writers, was influenced by the work of folklorist B. A. Botkin, who drew on oral traditions, popular culture, and personal narrative. Among these writers, class consciousness merged with traditional midwestern literary genres to create a "new democratic myth of concern." In Wixon's words, "Regional difference, social content and 'labor lore' were the basic elements of a new democratic myth of concern constructed by the radicals, who resurrected traditional values such as community and cooperation and reasserted others such as the right to open assembly."[16]

The Communist Party gave midwestern literary radicals a chance to publish their social critiques. Through John Reed Clubs and a network of presses, the Communist Party nurtured their work. Its commitment to workers, its organization of the unemployed, and its defense of the rights of African Americans impressed midwestern radicals such as Le Sueur. Because she resided in the Midwest, she could ignore the often bitter debates that engulfed the Communist Party on the East Coast. Unlike some of its East Coast membership, Le Sueur was not concerned with correct ideology. Instead, she focused on creating a "people's culture" that gave voice to those not traditionally represented in official histories and that would expose the underlying violence of monopoly capitalism.

Encouraged by the existence of a network of midwestern writers but discouraged by their reception by the publishing establishment in the East, Le Sueur tried to build a community of these writers. She helped develop the Midwestern Writers Conference and co-edited *The Midwest*, which for a brief period published struggling midwestern writers. *The Midwest* described its mission as "[drawing] on the living root of American culture." Le Sueur believed that the "living root" was not invented in the cultural warehouses of the Northeast but in the everyday lives of common people. She hoped the magazine would rally progressives living within a region that, like the nation as a whole, was becoming more conservative.[17]

Male proletarian writers located this "living root" in a masculine working class. They envisioned that this new proletarian writing would promote a working-class hero. As the "son of working class parents," this new writer "[wrote] in jets of exasperated feeling and [had] no time to polish his work. He [was] violent and sentimental by turns." This proletarian writing would be freed of "the nice waterish diet of emasculated, unsocial writing."[18] Both the writer and his writing would capture the pure masculinity of working-class culture. This masculinization of proletarian writing's subject marginalized the experiences of women.

In contrast to her male colleagues, Le Sueur looked to women's experiences to define proletarian writing. Consequently, her colleagues in the Communist Party sometimes accused her of violating the central tenet of proletarian writing, "proletarian realism," which attempted to describe workers' lives as they were, using as few words as possible and avoiding melodrama at all costs.[19] But Le Sueur found this style inadequate to convey the complexities of women's lives. Her work paid particular attention to the stories that women told her about themselves. The characters were often composites of women whom she had met and interviewed while living in Minneapolis. By telling poor and dispossessed women's stories, Le Sueur was aware that she was breaking new ground. When her grandmother discovered that Le Sueur was writing about her, she told Le Sueur, "I've spent my whole life trying to conceal [my life]"—a life that Le Sueur argued had made her grandmother "mute."[20] By telling the stories that women did not want told, Le Sueur believed that she could provide a voice for women such as her grandmother to describe the violence in their lives. Le Sueur's stories confronted controversial topics such as rape, domestic violence, and abortion, but she also found in mothering some hope for the future. She wanted her stories to help foster a woman's culture of creation and nurturance, where a communal sensibility could replace the individualist ethos of industrial capitalism.

Le Sueur's work described how women experienced poverty. She believed that women's experiences were different from men's and that women were left out of discussions on how to eradicate poverty. Again and again, Le Sueur emphasized that women went through poverty alone. Unlike men, who could move on when work was scarce, women were bound to place because they had the primary responsiblity for raising children. Such women's lives were often buried in statistics that "make unemployment abstract and not too uncomfortable."[21] By putting a human face on such statistics, Le Sueur hoped to make women's unemployment and poverty very uncomfortable.

Le Sueur's stories were typically drawn from the experiences of women whom she had met during her travels. The stories that make up her most famous work, *The Girl*, derived from the lives of women from the Workers' Alliance in St. Paul. Alternating between fiction and reportage, she emphasized that women were poor because they were left alone to raise their children and because they were invisible to social services and the labor movement. "You don't see women in bread lines," Le Sueur wrote, because, unlike men who have developed a public culture from the experience of poverty, a woman will "starve alone in a hall bedroom until she is thrown out, and then will sleep alone in some alley until she is picked up."[22] Le Sueur's characters learned to build their own public cultures around their unique experiences, especially mothering. In Le Sueur's romanticized view of the future, women would play a leading role in creating a community of caring, which, based in the values of procreating and maintaining life, would replace the culture of individualism that characterized monopoly capitalism.

In her stories and reportage, Le Sueur attempted to describe the effects that poverty had on the human spirit. In "Women on the Breadlines," a group of women wait in an employment office for jobs that never come. "There is a kind of humiliation in it," Le Sueur wrote about the process of applying for jobs that did not exist. "We look away from each other. We look at the floor. It's too terrible to see this animal terror in each other's eyes."[23] "Women on the Breadlines" attempts to answer critics of the left who argued that poverty was the result of individual weakness. The women whom Le Sueur described were hungry not because they were weak; indeed, they had remarkable resilience. They were hungry because they could not break the cycle of poverty. And because they were humiliated by their experiences, they would not reach out to each other. Only by sharing their stories, Le Sueur believed, would women learn to understand their experiences as a community problem rather than as an individual one.

Since the late nineteenth century, middle-class feminists had proposed expanding state services as a way of managing poverty. Le Sueur was skeptical of the welfare state and her stories often were stinging indictments of public and private charity. While she shared with social feminists the belief that motherhood gave women a special role in society, she did not agree with the politics of protection that emerged from that movement and helped shape the welfare state. Instead of nurturing women's aspirations and providing a safety net for their children, Le Sueur argued that social welfare, whether state or privately funded, sharpened poor women's marginality. "Charities take care of very few and only those that are called deserving," Le Sueur wrote. "The lone girl is under suspicion by the virgin women who dispense charity."[24] Like the WCTU of her grandmother's era, social welfare agencies were middle-class efforts to regulate the behavior of the poor. In particular, social service agencies targeted the sexual behavior of poor women. Le Sueur told stories of women whose eligibility for aid depended on their willingness to accept sterilization. The welfare state, she argued, was an extension of middle-class paternalism that attacked working-class families.

Le Sueur believed that the solution to women's poverty did not lie in social feminism's welfare programs but rather in the communal sensibility in working-class movements. As a middle-class writer, Le Sueur was aware of her status as an outsider in workers' movements. But unlike some middle-class intellectuals, she believed that middle-class writers had a responsibility to "stand for a belief."[25] Her job was to record a "people's culture," which "existed apart from and [was] opposed to dominant culture." "All culture [came] from the oppressed," Le Sueur wrote. "The oppressed [were] the only repository of culture in monopoly capitalism."[26] To participate in that culture, she believed that a middle-class writer must "proletarianize" him/herself by ridding him/herself of the individualist ethos of capitalism.[27]

Le Sueur describes her own troubled efforts to "proletarianize" herself in "I Was Marching," which also documents her participation in the 1934 teamsters' strike in Minneapolis. The strike, led by General Drivers Local 574, all but closed down Minneapolis's trucking industry. When other workers joined the strike, the city sat perilously close to a general strike that could have crippled the entire business community. As in many of the large strikes during the depression era, the police clashed violently with the strikers. On a day known in labor lore as "Black Friday," the police opened fire on strikers killing two and wounding sixty-seven, after which some of the men returned to the picket line armed. Le Sueur spent much of that day nursing injured strikers. Although the violence appalled her, the resolve of the strikers and their ultimate victory invigorated Le Sueur, who, like many members of the left, believed that such strikes exposed a fatal weakness in monopoly capitalism.

"I Was Marching" describes the narrator's transformation from a sympathetic middle-class observer to a participant in the strike:

> If you come from the middle class, words are likely to mean more than an event. You are likely to think about a thing, and the happening will be the size of a pin point and the words around a happening very large, distorting it queerly. It is a case of "Remembrance of Things Past" [a reference to Marcel

Proust]. When you are in the event, you are likely to have a distinctly individualistic attitude, to be only part there, and to care more for the happening afterwards than when it's happening. That is why it is hard for a person like myself and others to be in a strike.[28]

Participating in the strike forced the narrator to reassess her world view. "I felt I excelled in competing with others and I knew instantly that these people were NOT competing at all, that they were acting in a strange powerful trance of movement *together*."[29] While the narrator's first instinct is to offer her "special talents" to the strikers, she instead serves coffee and food to the workers. At this time, she realizes that she has "never before worked anonymously."[30] She learns from this experience that the joy of work is not the individual satisfaction of building a career but in a "communal sensibility," in participation in and building a self-sustaining community.

In the 1930s and early 1940s, Le Sueur saw the best hope for this communal sensibility in the Communist Party and its valorization of the worker. Despite the Communist Party's masculine ethos and failure to recognize the unique oppression of women, it provided for women like Le Sueur "a political theory and program of action to which she could commit herself."[31] Le Sueur's support, however, was not unqualified. She criticized the party for "beat[ing] the lyrical and emotional out of women" and for substituting workers' experiences with abstract theory in its analysis of workers' conditions. In turn, party members scolded Le Sueur for her lyrical style. Some party members also questioned Le Sueur's choice to have children. They feared that motherhood might distract her from her political work.[32]

Like many midwestern writers, Le Sueur Americanized the Communist Party's ideologies. While she accepted its basic philosophy, her critique of American society derived from the experiences of working people and from the social movements of her youth. She believed that the Communist Party nurtured a "progressive regionalism" that emphasized grass-roots democracy, anti-authoritarianism, and a Jeffersonian republicanism.[33] She rejected the party's harsher demands for conformity even as she defended it against its critics.

Le Sueur's search for a "progressive regionalism" led her to take advantage of the Works Progress Administration (WPA) and its sponsorship of writers. Under its sponsorship, she wrote a social history of the region. She recorded her own family's history in *Crusaders*. Le Sueur believed that the history of a people was found in the details of everyday life; she hoped to restore to the folk their historical legacy. Le Sueur was a conventional social historian who looked to the details of everyday life for the process of historical change. "It is only you who are making this history and can write the true story of it." Le Sueur wrote, "No matter what, you are a part of history. If you buy an orange or ride in a car or decide to have a baby, you are making history. History is a thing that everyone feels and some of us make it and many of us are living it right now."[34] In the words of critic Julia Mickenberg, Le Sueur wrote to reflect "upon the future of America's democratic promise [and] to demonstrate that those who built the nation's riches were its rightful inheritors."[35]

Le Sueur understood that the writing of history was a powerful weapon for both the oppressed and the oppressors. In the hands of the powerful, it could hide the contributions and struggles of the disinherited. She was especially concerned that women's history had been withheld from them. By writing about her mother and grandmother, Le Sueur attempted to restore their struggles to the historical record. She wrote of her mother:

> To those who remember her as an independent, aggressive, bold and brilliant woman it is difficult to understand that for each of these distinctions she had to fight most of society, public opinion and the laws of the land. Women especially would like to believe that her talents were God-given. But it was not so. Her anger, her strength, her determination, even her brilliance and her oratory were things she developed, often alone, and struggled and fought for, as much as [black abolitionist] Frederick Douglass had to struggle to even read. In Texas her husband divorced her on the grounds of dangerous thoughts gleaned from reading books![36]

Le Sueur believed that future generations should read history to understand the struggles of those who resisted the powerful. This legacy of resistance against exploitation, poverty, and despair, she argued, was the future generations' American inheritance.

The publication of a short-story collection in 1940 entitled *Salute to Spring* gained Le Sueur her greatest popularity. She supported American participation in World War II and wrote stories that captured the common soldier's experience. But with the war's end, the country entered into another period of conservatism. Ridding the nation of communism became the special mission of the House Un-American Activities Committee (HUAC). In the Senate, Joseph McCarthy stoked the fires of anticommunism with a relentless campaign against government workers and public figures whom he believed associated with Communists. Hollywood and the publishing industry blacklisted writers and performers suspected of disloyal behavior. Le Sueur and her family were continuously harassed by the FBI, and her daughter and son-in-law were called to testify before HUAC. Le Sueur was blacklisted, and publishers rejected her work and only consented to issue her children's books quietly. She made a modest living by teaching writing at the YWCA.

In the late 1960s the second women's movement took up her project of writing the histories of women. In its early stages, this history attempted to uncover the women writers of the past. Le Sueur's work found a new audience, and The Feminist Press published a collection of her short stories in 1982. Invigorated by the second women's movement, Le Sueur published *The Girl* and several new works. Many of her earlier ones have now been reissued. Most recently, the popular folk rock band The Indigo Girls immortalized Le Sueur for a new generation in their paean to college student activists, "Go." By the time that Le Sueur succumbed to a long illness at the age of ninety-six, a second generation of scholars and activists had restored her to the American literary canon as a quintessential social historian and proletarian writer.

Notes

1. Constance Coiner, *Better Red: The Writings and Resistance of Tillie Olsen and Meridel Le Sueur* (Urbana, IL, 1998), 81.

2. Douglas C. Wixon, *Worker-Writer in America: Jack Conroy and the Tradition of Midwestern Literary Radicalism, 1898–1990* (Urbana, IL, 1994), 147.

3. Meridel Le Sueur, *Crusaders* (New York, 1955), 11.

4. Ibid.

5. Ibid., 39–40.

6. Ibid., 46.

7. Mari Jo Buhle, *Women and American Socialism* (Urbana, IL, 1983).

8. Le Sueur, *Crusaders*, 52.

9. Elaine Hedges, "Introduction," in Meridel Le Sueur, *Ripening: Selected Works, 1927–1980* (Old Westbury, NY, 1982), 5.

10. Meridel Le Sueur, "Women Are Hungry," in ibid., 144.

11. Le Sueur, *Crusaders*, 39.

12. Elizabeth Faue, *Community of Struggle and Suffering: Women, Men, and the Labor Movement in Minnesota, 1915–1945* (Chapel Hill, NC, 1991), 59.

13. Ibid., 71.

14. Ibid., 111.

15. Wixon, *Worker-Writer in America*, 5.

16. Ibid., 147.

17. Julia Mickenberg, "Writing the Midwest: Meridel Le Sueur and the Making of a Radical Regional Tradition," in *Breaking Boundaries: New Perspectives on Women's Regional Writing*, ed. Sherrie A. Inness and Diana Royer (Iowa City, IA, 1997), 150.

18. Paula Rabinowitz, "Maternity as History: Gender and the Transformation of Genre in Meridel Le Sueur's *The Girl*," *Contemporary Literature* 29 (1988): 538.

19. Ibid., 539.

20. Mary Antoinette Lucy and Meridel Le Sueur quoted in Coiner, *Better Red*, 72, 123.

21. Le Sueur, "Women Are Hungry," 145.

22. Ibid.

23. Meridel Le Sueur, "Women on the Breadlines," in *Ripening*, 137.

24. Ibid., 141.

25. Le Sueur quoted in Hedges, "Introduction," 9.

26. Le Sueur quoted in Coiner, *Better Red*, 100.

27. Ibid., 93.

28. Meridel Le Sueur, "I Was Marching," in *Ripening*, 158.

29. Ibid., 159.

30. Ibid., 160.

31. Hedges, "Introduction," 14.

32. Ibid.

33. Wixon, *Worker-Writer in America*, 149.

34. Le Sueur quoted in Coiner, *Better Red*, 156.

35 Mickenberg, "Writing the Midwest," 152.

36. Le Sueur, *Crusaders*, 42.

Suggested Readings

Coiner, Constance. *Better Red: The Writing and Resistance of Tillie Olsen and Meridel Le Sueur*. Urbana, IL, 1998.

Faue, Elizabeth. *Community of Struggle and Suffering: Women, Men, and the Labor Movement in Minnesota, 1915–1945*. Chapel Hill, NC, 1991.

Le Sueur, Meridel. *Crusaders*. New York, 1955.

_____. *The Girl*. New York, 1986.

_____. *Ripening: Selected Work, 1927–1980*. Old Westbury, NY, 1982.

Mickenberg, Julia. "Communist in a Coonskin Cap? Meridel Le Sueur's Books for Children and the Reformulation of America's Cold War Frontier Epic," *Lion and the Unicorn: A Critical Journal of Children's Literature* 21 (January 1997): 59–85.

_____. "Writing the Midwest: Meridel Le Sueur and the Making of a Radical Regional Tradition." In *Breaking Boundaries: New Perspectives on Women's Regional Writing*, edited by Sherrie A. Inness and Diana Royer. Iowa City, IA, 1997.

Roberts, Nora Ruth. *Three Women Writers: Class and Gender in Meridel Le Sueur, Tillie Olsen, and Josephine Herbst*. New York, 1996.

Wixon, Douglas C. *Worker-Writer in America: Jack Conroy and the Tradition of Midwestern Literary Radicalism, 1898–1990*. Urbana, IL, 1994.

11

Gerald L. K. Smith
Political Activist, Candidate, and Preacher of Hate

Cynthia Clark Northrup

The United States has a long tradition of supporting evangelists, from George Whitefield during the Great Awakening of the eighteenth century to the televangelists of today. Some of these revivalist ministers, especially in the twentieth century, have found the lure of politics so irresistible that they have tried to use religion to influence political change. Today, leaders of the religious right are the most successful in this long line of activists.

Gerald L. K. Smith was a pioneer who helped to pave the way for the contemporary politically active religious leaders, even though most of them probably would have rejected his basic philosophy, especially his anti-Semitism and his opposition to the rights of African Americans. Even so, Smith was an important religious, and then political, leader in the period between the wars. He was an opportunist who attached himself to people— such as Huey Long—who agreed with him and were willing to tolerate his involvement. Before long, however, most political conservatives rejected him, and he found himself isolated. Near the end of his life he abandoned his political views and returned to religion.

Cynthia Northrup, a history faculty member at the University of Texas at Arlington, chronicles Smith's importance in this essay. A specialist in modern American history, she holds a Ph.D. in history from Texas Christian University. She currently is working on a four-book series dealing with U.S. tariff and trade policies.

Americans have gravitated traditionally toward strong, dynamic individuals who exude an air of self-confidence, especially during tumultuous times. The common-man qualities of Andrew Jackson persuaded many newly enfranchised voters to vault him into the presidency in 1828 as the nation adapted to the market revolution. The rugged individualism and fortitude of Theodore Roosevelt inspired patriotism in the public as the president enthusiastically led a reluctant and uncertain United States into an era of world domination. The poise and resolve of Ronald Reagan restored the spirit of the country after the Iranian hostage crisis, a prerequisite for the steadfast confrontation of communism that ended the Cold War.

Other effective communicators have enthralled the masses with their rhetoric, with some leaving a lasting impression on the nation's consciousness. Charles Finney sparked a revival movement that altered religion in America by calmly depicting, in vivid detail, the horrific consequences in store for the sinner who failed to repent. William Jennings Bryan took up many causes with his oratory to preserve traditional American values. Dr. Martin Luther King Jr. embued a generation of African Americans with the hope that his dream of equality could be achieved even as the nation struggled to deal with the assassination of President John F. Kennedy and America's continued involvement in the Vietnam conflict.

Just two months before the Spanish-American War, another great orator entered this world. Gerald Lyman Kenneth Smith, born in Pardeeville, Wisconsin, on the bright Sunday morning of February 27, 1898, followed in the footsteps of his father but exhibited a speaking talent far greater than Lyman Smith ever possessed. With a family steeped in the tradition of the Republican Party, as a youth Smith attended church regularly wherever congregations gathered to listen to his father, a third-generation fundamentalist preacher, proclaim the word of God. At the age of seven, Smith was baptized; and five years later he informed his family that preaching would be his chosen profession, a decision that pleased all of his loved ones. Although his family was poor and his father frequently ill, Smith remained in school while working odd jobs to help support the household. During these early years he displayed an eloquence evident through his participation in school debates and plays. For one particular oratory competition, Smith recited Bryan's "Cross of Gold" speech to the roaring applause of the audience.[1]

Before entering the ministry, Smith decided to further his education. In the spring of 1918 he graduated from Valparaiso University, a school for indigents in Indiana, and started applying to graduate schools where he hoped to earn his Masters degree in theology. During the summer he contracted nephritis, a severe kidney infection, and his plans to attend school in the fall faded as he was forced to move back to his parents' house in Viroqua. After a lengthy recovery that lasted almost a year, Smith accepted his first ministerial position as a temporary pastor in Soldier's Grove, Wisconsin. In the pulpit he found his calling. While at the Christian Church his oratory skills drew new congregants and so inspired original members that within a few months he raised enough money to pay off the $4,000 mortgage on the building.[2]

Smith's ambition, dedication, and brilliant speaking brought him recognition and success in the ministry. Shortly before marrying Elna Sorenson, Smith accepted a pastorate at the church in Beloit, Wisconsin, where he stayed for more than three years before his compulsive working led to a breakdown. After a three-month recovery he immediately accepted the responsibility of leading a larger church in Kansas, Illinois, and two years later became the minister of the Seventh Christian Church in Indianapolis, where he organized youth groups, attended night classes to earn his degree in theology, and increased the size of the congregation to 2,000 members after preaching his "Come to Jesus" sermon. Always searching for a bigger challenge, Smith agreed to work with a small group of college students meeting at the University Place Christian Church, helping them to develop and implement a twenty-five-year plan to build and finance a new sanctuary. In one year his dynamic sermons drew 1,600 new converts to his flock. In 1929, Elna contracted tuberculosis. Smith, after consulting specialists and inquiring about the best area for recovering patients, resigned his pulpit and moved with his wife to the pine hills of northwestern Louisiana, where his diligence and persuasive sermons helped increase the membership at King's Highway Christian Church by 356 people within the first two years. Despite the stock market crash in 1929 and the onset of the Great Depression, Smith continued to raise more contributions than ever. His exceptional oratorical skills brought him a significant number of invitations to speak at local clubs, civic meetings, and church groups, including the Chamber of Commerce, Rotary Club, Boy Scouts, YMCA, and area revivals. His charismatic personality attracted the praise of clergy from other faiths as well as of E. H. Williams of the American Federation of Labor and wealthy businessmen such as W. K. Henderson, who contributed to Huey Long's organization.[3]

Gradually, Smith shifted his focus from salvation to social reform, leading many of his parishioners to question his motives and his commitment to the church. The first sign of trouble appeared when Henderson financed the broadcast of Smith's radio sermons during which he voiced opposition to the corrupt practices of Standard Oil. By 1932 he had accepted an invitation to address the United States Olympic Committee in Los Angeles and also headed the local Community Chest fund. Members of the church objected to the amount of time that Smith spent on nonpastoral activities, especially after their minister began devoting a minimum amount of time and thought to the development of his homilies. Dedicated to assisting his parishioners, Smith found himself in the role of intermediary when several members asked for his help to save their homes from foreclosure by the Mutual Building Association, a company owned by other church members and a Jew named Philip Lieber. Smith called on Lieber, who refused to consider an extension of the notes until after Smith contacted Huey Long, the U.S. senator who controlled Louisiana politics. After receiving a call from Long, the banker cancelled the mortgage. While some of the church members thanked Smith for his involvement, others criticized him for interfering in private business matters, an area they deemed outside the purview of his position as the head of the church. Criticism over Smith's actions in this matter led the young crusader to resign.[4]

Smith and Long crossed paths again a few months later. Smith had decided to focus on humanitarian causes after leaving the ministry, and Long provided the opportunity for him to link his need and desire for recognition to a noble cause. In the midst of the Great Depression, Long devised a plan to help the poor masses who made up his power base, but he needed an organizer and spokesman to promote the idea. Smith, whose religious background disarmed many of Long's opponents and critics, formed the Share Our Wealth Society nationwide, calling for a maximum yearly individual earning of $1 million and an amassed fortune of no more than $5 million per person. Under the plan any excess amounts would be confiscated and redistributed; every family would receive a guaranteed income of $2,000 to $3,000 per year, free college tuition for qualified students, bonuses for veterans, and pensions for the elderly. Long spoke before many crowds, persuading them to support his program; those who backed him had their names placed on a mailing list. Smith spoke if Long had a scheduling conflict or was too exhausted to address the people himself. The positive response by the crowds to Smith's showmanship and dynamic appeal persuaded Long to employ Smith's gift of persuasion more frequently. Using a combination of mellow, reassuring tones with sudden shifts to violent, emotional pitches, Smith spoke to more than one million people throughout the South in 1934. Just four weeks after he assumed responsibility for communicating the message to the public, membership in the Share Our Wealth Society increased by 207,000 members. By January 1935, one year later, he had recruited 4.5 million Americans, and by July of that year the numbers had swelled to 7 million. With sweat soaking his shirt and running down his face, with his strong masculine presence dominating the audiences, and with the conviction of a hellfire-and-brimstone preacher, Smith persuaded the poor and the masses to support Huey Long, who would save the American people from their deep despair and uncertain future.[5]

At the height of his popularity as the right-hand man of a powerful and influential politician, Gerald Smith's world vaporized with the flash of a gun. In September 1935 an assassin murdered Long in the Louisiana capitol in Baton Rouge. After eulogizing his mentor, Smith attempted to assume leadership over the slain senator's followers, but the political contributors, particularly Seymour Weiss and Robert Maestri, reached a compromise with Franklin D. Roosevelt, agreeing to support the president's reelection bid in exchange for federal aid for Louisiana. Once the deal was concluded, Smith, who received word that his services were no longer required, attempted to obtain a copy of Long's mailing list to start his own organization. When he discovered that Weiss and Maestri had destroyed the names and addresses, he sought out other Long employees who might have the list, particularly Earle Christenberry, who had gone to work for Dr. Francis E. Townsend, another depression-era demagogue with a cure for the nation's problems.[6]

During the difficult economic times of the 1930s, Americans accepted the demagoguery and radicalism of a number of charismatic leaders with the hope that their ideas and programs would resolve the ever-deepening crisis. Smith joined the ranks of these nationally recognized personalities to find a replacement presidential candidate for his beloved Huey Long. In late 1935 he backed Eugene Talmadge, who supported the rights of the poor while accepting money from rich conservatives such as Pierre S. du Pont and Alfred P. Sloan, chairman of General Motors. Talmadge organized a convention to announce his intentions to run for the presidency and invited Smith to speak. When Smith received more applause from the crowds than he did, Talmadge severed the relationship and later withdrew altogether from the campaign.

Never discouraged, Smith located Christenberry at the headquarters of Dr. Townsend and within a matter of weeks worked himself into a position as adviser to the aging physician. Townsend advocated an "Old Age Revolving Pension" that guaranteed retirees over the age of sixty a monthly income of $200 from the government on condition that they spend the entire amount before the next month, thereby stimulating the economy; supporting earlier retirement that opened jobs for young workers; and increasing revenue for the government through a 2 percent sales tax. Smith persuaded Townsend to change the name of the program to the "Townsend Recovery Plan" and generated support for the idea. At the same time, Smith contacted Father Charles E.

Coughlin, a popular Catholic priest in Royal Oak, Michigan, who reached millions of listeners each week through his radio programs. Coughlin, who received thousands of letters and calls weekly, opposed the financial policies of Roosevelt; he particularly disagreed with the president on the use of silver to back U.S. currency—a strategy designed to reduce inflation and increase circulation.[7]

The triumvirate of Smith, Townsend, and Coughlin formed a new political party to oppose the reelection of Roosevelt in 1936. The Union Party chose Congressman William Lemke of North Dakota as its candidate and defined the party's platform as opposing inflation, assisting farmers, supporting a high protective tariff, and pursuing an isolationist foreign policy. The Townsend Recovery Plan formed the basis of the party's attitude concerning senior citizens. Coughlin's insistence on the use of silver dictated the economic policies of the organization, while Smith influenced social aspects such as free education for the poor and liberal labor policies. Although Smith and Coughlin employed their formidable speaking skills to arouse their supporters, they failed to develop a strong grassroots organization that would sustain the election. The Union Party candidate appeared on the ballot in only fourteen states, with an additional six states allowing for the candidate on a write-in basis.[8]

Weeks before the November election, Smith alienated himself from both the candidate and the other members of the triumvirate and ensured the failure of the party. On October 22, 1936, he announced that he personally would lead a group of more than 10 million followers against an "international plot to collectivize" the United States. Comparing Smith's strong nationalism to an American version of Nazism, Lemke, Townsend, and Coughlin severed all ties to Smith. Although Lemke received 891,858 votes, the disunity among the leaders, the lack of a strong labor base, and a reliance on anti-Roosevelt sentiment resulted in the dissolution of the Union Party in 1938.[9]

After the 1936 defeat, Smith experienced a political transformation. He moved to New York City where he formed an anti-Communist and anti-New Deal organization that he called the Committee of Ten Thousand, later to be known as the Committee of One Million. Members devoted their energies to investigating all Communist meetings and groups in an effort to preserve the right of private property, defend the Christian faith, and uphold the Constitution and democratic principles of the United States. Instead of poor people and the masses providing the financial support for the group, most of the funds originated from wealthy businessmen such as William Brown Bell of American Cyanamid, Charles Costa of Costa Trucking, members of the Pew family of Sun Oil, and Horace Dodge, the automobile magnate.[10]

When President Roosevelt announced his intention to seek an unprecedented third term, Smith devoted his energy to opposing FDR. In 1940, Smith chose Ohio's Governor John W. Bricker as the candidate whom he would support, but Bricker failed to win the Republican nomination. Then Smith decided to back Wendell Willkie, the Republican candidate, during the presidential campaign. After losing the election, Willkie toured the country promoting the idea that the United States should join a world organization, a concept that Smith adamantly opposed. Afterward, he determined to challenge any attempt by Willkie to seek the Republican nomination again in 1944.[11]

Just as Smith appeared to be settling down into a comfortable life based on his own popularity instead of relying on the fate of others, accusations concerning his motives and extremism derailed his movement once again. The first problem arose when Smith and Pat Powers, one of the partners of the Committee of One Million, disagreed over the direction of the group. Powers had been involved with its finances, and his separation from Smith negatively influenced fundraising efforts. Then a March of Time newsreel on Smith entitled "The Lunatic Fringe" portrayed him as a self-promoter concerned only with his own fame instead of with the plight of others. The documentary showed Smith practicing his speeches before a mirror, which led the producers to question whether he was a "man of destiny or merely a political windbag." The political fallout from the newsreel ended Smith's effectiveness in New York.[12]

In 1939, after moving to several towns in the Midwest, Smith and his wife settled in Detroit, where financial supporters such as Dodge breathed new life into his dying career. In addition to numerous offers to speak to local groups, Smith also obtained the financial backing necessary to produce a program carried on the forty-eight radio stations across the country that had previously aired Father Coughlin's sermons and speeches. Within a matter of months, Smith received more speaking invitations than he could accept, collected more than 250,000 names for his own mailing list, initiated a direct-mail program to address local issues, and offered a number of books to his followers. To promote his organization, he recruited volunteers, including such high-level government officials as Senator Robert R. Reynolds of North Carolina, Senator Arthur H. Vandenberg of Michigan, and Senator Burton K. Wheeler

Formal portrait of Gerald L. K. Smith. *Courtesy of Great Passion Play, Eureka Springs, Arkansas*

of Montana. In 1940, Smith reached 40 million listeners weekly who sent in contributions totaling $1,800 per week. By 1944 he was receiving more than $5,000 per week in donations.[13]

Instead of attacking the rich as he had done with Huey Long, Smith vilified Communists, labor unions, and Jews. According to Smith, labor unions acted as an instrument of the Communist Party in influencing workers to pursue a socialistic society. He particularly hated Walter Reuther of the United Auto Workers and his brother Vic who, according to Smith, had received instructions directly from Communist leaders during a visit to Moscow. His close ties with automobile moguls such as Dodge and Henry Ford distorted his views of labor.

Ford's distrust of Jews also influenced Smith, especially after he read Ford's book, *The International Jew*, which condemned Jewish bankers for the financial problems associated with the depression. Memories of another banker named Lieber from Shreveport convinced Smith that America should distance itself from Jewish financiers. Smith, who always blamed FDR for the assassination of Huey Long, argued that the president relied on too many Jews who filled the top positions in his administration—among them Bernard Baruch, Samuel Rosenman, and Supreme Court Justice Felix Frankfurter. Smith advocated a constitutional amendment that guaranteed the right of the American people to recall the president for unpatriotic acts such as filling cabinet positions with Jews.[14]

In 1942, Smith campaigned for a Senate seat from Michigan, but his failure as a political candidate altered his future once again. Campaigning with all the energy and heart that he could muster, he spoke to every group that extended an invitation. Broadcasting over loudspeakers mounted on trucks, he reached as many constituents as possible while his opponents in the Republican primary rarely made an appearance. His unsuccessful attempt to secure the Republican nomination devastated him, and the defeat was compounded by the unwillingness of the convention organizers to let him address the party members. His initial reaction—to run as a third-party candidate—turned to cynicism when his political backers pulled out. After several unsuccessful attempts to win an election by either supporting another candidate or by running for office himself, Smith turned his back on the political system.[15]

Between 1938 and 1942 he pursued an isolationist policy encouraging Congress and the American people to resist the temptation of fighting a war for the Jews and for the British empire. In July 1940 he delivered a petition to Congress calling for the government to outlaw communism and continue America's policy of neutrality. He argued against the Lend-Lease program, suggesting that the obvious benefits for the British would eventually draw the United States into the conflict. The antiwar rhetoric ended with the Japanese attack on Pearl Harbor in December 1941, and thereafter Smith, along with other isolationists, believed that the United States must defend its territory and honor.[16]

When Willkie opted not to run for president in 1944, Smith, more determined than ever to fight against a fourth term for FDR, searched for a suitable Republican candidate and threatened to back a third-party candidate under his America First Party if a conservative nominee was not selected at the Republican convention. His choices included the famous transatlantic pilot Charles A. Lindbergh, World War I flying hero Captain Eddie Rickenbacker, Senator Gerald P. Nye of North Dakota, *Chicago Tribune* publisher Colonel Robert McCormick, General Douglas MacArthur, now-retired Senator Reynolds, and Governor Thomas E. Dewey of New York. One by one he issued statements concerning the desirability of the men, but every one of them spurned Smith's support. Dewey stated that "the Gerald L. K. Smiths and their ilk must not for one moment be permitted to pollute the stream of American political life." Reacting to Dewey's comments after he received the Republican nomination, Smith called for a national convention in Detroit to select the America First candidate. On August 30 the delegates met and, not surprisingly, chose Smith to represent their party.[17]

The 1944 America First Party's platform reflected Smith's personal ideology; in fact, he had published the various planks in an issue of *The Cross and the Flag* prior to the convention. One of the important issues involved providing food for American citizens at home before sending supplies overseas to the French. Moreover, Smith argued that the time was right to "absorb Canada, buy Greenland, and accept strategic islands in the Pacific in lieu of payment of the allies' war debts." He also suggested that British and French territory be used for the creation of a homeland in Africa for American blacks, while some members of the party went so far as to propose that Jews in the United States be forced to leave the country. If some Jews could give a compelling reason why they should stay, then they would be automatically sterilized. Smith opposed this last measure and tabled the idea permanently. On election day he received a mere 1,781 votes. Although frustrated and disappointed, Smith rebounded quickly. Over the next several years he continued to look for a viable candidate to run in 1948.[18]

After World War II, Smith reverted to his isolationist position. He argued against joining the United Nations unless legislators insisted on ratifying the treaty along with the Connally Resolution, which reserved the right of Congress to confirm any foreign policy commitments made under the new organization. Smith also promoted the America First Party with the argument that Americans should place their interests before those of the rest of the world.[19]

During the immediate postwar years, Smith underwent several personal changes. In 1947 he and his family moved from Detroit to St. Louis and then to Tulsa, Oklahoma, where they purchased a house. In 1953 he toured California, where he resolved to establish his headquarters. Throughout his career, Smith had relied on his gift of oral communication, but for the rest of his life he focused on disseminating his ideas through the distribution of written literature, especially after the spread of television, a medium he always feared. As early as 1942 he published *The Cross and the Flag* for his followers who believed in the importance of both Christianity and the United States.[20]

As the election of 1948 approached, Smith actively involved himself in the selection of the Republican nominee once again. He was convinced that General Douglas MacArthur offered the best chance of defeating the incumbent, Harry S. Truman, who had assumed the office after FDR's death in 1945. At the Democratic convention many of the delegates, opposed to the position of the president on civil rights, walked out and later nominated their own candidate in Birmingham, Alabama. Smith attended the Dixiecrat convention and offered his support to J. Strom Thurmond, who promptly rejected Smith's endorsement. Angry over the rebuff, Smith announced that his own party, the Christian Nationalist Party, would meet in St. Louis on August 20. The delegates unanimously nominated Smith as their candidate and accepted a platform that was even more radical than the earlier one. The Christian Nationalists called for the deportation of blacks and Jews and the establishment of ghettoes for those who refused to leave; their homes would be confiscated and redistributed to returning veterans. All international agreements reached by FDR without open discussion would be rescinded. The Christian Nationalists won few votes, partly because Smith had spent four months of the campaign recovering from food poisoning and partly because he had alienated too many voters with his extreme positions and rhetoric.[21]

Throughout the 1950s, Americans accepted a societal conformity based on a distrust of communism, a strong faith in religion, an emphasis on family bonds, and an aversion to people and ideas that represented any deviation from the norm. Smith believed in the same values but to an extreme, especially as he grew older. During the congressional hearings on Un-American Activities, Smith supported investigations into the background of government officials and Hollywood actors, although he believed that congressmen such as Richard M. Nixon failed to conduct a thorough examination of Communists within the United States.

He defended Senator Joseph McCarthy for his stand against Communists even after his censure, although two of McCarthy's aides of Jewish descent disliked Smith for his anti-Semitic views. Smith believed, as did many Americans, that Jews remained a problem in this country. He traced their negative impact back to the Civil War when the Rothschilds supposedly assassinated Abraham Lincoln after he refused to borrow money from their banking house to finance the war. Twice, Smith led a movement to preserve Christianity in America in 1933 and 1942. He particularly distrusted Roosevelt and his cabinet, who, he believed, fought World War II primarily to establish the state of Israel. Smith's attitude toward civil rights remained consistent with his bigotry. He regarded blacks as inferior and claimed that those who refused to accept a dominant white society, such as Martin Luther King Jr., deceived their people into believing that they could achieve equality. Moral impropriety of any sort drew attacks by Smith, especially homosexuality and the sexual content of Hollywood films. Women who wore inmodest clothing, such as miniskirts, and who advocated abortion felt the sting of his criticism. He vehemently disapproved of the use of tobacco, alcohol, and drugs. The number of groups and actions that Smith publicly condemned earned him the title of "preacher of hate."[22]

Smith continued to write tracts and literature after his defeat in 1952 and planned for the next presidential campaign. In 1956 he ran again as the Christian Nationalist Party candidate against President Dwight D. Eisenhower, whom he referred to as a Swedish Jew. Still passionately anti-Communist and anti-Semitic, Smith emphasized his desire to maintain a society dominated by white Anglo-Saxon Protestants. He spoke out against the Supreme Court's decision in *Brown vs. Board of Education*, often referring to the judicial branch as a "nine-headed tyrant" after the appointment of Chief Justice Earl Warren, when rulings against school prayer and in favor of pornography and civil rights threatened his core beliefs. To preserve American independence he continually resisted efforts to strengthen the United Nations and encouraged legislators to restrict immigration. Although he received the nomination, Smith's name did not appear on any of the state ballots since he either missed the filing deadline or failed to meet other requirements.[23]

During the 1960s, Smith continued to support a number of candidates, but each time his endorsements were spurned or his choice lost. In 1960, Nixon alienated Smith by commenting "that there was no place for Gerald Smith and his followers in the Republican Party." Smith hated President Kennedy even more since the former Massachusetts senator espoused liberal views on social and political issues. In 1964, Smith initially backed George Wallace and then Barry Goldwater as the Republican nominee against Lyndon B. Johnson, who had assumed the presidency upon Kennedy's assassination. In 1968 his passionate dislike of the Kennedys forced him into campaigning against the nomination of Robert Kennedy. After Nixon won the election, Smith gradually accepted the president's foreign policy as the most realistic course to follow. The Soviet Union and Communist China had developed into formidable countries, and the appropriate method of dealing with them was not confrontation, but through trade and negotiation. Nixon never sought Smith's approval nor did he recognize Smith as an influencing factor during his presidency. Smith continually supported losers or individuals who rejected his endorsements since "he claimed to uphold principle, but his stance can be more accurately described as inflexible stubbornness. He never admitted that he could misjudge candidates and issues like other politicians and journalists." Smith pursued the presidency personally or through others "out of his own egotism and his neurosis, not because he could realistically appraise men and issues."[24]

Smith's popularity declined after the late 1940s for a number of reasons. The Jewish community realized that the most effective way of silencing him was to ignore him. Pressure placed on local newspapers, television, and radio stations restricted the amount of publicity given to Smith and his rallies. Protesters vanished, and the meetings were conducted with little fanfare. The less controversial that Smith appeared, the fewer the number of people who showed up. The strategy worked. In addition, television increased in popularity during the late 1950s and 1960s. Smith refused to adapt to the new technology and lost some of his audience as a result. During that same period his message grew stale. Times had changed, but Smith had not altered his message or his method.[25]

As Gerald Smith reached his sixty-fifth birthday, he reflected on his long career and contemplated a memorial suitable to leave the American people as his legacy. He toyed with the idea of erecting a traditional homestead site complete with log cabin but scuttled the idea when a genuine log house could not be purchased. In 1964 his business manager stumbled across an old Victorian home in the Ozarks called Penn Castle. The beautiful hand-carved, four-story stone structure contained fourteen rooms that Smith and his wife filled with antiques and keepsakes that they had collected during their travels. Situated in Eureka Springs, Arkansas, Penn Castle provided the Smiths with a quiet place to live in their retirement.[26]

Before long, Smith's boundless energy and continued need to promote a cause led the former minister to come full circle and once again devote his life to religious matters. Looking up from his home to the top of Magnetic Mountain, he envisioned a lasting shrine that would bear witness to his faith. He arranged for the purchase of the property, hired an architect, and raised the money for the construction of a seventy-foot-high statue called "the Christ of the Ozarks," which was dedicated on June 15, 1966. Within the next year, Smith added an amphitheater on the 167-acre complex where actors performed a Passion Play depicting the last days of Christ for the edification of visiting pilgrims. In 1971, under the direction of the Smith Foundation, two additional structures, the Christ Only Art Gallery and the Bible Museum, completed the project.[27]

During his later years, Smith experienced health problems that ultimately led to his death. In 1971 a virus caused severe pain in his neck. Three years later a blockage in his left nostril restricted his breathing. That same year he endured a bad case of influenza. In April 1975 he contracted phlebitis, which affected his ability to walk. In the fall he and his wife flew to California where he had another bout of the flu that led to pneumonia. In a weakened condition, Smith drew his last breath on April 15, 1976, after suffering a heart attack.[28]

Gerald Smith dedicated his entire life to communicating his beliefs to others and to leaving his mark on American society. While he professed his Christian faith, he attacked those in opposition to him. His anti-Semitism and racial bigotry encouraged many Americans to resist change during the early civil rights movement. His anticommunism and anti-New Deal rhetoric fueled the movements of other demagogues such as Senator McCarthy, Father Coughlin, and Dr. Townsend. He declared his hatred of President Roosevelt because of his socialist policies and because FDR placed Jews in top positions within his administration.

While some historians argue that Smith's fundamentalist background had a direct bearing on his extremism, a closer look reveals that his hatred began to flourish after the assassination of Huey Long. Turning his back on the ministry, he justified his actions by attending to the needy masses through the Share Our Wealth Society. After his humanitarian efforts ended with Long's death, Smith failed to find another cause worthy enough to keep a sense of guilt from developing. Throughout the majority of his life he fought against the evils that he believed threatened Christianity and the United States while waging a spiritual battle internally. At the end of his life he focused on Christ once again and appeared more at peace. The passionate hatred seemed to have subsided within both Gerald L. K. Smith and American society.

Notes

1. Glen Jeansonne, *Gerald L. K. Smith: Minister of Hate* (New Haven, CT, 1988), 11–19; Elna M. Smith and Charles F. Robertson, eds., *Besieged Patriot: Autobiographical Episodes Exposing Communism, Traitorism, and Zionism from the Life of Gerald L. K. Smith* (Eureka Springs, AR, 1978), 4, 5, 37, 74, 96, 114, 225, 255, 258, 291; Leo P. Ribuffo, *The Old Christian Right: The Protestant Far Right from the Great Depression to the Cold War* (Philadelphia, 1983), 128–30.

2. Ribuffo, *Christian Right*, 130; Jeansonne, *Smith*, 16–21.

3. Jeansonne, *Smith*, 19–28; Smith and Robertson, *Patriot*, 144–45; Ribuffo, *Christian Right*, 133–35; *Boston Globe*, September 20, 1935; Harriett T. Kane, *Louisiana Hayride: The American Rehearsal for Dictatorship, 1928–1936* (Gretna, LA, 1971), 151; David H. Bennett, *Demagogues in the Depression: American Radicals and the Union Party, 1932–1936* (New Brunswick, NJ, 1969), 115.

4. Jeansonne, *Smith*, 19–28; Ribuffo, *Christian Right*, 133–35.

5. Jeansonne, *Smith*, 33–41; Ribuffo, *Christian Right*, 135–40; Smith and Robertson, *Patriot*, 225.

6. Ribuffo, *Christian Right*, 140–44; Jeansonne, *Smith*, 41–54; Kane, *Louisiana Hayride*, 154–55, 180–99.

7. Ribuffo, *Christian Right*, 144–47; Jeansonne, *Smith*, 46–51; *New York Times*, January 27, 1936; Arthur M. Schlesinger Jr., *The Politics of Upheaval* (Boston, 1950), 521–22; *Detroit Free Press*, February 5, 1936; Bennett, *Demagogues*, 138; Abraham Holtzman, *The Townsend Movement: A Political Study* (New York, 1963), 171–72.

8. Ribuffo, *Christian Right*, 144–47; Jeansonne, *Smith*, 46–51.

9. Jeansonne, *Smith*, 51–63; Schlesinger, *Politics of Upheaval*, 526–58, 607–27; Alan Brinkley, *Voices of Protest: Huey Long, Father Coughlin, and the Great Depression* (New York, 1982), 91–94.

10. Jeansonne, *Smith*, 65; Ribuffo, *Christian Right*, 147–48; Smith and Robertson, *Patriot*, 36.

11. Ribuffo, *Christian Right*, 156–57; Jeansonne, *Smith*, 66–90.

12. Jeansonne, *Smith*, 66–67; Ribuffo, *Christian Right*, 145–46; Smith and Robertson, *Patriot*, 74–75; *New York Times*, March 19, 1939.

13. Ribuffo, *Christian Right*, 148–49; Smith and Robertson, *Patriot*, 36, 59, 107–8, 136; Jeansonne, *Smith*, 67–69; *Detroit News*, November 2, 1937.

14. Jeansonne, *Smith*, 70–76; Smith and Robertson, *Patriot*, 26, 48, 160–62; Nathaniel Weyl, *The Jew in American Politics* (New Rochelle, NY, 1968), 103; Ribuffo, *Christian Right*, 149–57.

15. Ribuffo, *Christian Right*, 159–62; *Detroit News*, September 13, 1942; Smith and Robertson, *Patriot*, 153–54.

16. Jeansonne, *Smith*, 80–100; Ribuffo, *Christian Right*, 159–66.

17. Jeansonne, *Smith*, 152–59; Smith and Robertson, *Patriot*, 157–58; *New York Post*, June 26, 1944.

18. Jeansonne, *Smith*, 152–59.

19. Ibid., 90–100; Smith and Robertson, *Patriot*, 316.

20. Jeansonne, *Smith*, 98–100.

21. Ibid., 92–100, 157–59; Smith and Robertson, *Patriot*, 37.

22. Jeansonne, *Smith*, 101–14; Smith and Robertson, *Patriot*, 178; Ribuffo, *Christian Right*, 165–70.

23. Ribuffo, *Christian Right*, 165–77; Jeansonne, *Smith*, 115–29.

24. Smith and Robertson, *Patriot*, 92; Jeansonne, *Smith*, 165–70.

25. Jeansonne, *Smith*, 206–8.

26. Ibid., 188–89.

27. Ibid., 188–213; John R. Starr, "Gerald L. K. Smith: From Politics to Passion," *Tulsa Daily World*, November 7, 1971.

28. Jeansonne, *Smith*, 309.

Suggested Readings

Bennett, David H. *Demagogues in the Depression, American Radicals and the Union Party, 1932–1936*. New Brunswick, NJ, 1969.

Brinkley, Alan. *Voices of Protest: Huey Long, Father Coughlin, and the Great Depression*. New York, 1982.

Holtzman, Abraham. *The Townsend Movement: A Political Study*. New York, 1963.

Jeansonne, Glen. *Gerald L. K. Smith: Minister of Hate*. New Haven, CT, 1988.

Kane, Harriett T. *Louisiana Hayride: The American Rehearsal for Dictatorship, 1928–1936*. Gretna, LA, 1971.

Ribuffo, Leo P. *The Old Christian Right: The Protestant Far Right from the Great Depression to the Cold War*. Philadelphia, 1983.

Schlesinger, Arthur M., Jr. *The Age of Roosevelt*, vol. 3, *The Politics of Upheaval*. Boston, 1950.

Smith, Elna M., and Charles F. Robertson, eds. *Besieged Patriot: Autobiographical Episodes Exposing Communism, Traitorism, and Zionism from the Life of Gerald L. K. Smith*. Eureka Springs, AR, 1978.

Weyl, Nathaniel. *The Jew in American Politics*. New Rochelle, NY, 1968.

12

Emma Tenayuca
Labor and Civil Rights Organizer
of 1930s San Antonio

Zaragosa Vargas

Emma Tenayuca was among the most important Mexican-American labor radicals and intellectuals of the Great Depression era. The leader of the
1938 pecan shellers' strike in San Antonio, Texas, she was a member of the
executive board of the Workers' Alliance of America and of the Communist
Party. In 1939, Emma, along with her husband, Homer Brooks, wrote "The
Mexican Question in the Southwest," the Communist Party's seminal statement on the position of Mexicans living in the United States.

Zaragosa Vargas, associate professor of history at the University of
California, Santa Barbara, is the author of *Proletarians of the North: Mexican
Industrial Workers in Detroit and the Midwest, 1917–1933* (1998), *Major Problems in Mexican American History* (1998), and *Forgotten Voices: Mexican
American Labor Organizers and Union Struggles in the Great Depression, 1929–
1942* (forthcoming). His articles and review essays have appeared in the *Pacific Historical Review, American Quarterly,* and *Science and Society.*

The problems of economic deprivation and mass unemployment generated by the Great Depression and the climate of hope and ideal-
ism created by the New Deal stirred Mexican workers to renew their
struggles to assert and protect their rights. Labor organizing by Mexican Americans took place in opposition to racial discrimination and
against the harsh treatment that accompanied the unionization attempts.
Out of these shared experiences a collective working-class identity
emerged that translated into unionization.

The participation by Mexican workers in the 1930s union movement was spurred by the passage of New Deal labor legislation, notably
Section 7a of the National Industrial Recovery Act (NIRA), which guaranteed collective bargaining rights. The National Recovery Administration (NRA) also proved beneficial. The creation of the Congress of
Industrial Organizations (CIO) in 1935 ushered in another wave of
labor organizing. The CIO union drives especially aided Mexican

workers, offering them unprecedented participation in the labor up-
surge of the 1937–38 period. Progressive CIO-sanctioned labor affilia-
tions actively sought Mexicans as members. The United Cannery,
Agricultural, Packing, and Allied Workers of America (UCAPAWA), the
Packinghouse Workers Organizing Committee (PWOC), the United
Auto Workers (UAW), and the Steel Workers Organizing Committee
(SWOC) recruited Mexicans in the drive to organize workers.[1]

This article traces the history of the participation of Texas Mexicans, or Tejanos, in the San Antonio labor movement during the Great
Depression. Its focus is on Emma Tenayuca, who played a key role in
the union effort in San Antonio. She was known as "La Pasionaria de
Tejas" because she helped her fellow San Antonio Mexicans infuse the
union movement with a communal spirit intrinsic to their own culture.
Moreover, Emma forged an identity from an understanding of the historical experiences of the Spanish-speaking people of the Southwest.[2]

Texas was home to 40 percent of the nation's Mexican population.
A pattern of Anglo jobs and Mexican jobs was maintained and was based
on the assumption "that the inferiority of the Mexican to the Anglo"
relegated Mexicans to the hardest and lowest paying ones.[3] In 1935 the
CIO challenged this unfair system of labor relations by proposing a
minimum wage and eight-hour workday, low-interest loans for the state's
landless farmers and agricultural workers, abolition of the poll tax, and
civil rights for Mexicans and blacks. Key CIO grassroots leaders in Texas
included Ruth Koenig, Elizabeth Benson, Manuela Solís Sager and her
husband James Sager, Juan Peña, and Emma Tenayuca and her husband
Homer Brooks. Although their numbers remained small, leftwing organizers were an important element in the 1930s Texas union campaigns.
They instilled confidence in and provided leadership for Mexican workers, assisted them in gaining higher wages and better working conditions, and led the fight against racial injustice in Texas.[4]

Early Mexican union activity in Texas took place in 1932 and 1933
in the form of strikes by garment and agricultural workers, and a statewide Mexican labor movement was launched in 1935. The Trade Union
Unity League (TUUL) was largely responsible for this early union activity. The union push culminated in a conference of Mexican labor
leaders in Corpus Christi out of which emerged the South Texas Agricultural Workers' Union (STAWU), an affiliate of the larger Texas Agricultural Workers' Union formed by TUUL. Unemployed Councils were
established in Texas urban centers under the slogans of "Don't Starve—
Fight" and "Work or Wages." The Unemployed Councils were orga-

nized into neighborhood, block, and city councils, and chapters of the Workers' Alliance were also set up. A major goal was bringing the union to the Rio Grande Valley in South Texas, a difficult task because of the region's strong anti-union and anti-Mexican atmosphere. A strike by STAWU centered in the onion fields outside Laredo, Texas.[5]

Staunch employer opposition in the form of legal sanctions and union-busting tactics ended this strike. Fearing that a U.S. government bridge would be dynamited or burned by striking farm workers, the district judge in Laredo called upon the state governor to open the highway. Texas Rangers were sent armed with rifles, pistols, and a machine gun to ensure that peace would be maintained. The workers feared the harsh consequences that continued labor agitation would bring to the local Mexicans and therefore ended their strike and returned to the fields. Texas labor activists next concentrated their efforts on behalf of San Antonio's Mexican workers. They collaborated with Emma Tenayuca, who had emerged as the leader and spokesperson for the city's West Side, home to the Spanish-speaking working classes.[6]

The onset of the depression limited the job options of the Mexican women who comprised 79 percent of the labor force in San Antonio's garment, cigar, and pecan-shelling factories. Employers met overhead expenses by maintaining low wages. Combined with bad working conditions, these low wages induced Mexican women to play an essential role in strike actions in the city. Clearly defined discriminatory patterns based on race and gender compounded the sweatshop conditions of the factories. For example, the garment industry hired Mexican women to sew clothing in their homes. The unfair piece-rate system resulted in entire families working for low wages. The women's garment and handkerchief makers comprised a workforce of 15,000 to 20,000 families who eked out their existence by doing piecework in unhealthy and overcrowded living environments. San Antonio's Mexican women garment workers derived few benefits from the New Deal wage and hour legislation because NRA minimum wage codes were set on an industry-wide basis. Sex differentials in wages were recognized and institutionalized by the federal government. Twenty-five percent of the codes adopted a lower wage rate for women. And just as women earned less than men, minority women earned less than white women. Thus, the NRA essentially institutionalized pay discrimination underscored by gender and racial inequality in the workplace.[7]

Other New Deal legislation penalized Texas's Mexican working classes and contributed further to their impoverishment. Through its "plow under" policy the Agricultural Adjustment Administration (AAA) eliminated one-third of the Texas cotton crop. This sharp reduction in acreage meant fewer jobs for Mexicans during the cotton planting and harvesting seasons. About 20,000 Mexicans left Texas on labor contracts, yet thousands more remained in the state. Without work, they flocked to cities such as San Antonio to obtain assistance or to seek jobs on New Deal projects, thereby contributing to the surplus labor force. However, Mexicans could not count on receiving government assistance; often the applicants were disqualified because they could not meet residency or citizenship requirements or because of discrimination. The jobless men and women represented a source of potential labor agitation, according to contemporary observers. Berkeley economist Paul S. Taylor prophesied, "These migratory hordes, unemployed three-quarters of the time, will be ripe for agitation, will storm State capitols for relief. . . . Field labor wage problems will interlock with relief burden problems."[8] Emma Tenayuca and a small group of labor and community activists were ready to take up the cause of these workers.

Emma had learned at a young age about the Ku Klux Klan, saw the circulars proclaiming "one hundred percent white Protestant Americans," and, because of the widespread racism, witnessed the repeated injustices meted out to San Antonio's Mexicans and blacks. Moreover, she was mindful of her *mestiza* heritage because family pride was instilled in her. The maternal side of the Tenayuca ancestry could be traced to the Spaniards who settled in northwestern Louisiana in the seventeenth century and later helped to colonize San Antonio. Native Americans comprised the family's paternal side. A strong Tejano identity merged with a deep-rooted Catholicism to produce in Emma Tenayuca her unique commitment to the cause of rectifying social injustice. Communist doctrine supplied the added dimension of class conflict to this worldview.[9]

Through discussions with her grandfather, who took her to San Antonio's Milam Park where radicals of divergent political persuasions presented their points of view, Emma was exposed to politics. She also read insatiably. The works of Henrik Ibsen and Emile Zola brought forth her compassion for the reality of human suffering. The young Tejana's social consciousness was honed in high school by several teachers who exposed this bright student to progressive writers and intellectuals. The materialism of Charles Darwin's *Origin of Species* made an impact. The avid young reader absorbed Charles and Mary Beard's sweeping history, *The Rise of American Civilization*, as well as Charles Beard's *An Economic Interpretation of the U.S. Constitution*, his retrospective exposé of the Founding Fathers. The writings of English socialists Beatrice and Sidney Webb, particularly their pioneering *History of Trade Unionism*, appealed to Emma's growing interest in the ways that workers have attempted to redress their social and economic grievances throughout modern history. This exposure led to Emma's political maturation and to the intellectual appeal of communism.[10]

Emma first encountered labor organizing in 1933 when several hundred San Antonio women cigar workers went on strike against the Fink Cigar Company. Their demands were union recognition, increased pay, and better working conditions. She watched these brave strikers taken to jail. The event had a personal impact because many of the striking women lived in Emma's neighborhood. She quickly learned that Mexican ethnic, family, and community networks played a crucial role in channeling the women's efforts in building and sustaining a union drive at the local level. When the striking cigar workers were arrested and jailed a second time, on this occasion for protesting against NRA compliance of wage increases and for improved working conditions, sixteen-year-old Emma went with the women. The Tejana high-school student had joined the labor movement.[11]

For Emma Tenayuca the Fink Cigar strike had another important dimension. The strike signaled the end of the power wielded by the political machine that ran San Antonio. Emma understood that in addition to their political agenda, city bosses worked in collusion with employers set on keeping Mexican workers as a reserve labor pool. She was aware that the San Antonio political machine perpetuated the rampant poverty in the city's West Side, where Mexicans lived in despicable, rundown shacks. Because of the West Side's rampant disease and malnutrition, San Antonio had the nation's highest tuberculosis and infant mortality rates.

Recently graduated from Breckinridge High School, Emma played a leading role in forming two locals of the International Ladies Garment Workers Union (ILGWU). But she was abruptly upstaged by ILGWU representative Rebecca Taylor, who took charge of local labor activities for the garment union at the behest of ILGWU national president David Dubinsky. Emma disliked Taylor, the daughter of a wealthy Texan, because she lacked an understanding of the specific needs of San Antonio's Mexican women garment workers. Emma also saw Taylor's shortcomings and resented her patronizing manner.[12]

In 1935, as secretary of the West Side Unemployed Council, Emma held mass meetings to protest the removal of the names of thousands of

Mexican families from the city's relief roles. As a Worker's Alliance representative, Emma helped the residents formulate their demands. The Workers' Alliance was fully bound to improving the plight of needy workers through the restoration of Works Progress Administration (WPA) projects, minimum wages of fifty cents per hour, a thirty-hour work week for unskilled labor, and the furnishing of clothing, school supplies, and free school lunches to children of all relief workers. The call for a revision of minimum wage guidelines was unprecedented, especially in the low-wage Southwest. More important, Emma requested an end to discrimination in the distribution of relief and of jobs on WPA projects. Hundreds of Mexican farm workers were dropped from relief rolls during the cotton-picking season. Cut off from any income, these laborers returned to the city of San Antonio and added to the problem of surging numbers of unemployed workers.[13]

By 1936, Emma was devoting much of her time to working with the Workers' Alliance. Her selfless efforts on behalf of the West Side barrio residents resulted in her appointment to the National Executive Committee of the Workers' Alliance of America in 1937. In June of that year she attended the National Convention of the Workers' Alliance in Milwaukee, Wisconsin. Emma voted with the other convention attendees for support of a congressional bill for relief work and for the passage of a resolution against war and fascism.[14]

Emma became the general secretary of at least ten Workers' Alliance chapters in San Antonio. In addition to writing to New Deal officials in Washington, she was completely absorbed by the door-to-door neighborhood work to help the West Side's needy Mexicans. Going without food or sleep subsequently led to her becoming sick with tuberculosis, and nervous exhaustion caused her eventual breakdown. Recuperated, though not fully cured of tuberculosis, Emma resumed waging her daily battle with San Antonio's police and with agents from the U.S. Immigration Service used by employers to intimidate Mexican WPA workers from joining the Workers' Alliance. Mexicans had trouble obtaining WPA relief because San Antonio's Relief Council would not certify them. Instead, relief case workers referred Mexican clients to agricultural work—first, to bring in the radish harvest, then celery, followed by cotton picking, which had resumed across the state. Upon their return to the city, the Texas Relief Commission advised the Mexican families that they were ineligible for WPA relief because they had been employed in the previous year.[15]

In charge of the activities of the San Antonio Workers' Alliance local chapters, and assisted by 300 followers, Emma mobilized picket lines, protests, and demonstrations against WPA cutbacks. She eventually led demonstrations by 10,000 unemployed workers and helped stage strikes for jobs, for minimum wage and hour laws, and, most important, for the right of Mexican workers to unionize without fear of deportation. About this time, Emma was coming under the influence of San Antonio's few Communists who dominated the Workers' Alliance. Though active in San Antonio since 1930, the Texas Communist Party was small; in 1937 there were a mere 409 members, and by the following year the number had grown only to 500. In 1937, Emma married Homer Brooks. Known in local party circles as the "Blue-eyed Boy," Brooks had been sent to Texas by the party as part of its southern strategy to recruit and support new members.[16]

Forty percent of the nation's pecans came from Texas, and the workers of the Southern Pecan Company owned by Julius Seligman shelled one-fourth of this crop. Machines had shelled pecans in San Antonio until 1926, when the process was converted to hand work because it was cheaper, owing to the large pool of Mexican labor on the city's West Side. The pecan-shelling industry was lucrative; like the garment industry, the jobs were subcontracted to Mexican families who worked in either the contractor's facilities or in their own homes. About 12,000 workers shelled pecans during the season that ran from November to March. The men, women, and children worked in sweatshop conditions. No skill was required, only speed and dexterity.[17]

Pecan shelling was done in 400 sheds scattered throughout the West Side. One hundred pecan shellers per shed worked on a subcontract basis. Paid five to six cents per pound for shelled pecans, a Mexican family—including the labor of children as young as six years of age— earned about $1 to $4 per week, or $192 annually. When combined with money from odd jobs their total income averaged $251 per year. The pecan shellers frequently were paid in food; for their week's work, they received a pound of coffee, rice, flour, or beans. Since San Antonio's pecan-shelling industry was considered an agricultural enterprise, employers such as Julius Seligman refused to recognize the NRA codes that fixed wages at $6 per day. San Antonio's Mexican pecan shellers first struck in 1934 to protest low wages, and the strike was settled through NRA arbitration. The issue of wages and unfair labor practices remained unresolved for almost four years. On January 31, 1938, San Antonio's pecan shellers organized as the Pecan Shellers Workers' Union and walked out against a 20 percent wage reduction, bad working conditions, and the notorious homework. Between 6,000 and 8,000 workers from 170 of the small pecan-shelling plants walked out to protest their meager earnings and the horrible working conditions. Though not a member of the Pecan Shellers Workers' Union, Emma Tenayuca had been a major voice calling for the walkout.[18]

The workers held meetings in lots adjacent to the pecan-shelling sheds on the West Side. Demonstrations took place at nearby local parks and at Milam Plaza. Most of the meetings drew hundreds and sometimes thousands of people. The leadership of the pecan shellers' movement was mixed; it included former Magónistas (followers of the Mexican anarchists Ricardo and Enrique Flores-Magón), socialists, and Communists such as Emma Tenayuca and Homer Brooks. The leaders used their oratory skills to politicize and propagandize among a largely uneducated population. Emma Tenayuca, a fine speaker, was able to convey the message that the crowd wanted most to hear.[19]

Support for the strike also came from Vicente Toledano's Confederación de Trabajadores Mexicanos (Confederation of Mexican Workers), or CTM. It had engaged in the strikes in South Texas, and CTM's union work extended to the rest of the Southwest, including Colorado's beet fields. A small pro-worker Catholic element was also active in the pecan strike. This support was short-lived; it lasted only for 1937, the year that the parish newspaper, *La Voz*, was taken over by the editor, who was not sympathetic to the strike.[20]

Emma was unanimously elected strike leader for San Antonio's pecan shellers. The striking workers respected her because of her unfailing support as a community leader and because she was a familiar and trusted resident of the West Side barrio. By now, field representatives of the national CIO had taken an interest in the strike, as had those of UCAPAWA, who had arrived in San Antonio to lend their support to the striking pecan shellers. One of the latter was Donald Henderson, UCAPAWA president and party member. The Texas state CIO wanted to make sure that the Communists would not gain control of the strike, so its own representatives were in San Antonio to stay informed of developments as well as provide assistance.[21]

Homer Brooks had initially taken control of strike operations. Emma was taking a leading role in the strike and was not hiding her Communist Party affiliation. Henderson reproached Emma, telling her, Brooks, and his other comrades that their "open ties" to the party blocked the favorable settlement of the strike by the CIO. This complaint seemed out of the ordinary to Emma, since she knew Henderson as a fellow party member. Apparently, the UCAPAWA official was following party orders specifying that membership be kept secret because the party's goal was to gain respectability among labor organizations.[22]

According to Emma, Henderson persuaded her to relinquish her leadership of the pecan shellers' strike to Luisa Moreno, who was brought in by Henderson from the East Coast. Henderson, Brooks, and Moreno knew one another. Before coming to San Antonio they had worked among Puerto Rican and Cuban-American garment and tobacco workers in New York and Philadelphia. All belonged to the Communist Party. The CIO had taken charge of the labor movement as soon as its field representatives entered the local scene in 1937. The UCAPAWA unionists who helped in the strike included Clyde Johnson and John Beasley. UCAPAWA moved to settle the strike through arbitration.[23]

Within several weeks of the pecan shellers' strike, the Texas Industrial Commission opened public hearings on the strikers' grievances and on the denial of the right of the pecan shellers to picket peacefully. The workers and the local pecan-shelling companies began labor negotiations. The demands were union recognition with full collective bargaining rights, restoration of pay previously cut, and an increase in workers' wages to maintain a reasonable living standard, and, of course, union recognition. The strike gains eroded within a few months when the pecan industry remechanized and displaced thousands of pecan shellers. Other contributing factors included the passage of the Fair Labor Standards Act by the U.S. Congress, which created a minimum wage of twenty-five cents, and the start of World War II, which halted Mexican participation in the Texas labor movement.[24]

A corrupt political ring that included Mayor C. K. Quinn and Chief of Police Owen Kilday ruled San Antonio. It had marked popular U.S. Congressman Maury Maverick for defeat. Kilday wanted to break the Pecan Shellers Workers' Union because the city bosses feared that if the pecan shellers were allowed to organize, they would gain political strength and bolster Maverick's reelection. To break the strike, Kilday made every effort to discredit Emma Tenayuca, Donald Henderson, and everyone else involved in assisting the pecan shellers to organize. Kilday overplayed their Communist connections. Organized labor, moreover, had another ally in the ILGWU's Rebecca Taylor, whose outspoken criticism of Emma kept organized labor suspicious of Emma's actual intentions. The Anglo and middle-class Mexican-American establishment, the League of United Latin American Citizens (LULAC), and the Catholic Church were all opposed to the strike. Organized labor had likewise disapproved of the picketing. Its newspaper, the *Weekly Dispatch*, branded the CIO leaders as Communist agitators.[25]

Kilday kept up a campaign of harassment. He denied the striking pecan shellers the right to picket and refused to recognize the strike as legal. Police attacked men, women, and children. The picketers were tear gassed, and from 30 to 175 workers were arrested daily and taken to jail and then released. Emma was jailed several times during the strike. She recalled that in the women's ward of the San Antonio City Jail as many as three dozen women and their children were placed in cells built to accommodate six people. When the incarcerated strikers protested against the overcrowded conditions, the jailors responded by turning fire hoses on them. Many of these prisoners were infected with tuberculosis, and the overcrowding contributed to the spread of the disease. Jails were filled beyond capacity, and hundreds of strikers were driven fifteen to twenty miles out of town and had to walk back to San Antonio.[26]

More than 1,000 strikers were eventually jailed on such trumped-up charges as obstructing sidewalks. To avoid arrest, Emma instructed picket captains to tell the workers not to make eye contact with the police, and, to those sick with tuberculosis, not to spit on the ground. Despite the onslaught by city officials, Emma held mass meetings daily.[27]

San Antonio's Mexicans were aware of the risks in their bid to unionize because of the presence of Immigration Service agents who were as ruthless as the local police. The Workers' Alliance in San Antonio made numerous attempts to prevent the repatriation of Mexicans engaged in labor activity who were not American citizens. This accomplishment resulted from the efforts of Emma Tenayuca. It was why the local Mexican working classes were able to make inroads in their unionizing campaigns.[28]

Emma's leadership proved invaluable in helping the Mexican working classes of San Antonio organize against relief cuts, discrimination, exploitation, and harassment by the Immigration Service. Her labor activities centered in San Antonio, but she kept well informed of events unfolding elsewhere in Texas. She traveled to Houston to attend labor meetings and also went to Laredo to assist local Mexican workers.[29]

Emma was one of an unknown and probably small number of Mexican Americans who, in the 1930s, chose membership in the Communist Party. As party members or sympathizers, Mexican Americans provided leadership for the jobless by leading marches on city halls, demanding relief in cash and jobs, calling for an end to racial discrimination, rallying against discrimination in WPA cutbacks and New Deal programs, and engaging in union drives, mass marches, land disputes, and relief bureau sit-ins.

Emma Tenayuca in June 1937 in a San Antonio jail. *Courtesy of the Institute of Texan Cultures, San Antonio, Texas*

In 1938 the Texas Communist Party nominated Emma as its candidate for Congress from San Antonio, and Homer Brooks as its candidate for governor. The lieutenant governor's nomination went to Cecil B. Robinet, an African-American civil rights activist from Houston.[30] By now, Emma was investing all her time and energy in the party. In 1939 she co-authored with Brooks "The Mexican Question in the Southwest," the first analysis of the issue of Mexican nationhood produced by a Mexican-American member of the Communist Party. Tenayuca and Brooks argued that the Southwest's Mexican Americans shared a common history, culture, and language, but that they did not represent an "oppressed national group" within the United States. Nor did they constitute a border segment of the nation of Mexico. Rather, the two Communists argued that Mexican Americans historically had evolved into separate communities in the

Southwest. Tenayuca and Brooks explicitly added, however, that the distinct Spanish-speaking communities were interconnected through a shared economic life and were inextricably linked to the Anglo populations of each separate community.[31]

The Tenayuca-Brooks article was printed in *The Communist*. It is doubtful that large numbers of Mexicans had access to these important formulations; and if they did, how many understood what was conveyed in the article? The two Texas Communists perhaps had a larger mission. The real purpose of "The Mexican Question in the Southwest" was probably to educate the party in this direction with regard to the Spanish-speaking workers of the region. During this Popular Front period, the Communist Party promoted its "unity against fascism" and made extra efforts to improve and expand its influence and membership among mostly second-generation workers such as Mexican Americans.[32]

In the summer of 1939 the Texas Communist Party held its state convention in San Antonio. The timing could not have been more perfect for Police Chief Kilday. He used the highly controversial event finally to bring about the downfall of his nemesis, Emma Tenayuca, who had helped to organize the party's convention. Consequently, a near riot ensued at Memorial Coliseum where another meeting by the Texas Communist Party was being held. The "one hundred percent Americanism" of San Antonio's citizens had pushed back the tide of communism in their city. However, what proved most opportune for Kilday in destroying Emma's credibility was the announcement on August 23 that the Soviet Union and Nazi Germany had signed a nonaggression pact that ushered in the German invasion of Poland. Emma learned about the Nazi-Soviet pact from reading the party's newspaper, *The Daily Worker*. Like many devoted American Communists who had put their faith in Soviet Russia, La Pasionaria was stunned by the news. It took her several weeks to recover from the betrayal.[33]

When Emma abandoned the Communist Party, she was unable to find work in San Antonio because she had been blacklisted and ostracized for her Communist activities. A Jewish garment manufacturer gave her a job sewing U.S. Army officers' uniforms. By now, she was divorced from Brooks. Rebuffed by the San Antonio community for her affiliation with communism, Emma left the city and went to San Francisco, California, where she enrolled at San Francisco State College (now San Francisco State University) and in a few years graduated magna cum laude. Fifteen years passed before Emma returned to her beloved hometown of San Antonio. Upon her return, she entered a Master's program in education at St. Mary's University and subsequently received this degree. She was alienated from her family for having embraced communism and because of her marriage to Homer. Stigmatized by divorce and raising her children alone, Emma once again embraced the Catholic faith. Ironically, the Catholic Church was her haven during the long years of the Red Scare.

The years of the Great Depression were a watershed for Mexican Americans. The New Deal was an unprecedented historical moment in that a major restructuring of the American economy occurred with the intrusion of the federal government into the marketplace. In turn, the New Deal changed the character of the American working-class experience by allowing the empowerment of workers and giving them a voice in improving workplace conditions. The optimism of the New Deal raised the expectations of a Spanish-speaking minority no longer feeling as powerless as it had during the earlier repatriation period.

Discrimination did not end for Mexican Americans in the New Deal years. Relief was not always forthcoming as they were bypassed in favor of Anglos. Employers often refused to hire Mexicans because of work cutbacks and wage reductions. Unless special efforts were made, employers favored Anglos over Mexicans. Once Mexican Americans obtained relief and demanded food, medical care, and clothes for their children, Anglos expressed fear that they would become dependent on this aid. Agribusiness frowned on relief assistance programs that benefited Mexicans because it denied them a valuable source of labor. And the government perpetuated seasonal migrant labor by manipulating relief jobs available to Mexican-American farm laborers so as to make them ineligible for assistance.[34]

As noted earlier, NRA codes did not cover agricultural work, and low wages were not eliminated because the government codes established pay scales based on previous levels. These codes perpetuated wage discrimination resulting from racial distinctions in job classifications. The New Deal programs in the Southwest were administered and controlled at the local level by Anglos who discriminated against Mexicans. Unemployed Mexican workers and those blacklisted for union activities were penalized and did not receive relief benefits.[35]

Mexican Americans, like African Americans, nonetheless pushed for racial equality and greater participation in the New Deal. In 1935, President Franklin D. Roosevelt issued Executive Order 7046, which banned discrimination on WPA projects; and in 1939, Mexican Americans benefited from a Civil Rights Section formed in the Justice Department. In

1941, Executive Order 8802 resulted in the creation of the Fair Employment Practices Commission, which opened the way for Mexican Americans into defense-related industries.[36]

By the late 1930s, Popular Front activities, such as the CIO drives and endorsement of ethnic associations like the Congress of Spanish-Speaking Peoples, occupied the efforts of America's Spanish-speaking working classes. Moreover, Mexican-American workers were being incorporated into the New Deal culture apparatus through jobs such as the Civilian Conservation Corps. The latter New Deal program prepared many Mexican Americans for entrance into military service by imbuing them with the spirit of Americanism. Those workers who remained out of uniform experienced a degree of democratization by the war mobilization of the late 1930s. The experiences of Mexican Americans during the Great Depression prepared them for the struggles of the World War II years.

The impact of the Great Depression and the broad and sweeping social legislation introduced by Roosevelt's New Deal greatly affected Mexicans. The contributions of Emma Tenayuca are a vital part of this history. She challenged a corporate enterprise and the power structure of the San Antonio city government through her call for equal pay for equal work for the city's Mexican Americans in an era of wage differentials. Emma Tenayuca helped to make the San Antonio pecan shellers' strike an important catalyst for subsequent strikes.

Notes

1. Foster Rhea Dulles and Melvyn Dubofsky, *Labor in America: A History* (Arlington Heights, IL, 1984), 258–62.

2. Green Peyton, *San Antonio: City in the Sun* (New York, 1946), 169.

3. Richard A. García, *Rise of the Mexican American Middle Class: San Antonio, 1929–1941* (College Station, TX, 1991), 58.

4. Don E. Carleton, *Red Scare! Right Wing Hysteria, Fifties Fanaticism, and Their Legacy in Texas* (Austin, TX, 1985), 27–28.

5. Roberto Calderón and Emilio Zamora, *Chicana Voices: Intersections of Class, Race, and Gender* (Austin, TX, 1986), 32.

6. J. R. Steelman, Commissioner of Conciliation, San Antonio, Texas, to H. L. Kerwin, U.S. Department of Labor, Washington, DC, April 20, 1935, Case File 182/326, Record Group 59, National Archives.

7. Ibid.

8. Lyndon Gayle Knippa, "San Antonio II: The Early New Deal," in *Texas Cities and the Great Depression*, ed. W. W. Newcomb (Austin, TX, 1973), 80.

9. Calderón and Zamora, *Chicana Voices*, 37–38.

10. Julia Kirk Blackwelder, *Women of the Depression: Caste and Culture in San Antonio, 1929–1939* (College Station, TX, 1984), 147; Peyton, *City in the Sun,* 169.

11. Blackwelder, *Women of the Depression,* 103–4; Calderón and Zamora, *Chicana Voices,* 33; García, *Rise of the Mexican American Middle Class,* 60.

12. Blackwelder, *Women of the Depression,* 145; Harvey Klehr, *The Heyday of American Communism: The Depression Decade* (New York, 1984), 50–56.

13. Telephone interview with Emma Tenayuca, February 20, 1990.

14. Franklin Folsom, *Impatient Armies of the Poor: The Story of Collective Action of the Unemployed, 1808–1942* (Niwot, CO, 1991), 422–23; Calderón and Zamora, *Chicana Voices,* 33.

15. *San Antonio Light,* June 30, 1937.

16. Carleton, *Red Scare!* 27–30; "La Pasionaria de Texas," *Time* (February 28, 1938): 17.

17. García, *Rise of the Mexican American Middle Class,* 55, 60–61; Knippa, "San Antonio II," 87.

18. Blackwelder, *Women of the Depression,* 141, 148–49; García, *Rise of the Mexican American Middle Class,* 62.

19. Blackwelder, *Women of the Depression,* 141.

20. Ibid.; Peyton, *City in the Sun,* 170.

21. Blackwelder, *Women of the Depression,* 141, 148–49.

22. Klehr, *The Heyday of American Communism,* 237, 312.

23. García, *Rise of the Mexican American Middle Class,* 63.

24. Blackwelder, *Women of the Depression,* 142.

25. García, *Rise of the Mexican American Middle Class,* 63.

26. Blackwelder, *Women of the Depression,* 141.

27. García, *Rise of the Mexican American Middle Class,* 63.

28. Author's interview with Emma Tenayuca, May 3, 1990, San Antonio, Texas.

29. Blackwelder, *Women of the Depression,* 147–48; Peyton, *City in the Sun,* 171; García, *Rise of the Mexican American Middle Class,* 64.

30. Carleton, *Red Scare!* 29.

31. David Montejano, *Anglos and Mexicans in the Making of Texas, 1836–1986* (Austin, TX, 1987), 117–19; Calderón and Zamora, *Chicana Voices,* 34–35.

32. See the article by Donald Henderson, "The Rural Masses and the Work of Our Party," *The Communist* (September 1935): 866–80.

33. Author's interview with Emma Tenayuca, May 5, 1990, San Antonio, Texas.

34. Sarah Deutsch, *No Separate Refuge: Culture, Class, and Gender on an Anglo-Hispanic Frontier in the American Southwest, 1880–1940* (New York, 1987), 175–78.

35. Ibid.

36. On the less than successful relationship between the FEPC and Mexican Americans in the Southwest during World War II see Cletus Daniel, *Chicano Workers and the Politics of Fairness: The FEPC in the Southwest, 1941–1945* (Austin, TX, 1991).

Suggested Readings

Blackwelder, Julia Kirk. *Women of the Depression: Caste and Culture in San Antonio, 1929–1939.* College Station, TX, 1984.

Calderón, Roberto, and Emilio Zamora. *Chicana Voices: Intersections of Class, Race, and Gender.* Austin, TX, 1986.

Carleton, Don E. *Red Scare! Right Wing Hysteria, Fifties Fanaticism, and Their Legacy in Texas.* Austin, TX, 1985.

Castañeda, Antonia I. "Women of Color and the Rewriting of History." *Pacific Historical Review* 61 (November 1992): 501–33.

Folsom, Franklin. *Impatient Armies of the Poor: The Story of Collective Action of the Unemployed, 1808–1942.* Niwot, CO, 1991.

García, Richard A. *Rise of the Mexican American Middle Class: San Antonio, 1929–1941.* College Station, TX, 1991.

Green, George N. "ILGWU in Texas, 1930–1970." *Journal of Mexican American History* 1 (Spring 1971): 144–69.

Kiser, George C. "Mexican American Labor, Before World War II." *Journal of Mexican American History* 2 (Spring 1972): 122–42.

Klehr, Harvey. *The Heyday of American Communism: The Depression Decade.* New York, 1984.

Montejano, David. *Anglos and Mexicans in the Making of Texas, 1836–1986.* Austin, TX, 1987.

Nelson Cisneros, Victor B. "La Clase Trabajadora en Tejas, 1920–1940." *Aztlán* 6 (Summer 1975): 239–65.

———. "UCAPAWA Organizing Activities in Texas, 1935–50." *Aztlán* 9 (1978): 71–84.

Peyton, Green. *San Antonio: City in the Sun.* New York, 1946.

Ríos Bustamante, Antonio. *Mexicans in the United States and the National Question: Current Polemics and Organizational Positions.* Santa Barbara, CA, 1978.

Rips, Geoffrey, and Emma Tenayuca. "Living History: Emma Tenayuca Tells Her Story." *Texas Observer* (October 28, 1983): 7–15.

13

Henry S. Aurand
Student, Teacher, and Practitioner
of U.S. Army Logistics

David J. Ulbrich

Studies of war almost always focus on the soldiers who fought and died, often as heroes. Behind the scenes, however, were legions of soldiers who organized the movement of supplies and other materials that were essential for the conduct of the war. Logistics became the name of the game in the twentieth century as the world entered the era of industrial warfare.

Henry S. Aurand is known to few people except the experts on World War II, yet he was one of those responsible for making the Allied victory possible. Transferring men, supplies, and weapons from one place to another may seem mundane, but Aurand's efficiency made the operation run smoothly. He was a product of the Progressive Era, especially because of his belief in the use of experts and his dedication to public service.

David J. Ulbrich is currently a doctoral student in military history at Temple University, Philadelphia, where he studies with Dr. Gregory Urwin. He published "Clarifying the Origins and Strategic Mission of the U.S. Marine Corps Defense Battalion, 1898–1941" in *War and Society* in 1999, and it received the 2000 Heinl Award from the Marine Corps Heritage Foundation. He extends his thanks to Robin Higham, Mark Parillo, and Donald Mrozek, all of Kansas State, for their assistance with this article. He also wishes to dedicate this article to his father, Richard W. Ulbrich, a bombardier with the U.S. Army Air Forces in World War II and a logistician with the U.S. Air Force and the Defense Department after the war.

Henry S. Aurand was born on April 21, 1894, in Shamokin in western Pennsylvania. In high school he earned high marks in mathematics and history, played the violin in the orchestra, and led the debate team. From early in his life, machines and especially railroads fascinated him, and thus his decision to pursue a degree in engineering was not surprising. He entered the United States Military Academy at West Point in 1911 and graduated twentieth out of 165 cadets in 1915. His class included Omar N. Bradley and Dwight D. Eisenhower. Aurand then spent his thirty-seven-year military career as a U.S. Army logistician, not leading American soldiers into battle but supplying and transporting them.

Although submerged in an unwieldy military bureaucracy, Aurand's career can be used as a springboard to understand the army and America from 1920 to 1945. During these years, Aurand studied the principles of logistics in the post-World War I years and later applied those principles during World War II. Simply put, logistics concentrates on the supply and transportation of military forces. The term "logistics" did not enter the army's everyday vocabulary until about 1940. Until then, terms such as "supply," "transportation," "subsistence," and "procurement" referred to different aspects of the more inclusive concept of logistics. Throughout his army career, Aurand gradually acquired considerable expertise in all facets of logistics. His experiences and activities also exemplified Progressive ideals such as efficient management and rational organization. His work ethic resembled that of a business executive or, perhaps more appropriately, that of a public servant such as Herbert Hoover.

Understanding logistics in the U.S. Army from 1920 to 1945 requires a brief discussion of World War I. From a logistical perspective, this conflict's difficulties served as haphazard case studies in mobilization, supply, and transportation. When the United States entered the war in 1917, one historian observed that the army was "shockingly unprepared."[1] It did not have enough soldiers, let alone enough well-trained and fully equipped soldiers. Worse still, no centralized authority existed to control all the aspects of logistics. Serious problems of planning, command, and control existed within the army.

After much bickering and infighting in 1917, all logistical responsibilities were consolidated under the Purchase, Storage, and Traffic Division, headed by George W. Goethals. In what would become a typical practice in America's military, Goethals was imported from the business world where he had gained experience and prestige from supervising the construction of the Panama Canal. Coordination of the nation's industrial mobilization fell to the War Industries Board; chaired by Bernard M. Baruch, a successful Wall Street speculator, this agency centralized and streamlined the war effort's management. Consequently, logistics in World War I grew more efficient, but peak efficiency was not achieved because the conflict drew to a close too soon.

The National Defense Act of 1920 reorganized the War Department and established the army's command structure for the interwar years. A year later, in 1921, a board under General James G. Harboard's direction met to determine the working relationships within the War Department and the General Staff. According to the Harboard Board's interpretation, the General Staff clearly supervised all army operations, small as they were, but planning was divided between the General Staff, headed by the Army Chief of Staff, and the assistant secretary of war. All strategic planning and logistics planning in a given theater of operations fell under the General Staff's authority. Specifically, the G-4 Division was created to deal with supply and transportation. The assistant secretary of war also controlled logistical planning in the zone of the interior, the area on the home front or far removed from fighting.

Mobilization planning was divided between the General Staff and the assistant secretary of war; the former concentrated on manpower, and the latter supervised all economic and industrial mobilization planning. However, the two did not coordinate with one another. Manpower requirements were not wedded to the equally important matter of material requirements. For example, serious problems arose because the General Staff refused to acknowledge the time needed for industrial and economic mobilization when formulating the strategic plans.

Major Henry S. Aurand understood all too well the problems within the army during the interwar years. Industrialization had affected modern warfare. Strategy grew more complex as the variables and contingencies of modern warfare increased. Fighting a large, industrialized conflict required a large, modern, and industrial logistical system. To be successful, the army had to be organized so as to encourage communication and cooperation between those strategic and logistical planners. Likewise, once the shooting started, Aurand realized that communication and cooperation must continue to occur between logistics officers and combat officers.

Although it may seem trivial to mention, Aurand did not have a marksmanship qualification in 1919. This fact may be significant. Because logisticians did not fight like "real soldiers," they were considered "technicians" and therefore not expected by combat troops to be proficient in the soldiers' most basic skill. Logisticians sat far behind the front lines and kept meticulous records. Aurand did not go to Europe with the American Expeditionary Force in World War I but stayed in the United States and served with the army's Coast Artillery. By the mid-1920s he resigned himself to the fact that he would be a logistics officer in a support arm such as Ordnance rather than a combat officer in the infantry, artillery, or cavalry.

Throughout the 1920s, Aurand distinguished himself as an ordnance officer. A chronic workaholic who was totally dedicated to his army duties, he consistently worked twelve-hour days and traveled much of the time. His long hours took a toll on his family life. In 1929 he and his wife of thirteen years divorced. This change drew him still further into his army duties. Indeed, Aurand eventually came to see logistics as his calling.

When he attempted to transfer out of Ordnance in 1921, the War Department denied his request because his services were "urgently required" and his superior officer was "very much pleased" with his performance.[2] Instead, to raise his level of expertise, Aurand received technical training in fields related to interior ballistics, the scientific study of expanding gases inside a gun barrel. A gun's trigger mechanism ignites the gunpowder, otherwise known as the propellant. The burning gunpowder produces expanding gases to exert pressure on the bullet, otherwise known as the projectile. These extreme pressures push the bullet down the gun barrel at speeds sometimes in excess of three thousand feet per second. Aurand took courses in advanced chemistry and mechanical engineering at the Massachusetts Institute of Technology.

After a decade of confusion under the National Defense Act of 1920, the assistant secretary of war finally recognized that any major war would take ten years of planning. With some preparation, some hoped that the army could avoid the logistical problems of World War I. The assistant secretary of war, therefore, sponsored the Industrial Mobilization Plans in 1930, several versions of which appeared in the decade that followed. According to the army's official history of army mobilization, the Industrial Mobilization Plans focused on "the total process of harnessing the nation's resources in time of emergency or war." The assistant secretary of war, however, did not actually exercise "total" control of the "process."[3] Manpower mobilization planning and strategic war planning remained the province of the Army Chief of Staff. Consequently, all interwar planning suffered from the same institutional shortcoming: noncommunication. The Army Chief of Staff refused to acknowledge that logistics, in this case manufacturing capacities, limited strategic or tactical planning. Although too unrealistic, the Industrial Mobilization Plans represented important theoretical exercises in attempting to grapple with economic and industrial mobilization problems.

During the Great Depression, Aurand had the rank of major, which he had held since July 1920. He spent 1930 and 1931 as a student at the Army War College, where his courses exposed him to strategic and tactical issues. Students at the War College specialized in one of five divisions: War Plans, G-1 (Personnel), G-2 (Intelligence), G-3 (Operations and Planning), or G-4 (Supply). The War College's faculty structure and course schedule adhered to these divisions. The curriculum separated into two parts: the Preparation for War course, which concentrated on war plans, and the Conduct of War course. In the latter, students simulated a battle or campaign against a fictitious, yet plausible, enemy. Although they existed, studies of logistics in these courses did not focus on the challenges of industrial or economic mobilization. On the contrary, supply and transportation at the battlefield or on campaign occupied much of G-4's time.

In 1933, Aurand returned to the War College to serve as an instructor in the G-4 (Supply) Division. When he arrived, strategy and tactics remained the primary focuses of the curriculum, just as they had been when he was a student. Selection of faculty and students overwhelmingly favored combat arms. Even in the War Plans Division, logistics did not occupy a high priority because all the instructors held posts in the combat arms. The course assignments concentrated on combat; field exercises studied the maneuvers and leadership styles of Civil War battles, while logistical matters received almost no exposure. In reaction, Aurand used his faculty position as a bully pulpit to preach the significance of logistics, including procurement, supply, transportation, and research development. Like Progressives in preceding decades, Aurand pushed hard to teach efficient management and rational organization in army logistics.

By 1936 the conservative War College slowly began to give serious consideration to economic and industrial mobilization. Prominent businessmen, including Wall Street's Bernard Baruch, lectured on matters such as corporate management and industrial mobilization. Such cross-fertilization of ideas between the corporate world and the military establishment benefited prewar mobilization plans and mobilization itself when World War II started.

In 1935, Aurand gave a lecture at the War College titled "Supply and Transportation in the Theater of Operations." This lecture, more than anything else, illustrated Aurand's philosophical understanding of his job. He articulated a principle of logistics: "Troops in action should never have to turn their backs on the enemy to fetch further supplies." Moreover, "troops should not be encumbered with supplies beyond immediate needs." Obviously, achieving a balance between too much and too little was a utopian goal, but Aurand argued that careful planning would increase the possibility of attaining that goal.[4] The high point of Aurand's lecture could be found in his arrangement of the five characteristics of a logistical system, in descending order of importance: certainty, simplicity, convenience, mobility, and flexibility. Aurand viewed the first two as psychological and the last three as physical. All five, he believed, were required for a truly successful system.[5] Progressive influences were apparent within Aurand's five characteristics.

During the mid-1930s, Aurand did not limit his saber rattling to the War College's classrooms. He also wrote memos to generals about such issues as distribution, communication, and inventory control. In one memo, Aurand echoed the recurring complaint that the National Defense Act of 1920 lacked coordination among the assistant secretary of war, the General Staff, and various bureaus such as Transportation or Ordnance. The possibility of miscommunications between the zone of the interior and the theater of operations worried Aurand because transportation was not clearly divided between the Ordnance Department and the Quartermaster Corps. These bureaus' autonomy confused the logistical system. Aurand's memos and reports often brought reprimands from his superiors. Yet, despite these reprimands, then-Lieutenant Colonel Aurand continued to be promoted and entrusted with greater responsibility because he was acknowledged as an expert organizer and manager.

By the late 1930s the army as an institution increasingly acknowledged the importance of logistical support for a possible war effort. From his mid-level position, Aurand suggested numerous reforms and new procedures. A few of his ideas eventually found their way up the chain of command and into army policy. When Aurand finished his tour at the War College in 1937, courses such as "Mobilization Problems" were being expanded to allow for more careful consideration of procurement, supply, and transportation. Other army officers as well as War Department administrators began to think in similar ways during the same period. In 1935 and 1937 the army's divided, complicated, and confused logistical system changed for the better. In these two years, President Franklin D. Roosevelt promoted General Malin Craig to Army Chief of Staff in 1935 and appointed Louis Johnson as assistant secretary of war in 1937. These top advisers to the secretary of war worked to streamline and centralize the army's logistical system.

After leaving the command of the War College to become the Army Chief of Staff, Malin Craig initiated comprehensive reforms in the army's command and logistical structures. For example, he restructured the army's infantry division to create a unit capable of independent functions. Craig also recognized the serious deficiency in coordinating strategy and logistics plans in noncombat arms. Previously, both had existed exclusive of one another; strategy was formulated irrespective of the logistical requirements to reach its objectives. Just as Aurand had been preaching for several years, Craig utilized the War College and other army education facilities to assess America's manufacturing and demographic capabilities to determine the feasibility of strategic planning.

In 1937 the second big step toward the coordination of strategy and logistics occurred when President Roosevelt appointed Louis Johnson as assistant secretary of war. To help stimulate cooperation between his office and the Army Chief of Staff, Johnson established an ad hoc, quasi-official advisory board to his office. Consisting of business leaders such as Baruch as well as younger talented businessmen, this board helped Johnson reorganize his own department and reach out to the General Staff. The reforms and informal cooperation between the General Staff and the assistant secretary of war culminated in the new 1936 and 1939 Industrial Mobilization Plans, the most realistic assessments of American military and industrial capabilities to date. Once again, Aurand had been calling for improvement in communication for years. Because of efforts by Craig and Johnson, logistics achieved a higher level of legitimacy in the army as a whole.

After completing his tour on the faculty at the War College in 1937, Aurand returned to the army's Ordnance Department. Typical of many officers of promise and talent, he had alternated between the army's educational system and practical duties. In this way, Aurand became not only a technical expert but also an experienced general manager. He worked in research and development at Picatinny Arsenal in New Jersey where he again focused on interior ballistics, his area of expertise in the 1920s. While at Picatinny, Aurand tested new designs and machinery for the army's artillery ammunition.

During his tour in the Ordnance Department, Aurand criticized the army's procurement system. He complained that effective communications did not exist between the manufacturer, the designer, and the combat arms. He cited his personal experience in ammunition development; the combat arms' requirements for a given caliber's ammunition efficiency were not made clear to the manufacturer. Aurand recommended that clear standards be established so that ordnance could place effective ammunition in the hands of soldiers. Moreover, he called for standardization of testing so the combat arms' forthcoming requirements could be measured and quantified.

As with the rest of the American military, low budgets plagued the Ordnance Department in general and Aurand at Picatinny Arsenal in particular. Difficulties were compounded by the fact that research and development entailed an expensive process of trial and error. Clever book-keeping compensated for budget deficits; but even so, feasibility studies for new equipment became backlogged because of insufficient funds. Civilian employees of the Ordnance Department suffered pay reductions and downsizing.

In 1938 the Ordnance Department experienced a fiscal windfall. The 1938 army appropriations bill had awarded a mere $25 million to Ordnance, barely enough to maintain its research and development program. However, in the 1939 bill, appropriations dramatically increased to $122 million. This budget growth signaled two changes in the army's understanding of logistics: the army started to appreciate the Ordnance Department's functions in design, manufacture, distribution, and maintenance of material; and this in turn aided mobilization planners who were attempting to project material requirements for a possible war.[6]

After his tour with the Ordnance Department ended in 1939, Aurand was selected as a student for the Army Industrial College, the advanced school for logisticians. His previous education and assignments pointed to the Industrial College as the capstone in his educational development. As a student at this school, Aurand honed his skills as a logistician, manager, and organizer. For the most part, however, the Industrial College remained outside the information loop running through the regular channels in the army. The school never overcame combat officers' perception of logistics "as an ancillary function that true warriors did not perform."[7] Logisticians had little to add to serious discussions of force organization, strategic planning, or tactical operations; instead, they handled industrial and economic mobilization on the home front and transportation to a given theater of operations.

As a student at the Industrial College, Aurand conducted several studies on logistics. He attempted to answer questions such as, "What are the divisions of a producing organization?" and "What are the functions of each?" Aurand's answers showed a sophisticated understanding of line-and-staff management.[8] These ideas did not remain on the proverbial drawing board; Aurand and his fellow students worked as consultants for businesses where real organizational, managerial, and logistical problems served as laboratories to test theories. To facilitate thinking about logistical issues among army officers, students at the Industrial College worked with business leaders to learn how to manage industrial and economic mobilization. Among other problems, lead times in research and development were considered in projecting military preparedness.

Henry S. Aurand speaking on the radio in support of the war effort on the home front, c.1943. *Courtesy of the Dwight D. Eisenhower Library, Abilene, Kansas*

Aurand learned that effective managers delegated both authority and responsibility to accomplish a task. For example, he made suggestions for a reorganization of the Trask Company, a manufacturing firm. Recognizing that staff or horizontal functions had to be differentiated from line or vertical decisions, Aurand recommended minimizing the number of line positions and maximizing the staff positions. Thus, the division managers could have the best of both worlds: more information from their advisers with which to make decisions, and less bureaucracy to follow through on their decisions. Aurand then made specific recommendations for consolidating or expanding various positions in the Trask Company. In similar studies, Industrial College students examined problems facing businesses and proposed solutions. Topics included cash flow, receivables, net worth, sales, inventory, net profit, and labor-management relations.

Germany's invasion of Poland in September 1939 started the downward slide to global war, and the fall of France and other events increased the American public's desire to be prepared for war, but not to intervene. The conflict caused several major changes in the War Department's structure that eventually centralized the authority as well as the responsibility for logistics. Even strategic planners increasingly considered the logistical requirements of fighting on the other side of the Atlantic and on the other side of the world.

In 1939, George C. Marshall was promoted to Army Chief of Staff, and he continued Craig's intensive program of logistical planning. With a realistic assessment of logistical goals in mind, the army finished the Protective Mobilization Plan in 1940. It contained some concrete estimates of manufacturing capabilities and manpower reserves. In particular, the Protective Mobilization Plan assigned certain products to be manufactured by particular factories. As a result, mobilization planners could envision timetables and budget requirements for equipping their million-man army. While it had certain tactical shortcomings, this new scheme did provide a good foundation for mobilization. It certainly included valuable input from Aurand and other logisticians.

The Industrial College helped to formulate the Protective Mobilization Plans by working to modify the previous Industrial Mobilization Plans. In November 1939, Aurand submitted a critical evaluation of the 1939 Industrial Mobilization Plan in which, predictably, he pointed to the confusion caused by the National Defense Act of 1920: "Separate points of view as to what agency should be created in time of peace to handle Industrial Mobilization." The "points of view" included those of the War Plans Division, the Ordnance Department, the Quartermaster Corps, and others. Each had multiple power bases within the General Staff and the assistant secretary of war's office, which could not be easily superseded by the others. So, despite reforms by Craig and Johnson, the army's infrastructure still negated centralization. In the final page of his evaluation, Aurand recommended that a revised 1939 Industrial Mobilization Plan prescribe the Joint Army and Navy Munitions Board as the "peacetime agency, which will coordinate the industrial efforts in time of war."[9]

Recommendations from Aurand had apparently found their way into army policy. Since its inception in 1922, logisticians such as Aurand had hoped that the Joint Army and Navy Munitions Board would become a catalyst to coordinate mobilization plans between the two services. Finally, in December 1939 the board received sanction from President Roosevelt himself to circumvent normal channels of mobilization and logistics planning within the War Department. This board assumed overall control of all mobilization plans for both. Indeed, it actively coordinated the economic and industrial mobilization of America during 1940 and 1941. As a result, military logisticians moved from merely planning procurement into a position of directing and managing procurement.

What Aurand, Craig, Johnson, Marshall, and Roosevelt could not do, the Japanese accomplished in a matter of hours on December 7, 1941. The attack galvanized public support for a war effort. No longer would there be problems with appropriations; the new challenge became mobilizing the resources to defeat the Axis powers. All the planning that had previously occupied so much of Aurand's time, not to mention thousands of other logisticians like him, had now come to fruition.

President Roosevelt recognized the need for efficient management and effective organization. In 1939 and 1940, respectively, the War Resources Board and the Council for National Defense had come into existence, but neither of these had the necessary mandate to be fully functional. Therefore, Roosevelt established the War Production Board in January 1942. Finally, this single "superagency" was given the power necessary to coordinate the ever-increasing complexities of the American economy, manpower, and industry. Shortly thereafter, Army Chief of Staff George C. Marshall reorganized the army by dividing all functions into three major commands: the Army Air Forces, the Army Ground Forces, and the Services of Supply (later renamed the Army Service Forces). With these reforms in place, the wheels of American industry could start turning. Aurand predictably found his way into the Services of Supply where he spent the war years. Almost two million American men and women in the army eventually worked for Service of Supply units during World War II.

Following his graduation from the Army Industrial College in 1940, Aurand moved to Washington to work for the General Staff as Chief of Requirements and Distribution. Then, in 1941, he assumed the position of Director of Defense Aid for the Lend-Lease program. Finally, in 1942 he moved to become secretary to the Combined Production and Resources Board. Aurand rose in rank to colonel in 1941 and then to brigadier general in 1942.

These three positions afforded him the opportunities to put his training and theoretical knowledge to practical use. Aurand acted as the army's senior liaison officer, who was responsible for balancing the material Allied needs with America's own material needs in preparation for war. He worked with both the British and American governments as well as their militaries. Because of the competing priorities, Aurand saw himself as being caught in a problematic "tug of war between mobilizing the U.S. army and giving guns to those who were killing Germans."[10] Despite his superior officer's disagreement, Director of Defense Aid Aurand favored a common pooling of American and British supplies to increase efficiency in resource allocation and distribution. Over the duration of World War II, the Lend-Lease program sent thousands of tanks and aircraft and millions of tons of gasoline and railway equipment to Great Britain and the Soviet Union. Without such support, neither nation would have been able to turn back the German onslaught.

As Chief of Requirements and Distribution, Director of Defense Aid, and secretary for the Combined Production and Resources Board, Aurand grew frustrated with army logistics. He carried on a crusade to remedy these shortcomings as evidenced in a 1941 report:

> The officers of the army who have come to grips with the manifold problems of supply are few and far between, and what is more important, have been neglected in promotion because they have been away from the command of combat units. Their one ambition, therefore, is to get away from supply duty. They fear the brand "supply man. . . ."
>
> Disaster alone, or at best, confusion a la 1898, awaits the first employment of our forces unless the war department takes immediate steps to organize them and itself on the basic of modern war, it is the tail—supply—that wags the dog.[11]

Aurand's words indicate the missionary zeal with which he called for an increased emphasis on logistics. The Japanese attack on Pearl Harbor in December 1941 reduced neither Aurand's frustration nor his zeal.

In the fall of 1942, Aurand left—or perhaps was exiled from—the center of power in Washington. His new assignment was in Chicago, where he excitedly took over command of the Sixth Service Command. A promotion to major general accompanied this transfer. He spent two years in the comfortable yet absolutely essential post. These two years in Chicago were stable for Aurand. He brought his second wife Betty, his young daughter Linda, and his widowed father Peter to live with him. Betty, in particular, understood Aurand's work habits and supported him despite some lengthy absences. She often wrote to him when he went to Europe and to China on his later wartime assignments.

The Sixth Service Command, comprised of Michigan, Illinois, Indiana, and Wisconsin, was one of nine regional logistics units in the country. Aurand immediately began redrawing the flow charts of his Sixth Service Command and trimming unnecessary positions. Harkening back to his studies at the War College, Aurand tried to decentralize authority among his subordinates by giving them more latitude with which to make decisions and less bureaucracy to follow through on their decisions. Consistent with his passion for rational organization and his trust in experts, Aurand brought in civilian advisers from the business world. These experienced people knew how to run complex organizations. The Sixth Service Command stabilized and ran more smoothly as a result of Aurand's structural reforms. To encourage innovation among his subordinates, he unveiled his "Think to Win" program, which allowed them to make suggestions about improving army logistics.

More than any other task, public relations occupied the majority of his time. He hosted weekly radio talk shows, "The General's Review" and "21 Stars." In various public addresses, Aurand explained the importance of logistics. Excerpts from a speech to the American Legion in 1943 illustrate his emphasis on logistics: "When a democracy wages total war, it must overcome four distinct bottlenecks before its military force can be utilized in full power against the enemy." The four were industrial manufacturing, raw materials, manpower, and transportation. Aurand believed that only the first bottleneck had been "well cleared"; the remaining three had yet to be "broken" or "cleared."[12] In addition, he used public forums to promote the army's image, raise morale among troops, and warn against leaking secrets to the enemy.

For his "exceptionally meritorious and distinguished services" in Chicago, Aurand was given the Distinguished Service Medal, the army's second-highest award for noncombatant duties. The citation for this medal offers testimony to his effective methods and to his significant achievements:

General Aurand, through able, aggressive leadership, skillful planning and efficient guidance, succeeded in bringing the command to a superior plane of efficiency. In view of the large number of army installations located within this command, as well as the extensive war production facilities established there, the problems of the Sixth Service Command were exceptionally varied, and the responsibilities of the Commanding General extremely heavy. In the successful solution of these problems, General Aurand demonstrated sound judgment, great foresight, and marked executive ability and keen devotion to duty.[13]

Although Aurand derived much satisfaction from his duties with the Sixth Service Command, he longed for the opportunity to go overseas. His wish was granted in October 1944 when he transferred to the European theater of operations. For about two months, Aurand worked directly for General Eisenhower, his former classmate at West Point, to solve a chronic problem of ammunition shortages. In December, Aurand moved to another assignment as commanding officer of the Normandy Base Section. His new command consisted of the ports of Cherbourg, Le Havre, and Rouen on the French coast of the English Channel. The ammunition, food, fuel, and equipment required for the hundreds of thousands of Allied soldiers sweeping across Europe passed through these ports. For example, the Allies disembarked 10,000 tons of cargo each day at Cherbourg alone beginning in August 1944.

Commanding the Normandy Base Section was the task for which Aurand had spent twenty-nine years of preparation. As with his previous commands, he quickly set about raising the morale as well as the *esprit de corps* of his soldiers. Though not front-line combat troops, they made essential contributions to defeating the German forces. Aurand also set about eliminating bottlenecks in the supply lines. Ideally, equipment was disembarked at one of the ports; then it was transported by rail to supply depots near the front; and last, trucks hauled the equipment to the area of fighting. In reality, however, the Allied forces drove across France too quickly. Neither the rail system nor the truck convoys could keep up with the demand. Consequently, much-needed supplies sat in bottlenecks on the docks in port or at depots near the front.

After becoming acquainted with his staff and upon touring facilities, Aurand delegated authority and responsibility to his subordinates and checked up on their progress at staff meetings. His subordinates nicknamed him the "Great Conferrer" because he held so many meetings and conferences. As a practical matter, Aurand eliminated the bottlenecks at the ports by having equipment loaded directly from the ships to railroad cars, thus allowing more trucks to be sent to the front. Even when the Germans began the Battle of the Bulge on December 16, 1944, Aurand's Normandy Base Section more than picked up the slack for the extra manpower, ammunition, fuel, and equipment needed to turn back the German assault. Eventually, the three ports, the railroads, and the trucks of the Normandy Base Section handled some 25,000 tons of supplies per day; tens of thousands of soldiers worked tirelessly under Aurand to accomplish this feat. In all, he succeeded to such a degree in making his command an efficiently managed and rationally organized unit that he was left with little to do except periodically go on tours or hold staff meetings. For his efforts, he was awarded an Oak Leaf Cluster for his Distinguished Service Medal. The citation spoke of Aurand's "rare leadership and superior management" with which he supervised an "efficient operation."[14]

In May 1945, Aurand left his post with the Normandy Base Section to become commanding general of Service and Supply in China. This position—the "Allied Grocer" of China[15]—entailed supplying the army units there and continuing to help supply China's millions of soldiers. This proved to be no easy task, especially because China remained in the age of human and animal power rather than the age of steam and gasoline power as in Europe. To complicate matters, Aurand contended with long distances as well as the constant antagonism between the Communist Chinese forces and the Nationalist Chinese. After V-J Day in August 1945, his priorities turned to downsizing American forces and leaving China altogether. As with his previous commands, Aurand negotiated around political, administrative, and military pitfalls to establish an efficiently managed supply organization.

Following World War II, Aurand did not retire and enter academia as he had expected. Instead, he was promoted to lieutenant general and spent two years in several assignments at home and abroad. Then, from January 1948 until March 1949, he served as the Director of Service, Supply, and Procurement of the U.S. Army General Staff. Aurand's title soon changed to Director of Logistics, the only such position in army history. He spent his last tour of duty as commanding general of army forces in the Pacific from 1949 until his retirement in August 1952. He died on June 18, 1980.

As an army logistics officer from 1920 to 1945, Henry S. Aurand critiqued the army's dysfunctional logistics, learned rational organization theories, preached the need for realistic mobilization planning, and ultimately put his theoretical knowledge to practical use as a logistics officer during World War II. All the while, he acted more like a Progressive businessman or public servant than an army officer. Aurand came to realize that because warfare had become much more complex in an industrial age, good managers were as important as heroic combat leaders. Perhaps General Eisenhower and General George S. Patton can be added to this argument. Eisenhower, the great organizer and administrator, may have been more important to the Allied victory in Europe than was Patton, the great battlefield commander. Eisenhower's way of thinking was similar to that of Henry S. Aurand.

Notes

1. Phyllis A. Zimmerman, *The Neck of the Bottle: George W. Goethals and the Reorganization of the U.S. Army Supply System, 1917–1918* (College Station, TX, 1992), 3–7.

2. H. R. Kuntz to Henry S. Aurand, March 9, 1921, Memo to Aurand, June 20, 1922, both in Henry S. Aurand Personal Papers Collection, Box 1, Eisenhower Library and Archives, Abilene, Kansas (hereafter cited as Aurand Papers).

3. R. Elberton Smith, *The Army and Economic Mobilization* (Washington, DC, 1959), 46.

4. "Supply and Transportation in the Theater of Operations," March 1, 1935, Box 58, Aurand Papers.

5. Ibid.

6. Stetson Conn and Bryon Fairchild, *The Framework of Hemispheric Defense* (Washington, DC, 1960), 40–43.

7. Alfred Gough, "Origins of the Army Industrial College: Military-Business Tensions after World War I," *Armed Forces and Society* 16 (1991): 268–71.

8. Memo from Aurand to the President of Trask Company, November 24, 1939, Box 58, Aurand Papers.

9. "Industrial Mobilization Plan," c. 1939, Box 58, Aurand Papers.

10. Henry S. Aurand, interview with William Morrison Jr., April 5–6, 21–22, May 3–7, 1974, Eisenhower Library, in John Russell Reese, "Supply Man: The Army Life of Lieutenant General Henry S. Aurand, 1915–1952" (Ph.D. diss., Kansas State University, 1984), 40–41.

11. Untitled report, n. d. [c. September 1941], Box 10, Aurand Papers.

12. "The Supply Problem of the Army," November 13, 1943, Box 65, Aurand Papers.

13. "Henry S. Aurand," citation, December 1944, Box 58, Aurand Papers.

14. "Henry S. Aurand," citation, May 1945, Box 58, Aurand Papers.

15. *Chicago Tribune*, n.d., Box 27, Aurand Papers, in Reese, "Supply Man," 136.

Suggested Readings

Brinkley, Alan. *The End of Reform: New Deal Liberalism in Recession and War.* New York, 1995.

Gough, Alfred. "Origins of the Army Industrial College: Military-Business Tensions after World War I." *Armed Forces and Society* 16 (1991): 259–76.

Hawley, Ellis W. *The Great War and the Search for Modern Order: A History for the American People and Their Institutions, 1917–1933.* 2d ed. New York, 1992.

Huston, James A. *Sinews of War: Army Logistics, 1775–1953.* Washington, DC, 1966.

Kennedy, David M. *Freedom from Fear: The American People in Depression and War, 1929–1945.* New York, 1999.

Koistinen, Paul A. C. *Planning for Peace, Preparing for War: The Political Economy of American Warfare, 1930–1939.* Lawrence, KS, 1998.

Leighton, Richard, and Robert W. Coakley. *Global Logistics and Strategy, 1940–1943.* Washington, DC, 1955.

Ohl, John Kennedy. *Supplying the Troops: General Somervell and American Logistics in World War II.* Dekalb, IL, 1994.

Reese, John Russell. "Supply Man: The Army Life of Lieutenant General Henry S. Aurand, 1915–1952." Ph.D. dissertation, Kansas State University, 1984.

Ulbrich, David J. "Logistics Need Practice: Comparing the Pre-War Military Careers of Montgomery Meigs and Henry Aurand." *Logistics Spectrum* 34 (2000): 32–34.

Weigley, Russell F. *History of the United States Army.* Bloomington, IN, 1984.

Zimmerman, Phyllis A. *The Neck of the Bottle: George W. Goethals and the Reorganization of the U.S. Army Supply System, 1917–1918.* College Station, TX, 1992.

14

Oveta Culp Hobby
Director of the Wartime Women's Army Corps

Michael S. Casey

Many people today view women's fledgling steps toward full equality in the military as a symbolic indicator of the progress of women's liberation. The first steps to incorporate them into the military occurred during World War II. A special woman was required to head the newly established and highly controversial Women's Auxiliary Army Corps (WAAC), later the Women's Army Corps (WAC). Oveta Culp Hobby was the logical choice. A Texan, she came from a wealthy, elite background and brought respectable conservative credentials with her when she packed for Washington to begin this bold experiment. No social radical, Hobby nevertheless waged an aggressive battle for "serious recognition" for women in the military and was a leader in integrating the officer corps. Her successful administration of the WAC eventually led to an equally sensitive position after the war. In 1953, President Eisenhower appointed Hobby the first secretary of Health, Education, and Welfare, only the second woman (after Frances Perkins) to hold a cabinet office.

Michael Casey has painted a revealing portrait of this pioneering woman. Casey teaches American history and humanities at Graceland University in Lamoni, Iowa. His academic specialty is American military and naval history. As a commander in the U.S. Navy, Casey was formerly a faculty member at the Naval War College. Upon retirement from active naval service, he joined the administration and faculty of Graceland, where he also serves as a vice provost and as the dean of the College of Professional Studies. Casey holds a Ph.D. from Salve Regina University, Newport, Rhode Island.

O veta Culp Hobby was an often-controversial trailblazer who provided exemplary leadership to American women of the 1940s and 1950s as they entered professional fields that were previously the sole purview of men. Already a successful newspaperwoman, Oveta headed the Women's Army Corps (WAC) from its inception through the Second World War. Only the second woman to hold a cabinet-level appointment, she became the first secretary of the new Department of Health, Education, and Welfare (HEW) under President Dwight D. Eisenhower. Her service to the nation during these decades was perhaps

unsurpassed by any other woman in the United States. Through repeated success in a "man's world," Oveta set an inspirational example
for millions of women who were hoping to enter public service or the
business sector.

Her competence in these roles was always under close scrutiny. She
often drew severe criticism, in some cases due solely to her gender. Powerful men in the military, politics, and throughout the country believed
that a woman's place was in the home. Many women were themselves
uncertain about Oveta and what she accomplished, and she served as a
lightning rod for such disagreement. Her ability to keep her composure
in the face of vocal and often mean-spirited disapproval attests to her
professionalism. Though recognized late in life for her many contributions to her country, Oveta is often overlooked today when the modern
women's movement is discussed.

Oveta Culp was born on January 19, 1905, in Killeen, Texas. Emma
Hoover Culp, her mother, was a supporter of the contemporary movement for women's rights. Her father, Isaac William Culp, practiced law
and was active in state politics. Oveta was the second of seven children.
Her name, from a Native American word for "forget," was chosen because it rhymed with the name of her sister, Juanita.[1] Oveta was her
father's favorite child. Although he pampered her, he failed to spoil her
readiness for hard work.

Oveta attended public school, though sometimes private tutoring
augmented her education. Highly competitive and an excellent student,
she usually won the spelling bees. Not surprisingly, she was an avid
reader. Every Sunday her parents had to pry a book from her hands to
get her ready in time for church. She graduated at the top of her high-
school class. Her thirst for knowledge presaged the self-taught nature of
her preparation for later careers in business, the military, and government. Initially, her goal was to be a lawyer, having acquired a penchant
for law from the hours spent in her father's office. She loved to listen to
discussions of legal and political matters. Oveta spent one year at Mary
Hardin-Baylor College while her father served his initial term in the
Texas House of Representatives. She subsequently studied at the University of Texas Law School.

Oveta worked as a legal clerk with the Texas Banking Department
where she codified banking laws. In 1930 she became an assistant to
Houston's city attorney and broadened her experience. Perhaps because
of her fascination with her father's career in the Texas House, Oveta
became interested in parliamentary procedure. Her subsequent appoint-

ment as clerk for the judiciary committee of the legislature afforded her an opportunity to study the subject. Learning all she could about that complicated field, she became a subject matter expert. Although her father's connections did not hurt her candidacy, Oveta earned the position of Parliamentarian to the House, holding that post off and on for eight years between 1925 and 1941.

At twenty-four, Oveta ran for the state legislature from Harris County. Her opponent, backed by the Ku Klux Klan, accused her of being a blatant "parliamentarian," an impossible charge to refute. Whether the voters actually understood the true meaning of the accusation, the label cast doubt and probably cost her the election. Oveta was philosophical about the experience, learning much about herself and the political process as well as the important use of information to shape public opinion. Although she would never again run for elected office, Oveta became increasingly active in local, state, and national politics. Moreover, the crucial lesson about public relations would propel her to national prominence during the war years.

As secretary of the Women's Democratic Club, Oveta played a vital role in local politics. The Democratic National Convention, held in Houston in 1928, exposed her to a broader segment of the body politic and boosted her reputation as a dynamic and tireless party organizer. She served as state president of the League of Women Voters. As she would throughout her life, Oveta stayed active in the Episcopal Church.

Oveta soon embarked on a new career—the newspaper business. The president of the *Houston Post* was Will Hobby, former governor of Texas and a friend of Oveta's father. He, a widower in his fifties, and Oveta, in her twenties, became close friends. After a lengthy courtship the couple married on February 23, 1931. Oveta was not marrying into wealth and leisure, as she well knew. Will faced bankruptcy when the two were married, having invested heavily in an insurance company that subsequently failed. That the Hobby fortune was soon restored was largely due to Oveta's hard work and business savvy. Referred to as the "Hobby Team," Oveta and Will, over the following decades, worked together and invested shrewdly to build a communications empire.

Beginning as a research editor at the *Houston Post*, Oveta began to work her way to the top through self-study and diligence. She became the paper's literary editor, holding that position from 1933 to 1936. Oveta was unstoppable. Injured in a horseback riding accident, she continued her daily routine while wearing a neck brace.[2] In 1936, Oveta advanced to associate editor, where she gave the women of Texas the kind of news they wanted. She was aware of the typical male reaction to these initiatives but did not let such criticism stop her. She was able to shake off personal attacks, trusting in the inherent correctness of her decisions. Oveta would demonstrate this thick skin repeatedly during her military and governmental service.

Oveta redirected efforts by the *Post* to ensure that news of Houston's African-American community found its way into print, since this segment of the local populace had been largely ignored in the past. Under her stewardship, the *Post* featured stories about the contributions of local blacks to the region. In this effort, Oveta was several decades ahead of many other editors and publishers across America's South.

In 1938 the chairman of the newspaper's board, J. E. Josey, created the position of executive vice president specifically for Oveta to reflect the role that she had invented. From there, she ran the daily operation of the newspaper while her husband focused on other businesses, specifically banking and a growing radio empire. Oveta reorganized the administrative structure of the entire news organization to improve communications and foster efficiency. She revised the layout of the paper, to give it a more contemporary look. Oveta simultaneously served as executive director of radio station KPRC and as director of the National Bank of Cleburne, other parts of the couple's holdings.

Given the pace at which Oveta was building her reputation as an astute businesswoman, she nevertheless found the time to have two children during these years. William Pettus Hobby Jr. was born in 1932; Jessica Oveta Hobby followed in 1937. Oveta often was asked about the challenges of running a household and raising children while pursuing a successful business career. Characteristically, she downplayed her accomplishments.

Capitalizing on past experience, Oveta wrote a syndicated column for the *Post* that put parliamentary procedure into terms understandable by the general public. In 1937 she authored *Mr. Chairman*, a textbook that became the definitive reference on the subject throughout the region. Busy with such projects, Oveta had no way of knowing that an opportunity to serve her country would soon knock at her door and take her away from the familiar offices of the *Post*.

In July 1941, Oveta went to Washington in an official capacity with the War Department's Bureau of Public Relations. As events in Europe and the Pacific heated up, and American involvement in the war became likely, Oveta's task was to organize a Women's Interest Section for an important mission—to ensure that American wives and mothers were at ease regarding the welfare of their husbands and sons in the military. Through featured articles and stories, she kept civilian women informed of the men's comfort, health, and recreational opportunities, thus ensuring that popular support for militarization on the home front did not waver. This position paid only the token sum of one dollar per year.

Although Jessica joined her in Washington, Oveta missed William and Will, who remained in Houston. Nevertheless, Oveta was committed to the mission and convinced that her contribution to the nation was worth the personal sacrifice. Her homesickness was not reflected in her performance. In this key position, she worked on a daily basis with top policymakers, particularly General George C. Marshall, the army's senior officer, who was impressed by Oveta's can-do spirit and remained her mentor during the war years. Known to her subordinates as the "Charming Chief," Oveta would receive unwavering professional support from Marshall in the trying times ahead.

Immediately after Pearl Harbor, Marshall asked Oveta to commence detailed planning for a women's unit for the army. Oveta worked intimately with Congresswoman Edith Nourse Rogers in drafting the legislation for this controversial proposal. Oveta's congressional testimony during hearings regarding the role of women in the armed forces was twofold: the army needed women in uniform immediately to free men for combat, and to put them there required central coordination. Oveta sometimes slipped from sight during the intense politicking that accompanied the final adoption of the concept, but she worked intensely in the background for legislative approval.

When Congress created the Women's Auxiliary Army Corps (WAAC) on May 12, 1942, selection of its commander became the highest priority. *Time* magazine prophesied that Oveta would get the job, considering how capably she had handled her responsibilities with the Women's Interest Section. Her selection was far from certain, however, given the political realities of wartime Washington, although her references included nine of the most successful business and professional women in the country. Several lists of official and unofficial candidates were submitted to the army's chain of command. The army's staff narrowed the choices to three candidates, with Oveta's name heading the list. Representative Rogers's list of proposed directors was shorter still—Oveta Hobby. While the official selection by Henry Stimson, the secretary of war, was delayed by lobbying from political factions, Marshall unofficially moved Oveta into the new position to start work on the critical tasks that lay ahead while awaiting the secretary's final approval.

President Franklin D. Roosevelt signed the act forming the corps on May 15. The next day, Oveta was sworn in as director of the WAAC by Secretary Stimson.

An "auxiliary" force, the WAAC was not officially in the regular army; and, as director, Oveta received the equivalent rank of only a colonel. More important to the ultimate success of the endeavor, however, was the fact that Oveta had the same access to Marshall and other top men typically enjoyed only by general officers. Before she was in the job very long, however, she ran headlong into the army's parochial internal politics that made her task more difficult than expected.

Because the WAAC was not an integral part of the army, U.S. Army regulations could not be used to govern it. Oveta drafted a set of WAAC regulations patterned on those of the army. Without benefit of military experience, Oveta anticipated the many contingencies inherent in a large military force and imposed high standards for her new corps. Because of her standards, the average age of incoming WAAC officers was thirty; more than 40 percent were college graduates. Enlisted WAACs averaged twenty-four years of age; more than 60 percent were high-school graduates.[3] Oveta's charges vastly exceeded the educational norms for the regular army under the draft. In spite of these high standards, the annual goal of 25,000 WAACs was reached in only six months and was subsequently raised to 150,000 women.

Although the public laughed at the very idea of "GI Janes," Oveta avowed that military service was a "serious job for serious women." She even asked photographers not to take her picture while she was smiling so as not to detract from the dignity of the WAAC. It was slow going, but she began to win over male officers and congressmen to her position. Her opinions were clearly stated and unswervingly followed. Her women would receive the same training as men and would be held to the same standards. Over the objections of male officers who believed that women could not endure the rigors of basic training, Oveta set out to prove otherwise. She established a WAAC Training Center at Fort Des Moines in Iowa, where a strict regimen ensured that the first WAACs were ready for army life. While some candidates were surprised at the no-nonsense training, they accepted it readily. Morale within WAAC ranks soared despite the many hardships.

Women were soon clamoring to undergo training. Oveta herself was determined to do so to gain a better understanding of military life for the average WAAC. As each senior officer disapproved her request for training, she immediately appealed to his superior officer. Eventually, she applied directly to General Marshall, who was sympathetic but unswayed. Army protocol did not permit the WAAC's senior officer to take part in basic training. Moreover, Oveta was too valuable in her post at the top to be spared.

By mid-1945, when Oveta finally stepped down as commander, there had been about 200,000 women in the corps, ten times as many troops as commanded by the typical male general officer. Clearly, one of her strengths was building and managing a large organization. Although she visited England to learn from the British experience (the Women's Royal Army Corps, or WRAC), most of what she accomplished was due to her own abilities.

One of Oveta's earliest policy decisions was as important as any that were to follow. She insisted that her corps would avoid cronyism. Army recruiters, not Oveta or her staff, would select the first cadre of prospective WAAC officers. After the first cohort graduated from the WAAC Officers Candidate School, subsequent officers would be selected from enlisted personnel. WAACs were to become officers based on merit, not on a connection with a prominent political or military person. Oveta personally benefited from this policy of "no direct appointments"; it ensured that no political or military appointees were forced onto her staff.

Similarly, Oveta directed that African-American women be appointed to the WAAC at both the officer and enlisted levels in accordance with the proportion of blacks in the regular army. This move disappointed some and surprised many in the army and across the nation. Full integration of blacks into the armed forces was years away, and Oveta's decision was not universally popular. Not only was this move the right thing to do, but it also effectively disarmed her first critics. The National Negro Council and the National Council of Negro Women had lobbied for black educator Mary McLeod Bethune as director, fearing that a WAAC director from the South would not ensure fair treatment of African Americans in the new organization. When forty of the first 450 officer candidates selected were black women, that criticism stopped.

Placed in their social context, Oveta's racial policies were ahead of the times. The regular army segregated black men almost totally. In the WAAC, Oveta moved to redress the situation. Encouraged by pressure put on the army by the National Association for the Advancement of Colored People (NAACP), Oveta largely desegregated WAACs among the officer ranks in late 1942. At the enlisted level, the WAAC continued to segregate, in theory to avoid racial disharmony.

Another major policy decision was soon at hand. Male officers believed that when a WAAC became pregnant, she should immediately be dismissed with a dishonorable discharge. Oveta was equally insistent; to do so would constitute unfair treatment. She did not excuse fraternization; she simply believed that not all blame should fall on the woman. The army did not dishonorably discharge male soldiers for their roles in such inappropriate behavior, she noted. While the acrimonious debate won her few friends among the army's upper echelons, Oveta did win the argument. WAACs would henceforth receive an honorable discharge when separated from the service by reason of pregnancy.

Few people in America initially took the WAAC seriously. At her first press conference, Oveta was asked frivolous questions about girdles and nail polish. That many of these questions came from female reporters was probably disheartening. It took a conspicuous effort on her part to refocus correspondents on important matters: the WAAC existed to free men for combat; whenever feasible, WAACs would adhere to army regulations and traditions; women selected for service in the WAAC would meet consistent standards of age (21–45), character, experience, adaptability, personality, bearing, and appearance.

Despite Oveta's efforts to establish a solid reputation for military professionalism, a campaign of outright slander against the women's service soon broke out. Gossip, innuendo, and downright lies, fed by soldiers and civilians for various reasons, spread the word that all WAACs were lesbians, prostitutes who corrupted the morals of American manhood, or pregnant women who shirked their duties. Destructive stories were spread by many in the media who chose to sensationalize WAAC-related "news."

A nationally syndicated newspaper column repeatedly but incorrectly reported that WAACs were issued contraceptives for their role in keeping up the morale of male soldiers.[4] Although women became pregnant every day in the civilian world, when the media learned of a pregnant WAAC, it made the headlines. Fraternization and bigamous relationships were given equally lurid coverage, with the blame invariably placed on the WAAC rather than on her male counterpart. Radio evangelists, who considered women in uniform to be an abomination, called upon the government to disband the organization.[5] Almost nationwide, WAACs were labeled as promiscuous, "fallen" women. Oveta had a first-rate public relations disaster on her hands.

Her response was swift, if not universally successful. With help from General Marshall, President Roosevelt, and First Lady Eleanor Roosevelt, she issued repeated public denials of the vicious and unfounded rumors. Official investigations were conducted immediately whenever such accusations were made. Almost invariably, no basis to the charges was discovered. Nevertheless, the "Whispering Campaign," as it came to be known, undermined the morale of many women in the WAAC. Knowing that the British had dealt with similar slander campaigns during both World Wars when women served in uniform made Oveta philosophical. By war's end, hard data finally confirmed, for the years 1942 to 1945, that the number of WAAC pregnancies was one-seventeenth the total of pregnancies in the civilian sector.[6]

Throughout her "trial by fire," Oveta kept her composure, although the experience took its toll. Her unrelenting responsibilities weighed heavily upon her, as evidenced by the premature graying of her hair. Oveta continued to exemplify the professional female military officer, however, and ensured that her troops strived to meet the same standards. Investigations during the slander campaign had found that misbehavior of civilian women wearing clothes remotely similar to WAAC uniforms was regularly blamed on the WAACs. Oveta wore her uniform, topped off by the "Hobby hat," the official WAAC cap, with pride. (Later, in the 1950s, she was named one of America's best-dressed women.)

At the outset, WAACs were confined to sixty-two specific noncombatant jobs, including typist, clerk, dental hygienist, chauffeur, cook, and baker. Through constant lobbying inside the army and in Congress, Oveta made more jobs available to her WAACs. By war's end, women served in 239 different billets, greatly enhancing their wartime contributions and their postwar employability. The final list of occupational specialties for WACs included weather observer, intelligence analyst, aerial photographer, and heavy equipment operator.

In late 1942, Oveta and Representative Rogers drafted a bill proposing full military status for the WAAC. Marshall approved of the proposed legislation, but it took six months to proceed through Congress. In mid-1943 conversion of the auxiliary corps to an official branch of the army gained congressional approval, and President Roosevelt signed the act establishing the Women's Army Corps (WAC) on July 1, 1943. Although this change of status provided an opportunity for her to step down from her beleaguered post, Oveta was committed to going the distance. She accepted the proffered rank of U.S. Army colonel. Other WAAC members also faced a tough decision. The smear campaign caused concern at the upper levels of the army that thousands of WAACs would choose discharge rather than enlist in the new organization.

Oveta's approach, as always, was pragmatic and correct. She was opposed to compelling WAACs to enlist in the regular army. She firmly believed that it would be better to have a smaller corps of women who wanted to serve than a larger force of involuntary personnel. Over the ninety-day conversion to regular army status, Oveta's office oversaw the entire process, keeping it on track and ensuring that the new WAC would be ready to accomplish its wartime mission.

Although Oveta had long sought regular army status for her corps, the new command arrangements initially hampered her effectiveness. Now an "adviser" to the secretary of the army, Oveta had less direct control over WAC affairs. Individual unit leaders, all men, now had authority over WAC personnel under their command. Since Oveta could communicate directly with major commanders, she could still monitor the situation, but correcting inequities or inappropriate utilization of WAC personnel was problematic.

Another setback occurred almost simultaneously. The regular army assumed complete responsibility for WAAC recruiting, including setting of policy. In January 1943, over Oveta's objections, the army lowered entry standards to encourage enlistments, primarily because of the stiff competition from the Navy's WAVES as well as from the women's branches of the Marines and Coast Guard. After collecting hard data, Oveta could demonstrate the negative effect on the WAAC from the lower standards. Unskilled and often untrainable women had replaced the top-notch recruits of the past; discipline problems were up forcewide. Oveta persuaded Marshall to restore the higher standards. In April 1943 he delegated WAAC recruiting policies and procedures to Oveta.

By late 1944, with the end of the war predicted, planning for the postwar army and demobilization of the WAC began in earnest. While Oveta had once advocated the unpopular measure of drafting women during the war, she took the opposite approach with regard to termination of the war effort. When army staff officers made a strong case for early demobilization of combat troops, while WACs filled administrative positions, Oveta recommended that WACs should be discharged immediately after the war. She was anxious to see them make a rapid return to civilian life to reconstitute the American family after the disruption of the war. At the same time, she sought to ensure that women who had served honorably in uniform could find a job in the civilian sector. Since female veterans did not have the same reemployment rights as their male counterparts, Oveta realized that servicewomen might end up facing severe financial hardships if they were kept in uniform longer than absolutely necessary.

On December 31, 1944, as a result of her exemplary performance as director of the WAC, Colonel Oveta Hobby was awarded the Distinguished Service Medal, the first army woman to receive this, the third highest decoration in the U.S. Army. The ceremony masked the fact that Oveta was exhausted by her nonstop schedule. Her military responsibilities had grown exponentially during the war, and it was almost inevitable that the process would begin to wear her down. Fatigue led to repeated illnesses. Her subordinates filled in for her during several extended periods in early 1945. Even though she was under serious consideration for promotion to brigadier general, the first woman ever proposed for that rank, Oveta resigned her commission in July 1945 and returned to Houston. By handpicking her replacement, Col. Westray Battle Boyce, Oveta ensured that her proposals for the postwar period would receive due consideration after she was gone.

Characteristically, Oveta Hobby, the first female "old soldier," did not simply "fade away" upon release from active duty. She redoubled her efforts with the family businesses in Texas where she again became active in state politics and was mentioned as a possible Democratic candidate for governor. Further, Oveta was appointed to the United Nations Conference on Freedom of Information held in Geneva in 1948. She became the first female director of the American Society of Newspaper Editors and the president of the Southern Newspaper Publishers Association. Her liberal views on women and minorities had an important, if indirect, impact on the social opinions of key media figures as the United States entered the 1950s and the opening of the Civil Rights Era. She subsequently sat on the board of regents of Texas State Teachers College, was awarded honorary degrees from several universities, and was chosen as the "Outstanding Texas Woman" in 1951.

Oveta sat on the President's Bipartisan Committee on the Organization of the Executive Branch and was a valuable member of the board of directors of the Citizens Committee for the Hoover Report on governmental reorganization. These posts afforded her excellent insight into the role of a modernized federal government. Back in Houston, Oveta threw her considerable energies behind Dwight Eisenhower's presidential campaign. Her high-visibility support delivered Texas for Eisenhower, and Texas was crucial to his victory at the national level. President Eisenhower rewarded Oveta by naming her to head the Federal Security

Agency (FSA), which oversaw the health, education, and economic security of individual citizens. The Senate approved her appointment as FSA administrator on January 21, 1953. Subordinate agencies under her charge included the Public Health Service, Food and Drug Administration, Office of Education, and the Bureau of Old Age and Survivors Insurance.

This agency soon was expanded and elevated to become the Department of Health, Education, and Welfare (HEW), and Oveta took the oath of office before President Eisenhower on April 11, 1953. As the secretary of this new federal department, Oveta was the first woman to serve in a cabinet post since Frances Perkins, President Roosevelt's secretary of labor, and only the second woman overall. Rather than the address "Madam Secretary," Oveta preferred "Mrs. Secretary," which she thought sounded more typically American. Her powder-blue official government limousine was easy to spot on the streets of Washington, and she maintained as high-profile a role as secretary as she had as director of the WAC.

In the midst of the decade's Red Scare, Oveta, a staunch anti-Communist, aggressively enforced strict loyalty and security standards at HEW, dismissing several hundred government employees. Strongly opposed to socialized medicine, she instead advocated a comprehensive but complex and expensive health "reinsurance" plan through which the federal government would help to underwrite public health insurance coverage. After an exhausting political battle, the plans for the defeated program had to be dropped.

The most controversial event during her tenure came from the discovery of a polio vaccine by Dr. Jonas Salk. Nationwide, parents were clamoring for the inoculations needed to protect their children from the scourge of polio. HEW was responsible for procuring sufficient vaccine so that, as President Eisenhower had promised the voters, every child in America would be inoculated. Unfortunately, since no mechanism to produce and distribute the vaccine was in place, Oveta's HEW was ill prepared for the massive undertaking. Administrative shortcomings within the agency hampered production and delivery. When someone discovered that some batches of the vaccine produced by government contractors were contaminated, frantic politicians and voters immediately sought a scapegoat, and HEW Secretary Oveta Hobby became the object of their displeasure.

Oveta and her staff worked desperately to meet the demands for the vaccine. She employed virtually all of her public relations skills to as-

sure the public that HEW was handling the difficult situation professionally. President Eisenhower refused to dismiss her, despite the many
calls for her firing. Oveta recognized that she lacked the influential
Washington allies needed to weather the political storm, but she was
loath to quit her post. When Will Hobby suddenly became ill, however,
she realized that the best course of action was to return home to care for
her husband. When Oveta resigned as HEW Secretary in July 1955,
one of her fellow cabinet members stated that the "best man" in the
cabinet had been lost![7]

Back home again, Oveta resumed what was, for her, business as
usual: the management of the huge Hobby communications empire.
Because of Will's illness, during the years leading up his death in 1964
the Hobby Team was essentially down to one; Oveta managed the entire conglomerate. His death failed to slow her down. Her business acu-
men was highly valued, and by the mid-1960s she served on the boards
of General Foods Corporation and the Mutual Insurance Corporation.
In 1967, *Harper's Bazaar* magazine named her one of its "100 American
Women of Accomplishment."

President Lyndon B. Johnson placed her on the board of the Corporation for Public Broadcasting in 1968. Other calls to serve her nation included the President's Commission on Selective Service and the
Vietnam Health Task Force sponsored by HEW. In October 1978, Oveta
was presented with the George C. Marshall Medal for Public Service for
"selfless and outstanding service," the nineteenth recipient of the award
and the first woman so honored. Slowly, Oveta became less active in
business affairs. On August 16, 1995, Oveta Culp Hobby died, surrounded by friends and family as well as by the antiques, paintings, and
rare books that she had carefully collected throughout her life.

During her military and government careers, Oveta Culp Hobby
drew both praise and criticism. Each was, at times, justified, but her
detractors often outshouted her supporters, leaving an overall negative
opinion about her in the minds of many Americans. That is unfortunate. By no means can critics negate the overwhelmingly positive nature of Oveta's contribution to American life. With the war years, women
began to play significantly more active roles in society than before.

Oveta was at the forefront of that advance. First, through her high-
profile success in a man's world, she set a stellar personal example for
other women. Second, and more important, she took America's women
by the hands and led them along the path she had blazed. Several hundred thousand women served in the WAC during the war years, making

an irreplaceable contribution to the Allied victory. When the war ended, some of these women remained in the army, thus solidifying woman's place in the armed services. Most WACs returned to civilian life where they continued to set examples of pride and determination in the face of social and economic obstacles. That groundswell eventually became the modern women's movement, and Oveta Culp Hobby arguably made the first splash.

Notes

1. Ann Fears Crawford and Crystal Sasse Ragsdale, *Women in Texas: Their Lives, Their Experiences, Their Accomplishments* (Burnet, TX, 1982), 249.
2. Ibid., 252.
3. Bettie J. Morden, *The Women's Army Corps, 1945–1978* (Washington, DC, 1990), 7–8.
4. Mattie E. Treadwell, *The United States Army in World War II Special Studies: The Women's Army Corps* (Washington, DC, 1954), 201–2.
5. Ibid., 197.
6. Morden, *Women's Army Corps*, 16.
7. Kelly King Howes, *World War II Biographies* (Detroit, MI, 1999), 120.

Suggested Readings

Adams, Sherman. *Firsthand Report: The Story of the Eisenhower Administration.* New York, 1961.

Crawford, Ann Fears, and Crystal Sasse Ragsdale. *Women in Texas: Their Lives, Their Experiences, Their Accomplishments.* Burnet, TX, 1982.

Eisenhower, Dwight D. *The White House Years: Mandate for Change, 1953–1956.* Garden City, NY, 1963.

Holm, Jeanne. *Women in the Military: An Unfinished Revolution.* Novato, CA, 1982.

Howes, Kelly King. *World War II Biographies.* Detroit, MI, 1999.

Hurt, Harry, III. "The Last of the Great Ladies." *Texas Monthly* (October 1978): 143.

Miles, Rufus E., Jr. *The Department of Health, Education, and Welfare.* New York, 1974.

Quester, George H. "The Problem." In *Female Soldiers—Combatants or Noncombatants: Historical and Contemporary Perspectives,* edited by Nancy Loring Goldman. Westport, CT, 1982.

Treadwell, Mattie E. *The United States Army in World War II Special Studies: The Women's Army Corps.* Washington, DC, 1954.

15

Ernie Pyle
From a "Worm's-Eye View"

Donald W. Whisenhunt

Ernest "Ernie" Pyle was the most famous American war correspondent of World War II. An average person from the Midwest who never saw himself as a celebrity, Pyle is remembered for his columns about the everyday life of the average American soldier. He almost never wrote about officers, and he seldom included graphic details about battles, injuries, and destruction. His columns, published in as many as 300 newspapers, endeared him both to the men in the field and to their families at home. Even people without loved ones in the war could relate to Pyle's stories. He was one of the few journalists to die in the war, killed by a Japanese machine gunner. Therefore, no one can know what kind of career he might have had if he had lived beyond his forty-five years.

Donald W. Whisenhunt, editor of this volume, specializes in studying the period between the wars. He is professor of history at Western Washington University. His most recent books are *Poetry of the People: Poems to the President, 1929–1945* (1996), *Tent Show: Arthur Names and His "Famous" Players* (2000), and *It Seems to Me: Selected Letters of Eleanor Roosevelt* (2001).

"I have known no finer man, no finer soldier than he," said General Omar Bradley of Ernie Pyle.[1] President Henry S. Truman added, "No man in this war has told the story of the American fighting man as American fighting men wanted it told. . . . He deserves the gratitude of all his countrymen."[2] *American Decades* stated that he was "the most famous war correspondent the United States ever produced."[3] Others said that he "was arguably the best-known and best-loved American war correspondent" and "did everything with the G.I.s except shoot a gun."[4] J. W. Raper of the *Cleveland Press* called Pyle "just about the best reporter in the United States."[5] *The Encyclopedia of American Journalism* described him as the "greatest American war correspondent."[6] Despite the high praise that poured forth at the time of his death on the battlefield in 1945 to the assessments of historians in subsequent years, a review of his life reveals him to be an average American who rose to the heights of success through good luck and sheer talent.

Because of the nature of World War II and the sentiment at the time that this conflict was a fight for survival, this period produced famous people—heroes, one might say—who might not have otherwise risen to the level of public consciousness. One only has to think of Bill Mauldin, another journalist, who made his reputation as a cartoonist who immortalized the common soldiers in the trenches with his characters, Willie and Joe. Whereas Mauldin told the soldiers' story through drawings, Pyle dealt in prose. Unlike most of the other correspondents of the war who made names for themselves, Pyle concentrated on the average soldier in the field. Seldom did Pyle write about generals or high-ranking politicians. He told a story that resonated with the American people and made the war real to them. Ernie Pyle was truly the GI's writer and friend.

Newspapers in World War II were one of the most important means by which the home front kept abreast of events in the various theaters of war. Television was not available to the public yet; radio was the only real competition to the newspaper, along with *Life* magazine and movie newsreels. The newspaper had matured through many wars to report firsthand what was going on. Pyle added a human touch to the war story, and in the process he touched the lives of millions of people.

Ernest Taylor Pyle was born in a farmhouse near Dana, Indiana, on August 3, 1900. His ancestors on both sides of the family were mostly Scottish and English; he grew up a Methodist. The major influences on the young Pyle were his mother, Maria—usually called Marie—and her sister Mary. Pyle was slight in stature, red headed, and shy.[7]

Farm life held no attraction for him. At age nine his father introduced him to farm work, especially how to use the harrow and to plow behind a horse. Pyle came to despise horses and all they represented. He recalled, "I worked like a horse," something he said he would never do again. Even when he was traveling around the country as a roving reporter, he refused to stay at farmhouses that rented rooms because "I've had enough of farms."[8]

When the United States entered World War I in 1917, Pyle was desperate to get involved, but he was too young by about a year. He was able to join the naval reserve, but a month later the armistice was signed. With few other options, young Ernie enrolled in Indiana University where he majored in journalism because classmates told him that it was "a breeze."[9] One of Pyle's biographers, however, says that he majored in economics because journalism courses were not open to freshmen, even though journalism occupied his mind most of the time.[10]

In college he had periods of "mental lowness . . . when he was certain he wasn't worth a damn."[11] Despite his low self-esteem and his shyness, Pyle made friends and eventually spent most of his time at Indiana University on the student newspaper, the *Daily Student*. One semester before graduation he left college to take a reporting job with a small newspaper in La Porte, Indiana. Only a few months passed before he moved to the *Washington Daily News* where he was a copy editor. This paper was part of the Scripps-Howard chain, with which Pyle spent the greater part of his career.

Pyle soon tired of this work; a short attention span would characterize his future life. While in Washington he met Geraldine ("Jerry") Siebolds, a young woman from Minnesota who had adopted the bohemian lifestyle common among many young people during the Roaring Twenties. Jerry proved to have serious emotional and mental problems that plagued the couple for the rest of their lives. Ernie and Jerry were married in 1925.[12] Shortly afterward, they both quit their jobs and took off on a 9,000-mile drive around the country. Returning to the East and settling in New York, Pyle went to work again as a copy editor, this time for the *Evening World* and then the *Evening Post*.

Before long they were back in Washington where Pyle worked as wire editor, reading the teletype and telegraph. There he started the first daily aviation column in the United States. In the wake of Charles Lindbergh's transatlantic flight in 1927, Americans were fascinated by air travel. So was Pyle; he took advantage of this opportunity to free himself from the daily grind of a desk job and to write something he really cared about.

In 1932, Pyle was named managing editor of the *Daily News*, but that job lasted only three years. Feeling constrained by the daily routine, he gladly gave up this position to become a roving reporter for Scripps-Howard. This change was ideal for Pyle. He crisscrossed the continental United States, then going as far as Alaska and Hawaii and all the way to South America. He once wrote that he had stayed in more than 800 hotels, "flown in sixty-six different airplanes, ridden on twenty-nine different boats, walked two hundred miles, gone through five sets of tires and put out approximately $2,500 in tips."[13] During this time he filed six syndicated columns per week.[14]

Then came World War II. After Hitler's invasion of Poland on September 1, 1939, Americans paid more attention to the events in

Europe, particularly in England after the Battle of Britain began. At first, Pyle did not have a special interest in those events, but, like everyone else, his focus gradually moved overseas. Finally, in late 1940 he decided he had to go to London to see firsthand what was going on.

He left Jerry in Albuquerque, which they had discovered in their travels and where they had built a house. He was somewhat uncertain about what might happen to her. Jerry's emotional problems had escalated into clinical depression, which resulted in her addiction to alcohol, sedatives, and amphetamines. Her condition occasionally improved, but she never fully recovered. Moreover, he was suffering from influenza and possibly anemia when he left for England.[15] Various ailments came to be a pattern for the rest of his life. He was a small man, usually weighing less than 140 pounds and subject to illness. He later described his wife's setbacks in letters to friends and family from the front.

Pyle's experience in London was little different from that of other war correspondents on the surface, but his columns were not run of the mill. Some of them were almost poetic in tone, even though they described horrible conditions. After the firebombing of London on December 29, he wrote "even though I must bite my tongue in shame for saying it—[it] was the most beautiful sight I have ever seen," a night when "London was ringed and stabbed with fire." In the attack "there was something inspiring in the savagery of it."[16] He told of how Londoners coped with nighttime bombing, the shelters, and the British struggle to carry on the war.[17] Some of his stories were so graphic and emotional that after they were published in the States they were cabled back to England for British readers.[18] He wrote about American GIs training in England for an invasion of Europe; he described their boredom, their dreams, and the culture shock in their interaction with British citizens who were overwhelmed by the foreigners.

Pyle returned to the United States in the summer of 1941, exhausted and convinced that his work was not very good. The Scripps-Howard Alliance was confident enough to publish a volume of his columns, *Ernie Pyle in England* (1941). His time at home was difficult and unpleasant, however. His wife's emotional condition had worsened, and he took a leave of absence to be with her. When she told him that she wanted to have a child, Pyle did not respond favorably, and she had a relapse. She would get better for awhile but then sink into depression again. The two of them decided to divorce, hoping that the shock of such a decision might help Jerry. If she got better, they could remarry later. In April 1942 the divorce became final.[19]

By 1942 the United States was in the war. Pyle felt the pull to get back to Europe, into the thick of action. Despite the divorce, he was reluctant to leave Jerry. His lack of confidence in his own ability continued but now was intensified by his fear of dying. In August he wrote to his friend Lee Miller, "Today is my birthday. Just an old broken-down, washed-up 42-year-old sonovabitch. . . . Wonder if I'll ever be 43, and if so why?"[20] In June, Pyle returned to England. For four months he dispatched columns from England and Ireland. In November he embarked by convoy to North Africa where the American invasion had begun only a few days earlier.

Pyle did not go immediately to the front in North Africa. Instead, he stayed behind, in Oran in Algeria, getting accustomed to the area, becoming familiar with censorship policy, and getting to know some of the low-level army bureaucrats. By chance he became aware of a major story and was able to sneak it through the censorship web—a feat that is still not totally understood. The American public was being led to believe that the North African campaign was easy, "that our losses have been practically nil; that the French here love us to death, and that all German influence has been cleaned out."[21] Furthermore, the United States was allowing French collaborators with the Nazis or outright French Nazis to do as they pleased. Pyle was outraged: "Our fundamental policy still is one of soft-gloving snakes in our midst." He said that this attitude amazed the loyal French: "Our enemies see it, laugh, and call us soft. Both sides are puzzled by a country at war which still lets enemies run loose to work against it."[22]

Pyle's work in North Africa, as it was in London, continued to be interrupted by his concern about Jerry. He wrote her in December 1942 suggesting that they remarry by proxy. He sent his proxy to the Mother Superior at St. Joseph's Hospital in Albuquerque where Jerry was a patient, but there was no immediate response. Not until March 1943, while traveling in Accra in the Gold Coast of Africa, did Pyle receive a cable telling him that he was remarried.[23]

Throughout his wartime experience Pyle felt most comfortable around ordinary soldiers. He wrote about their daily lives, not only battles and victories; about planes that did not make it back from bombing runs and those that barely managed to return; about eating from tin plates, lack of bathing facilities, and the mud and the heat and the cold. Back home in the States, people read his columns as if they were reading letters from their own loved ones in the battle zones. Still, self-doubt and depression plagued him. In a letter to Jerry he said, "I'm sad at not being able to do a wonderful job with the column. . . . I guess the

Ernie Pyle at the battlefront. *Courtesy of the Ernie Pyle State Historic Site, Dana, Indiana*

last struggling vestige of my will to write has finally gone." He thought that his columns were lifeless, "although I am really in a section where everything is exciting and interesting." The readers had no such doubts. By the middle of the war, his columns were carried in at least 300 newspapers in the United States.[24] In 1943, Pyle's North African columns were published in America under the title, *Here Is Your War.* That and another volume of columns, *Brave Men,* became the basis for a movie, *The Story of G.I. Joe,* which was released in 1945.

While in North Africa, Pyle adjusted to the role that the military expected correspondents to play. In earlier wars, reporters were considered a necessary evil whose access should be limited. By World War II, the military had become aware of the propaganda value of the news reporters and catered to their needs. While the army provided certain information to the newsmen, the reporters were also expected to be "a part of the team" who would help win the war. Because Pyle, never a maverick, wrote almost entirely about the daily lives of the "the goddamned infantry," he seldom had any conflicts of conscience about being a "mouthpiece" for the military.[25]

After the North African campaign, Pyle went to Italy for the invasion of Sicily. This was the largest seaborne invasion up to that time, involving some 2,000 British and American vessels. Pyle stayed on the USS *Biscayne* for ten days after the invasion, but then he went ashore. His fears and insecurities surfaced again. Certainly part of Ernie's depression and self-doubt had to do with real health problems, one of which was persistent anemia, compounded by his genuine fear of dying in war.[26] In Sicily he wrote Jerry, "I find myself more and more reluctant to repeat and repeat the old process of getting shot at."[27] Despite his fear and his constant complaining, his work continued to improve and his following of readers increased.

Pyle, once ashore, rushed to catch up with General George S. Patton's Seventh Army, which had broken out of the beachhead and moved about a hundred miles inland. Pyle then was stricken with a real illness, even though the doctors were never able to diagnose it exactly. It may have been malaria, dysentery, or "battlefield fever"—exhaustion, lack of sleep, poor food, and the normal tensions of the battlefront. He spent about a week in the hospital and then was back with the troops. Pyle was in Sicily when Patton slapped two soldiers. Pyle was not present, but he knew all about the notorious incident. Yet he did not write about it. He detested Patton, but rather than criticize him, Pyle chose instead to praise General Bradley.[28]

The pressure that Pyle faced in North Africa and then Sicily was enough for him. He decided to go home. After being overseas for 427 days, he was not sure that he could tell the war story fairly and accurately. After his return he told his readers, somewhat apologetically, "Through repetition, I had worn clear down to the nub of my ability to weigh and describe. . . . I had come to despise and be revolted by war clear of any logical proportion. I couldn't find the Four Freedoms among the dead men."[29]

The time at home was a mixed blessing. Almost at once, his friend and agent, Lee Miller, handed him a proposal for a Hollywood movie about his experiences. The studio had hired the young Arthur Miller, later to be much more famous, to write the screenplay. Miller did not work out, but a screenplay was finally written by someone else and the movie was made. Pyle approved the script after some haggling with the producers, and he eventually approved of the actor, Burgess Meredith, hired to play him. Pyle did not live to see the movie completed. At the Washington premiere, Jerry Pyle was presented with Ernie's posthumous Medal of Merit.[30]

His relationship with his wife continued to be rocky after his return to the States. While in Washington, he encountered Moran Livingstone, the wife of another reporter whom he had known earlier and to whom he had unsuccessfully made advances. This time was different. Both Pyle and Livingstone were in struggling marriages, and they had a brief affair. Pyle had been plagued with impotence for a number of years, but he apparently overcame the problem here.[31] Neither of them thought much about the affair, apparently, but Pyle did write to her several times from overseas.

One day while he was with Livingstone, his phone rang. It was Malvina Thompson, the secretary to Eleanor Roosevelt, inviting him to tea with the First Lady at five o'clock that afternoon. Pyle was happy to meet with Mrs. Roosevelt, but he was embarrassed because his only good suit was in London. All he had with him was a sports jacket out at the elbows, "and I mean *out*." Miss Thompson replied that "if Mr. Pyle didn't care about his elbows, neither did Mrs. Roosevelt." The meeting lasted fifty minutes. Miss Thompson sat in, saying that this was one tea she was not about to miss. Mrs. Roosevelt and Pyle compared their experiences writing newspaper columns. It took the First Lady about thirty minutes to dictate her column. When Pyle said that it took him about half a day to write one, she responded, "But you write a much better column than I do."

She told him about her recent trip to the Pacific where some of the servicemen felt neglected because of the attention paid by most of the world to the fighting in Europe. She wondered if he planned to go to the Pacific theater. Pyle said that he had considered it, but he and his editors thought it was best to return to Europe for now. Her enthusiasm for the Pacific war almost convinced him to change his mind. Pyle was much impressed with Mrs. Roosevelt's intensity and her interest in him. He understood why she generated such passion among supporters and detractors alike.[32]

By December 1943, Pyle was back on the Italian mainland to cover the difficult fight that the Allies were waging in their march up the peninsula. Here he wrote his most famous column, on the death of Henry T. Waskow of Belton, Texas. It was a moving account of how the men in the unit reacted when the popular captain was killed in action. It was front-page news across the country, and the *Washington Daily News* devoted its entire front page to the column.[33]

Pyle told his readers that he had known a lot of officers who were respected by their men, "but never have I crossed the trail of any man as beloved as Captain Henry T. Waskow, of Belton, Texas." Waskow was a young officer in his twenties who had been with his company before it left the States. Pyle explained how he was present when Waskow's body was brought down off the mountain: "Dead men had been coming down the mountain all evening, lashed on the back of mules. They came lying belly-down across the wooden pack-saddles, their heads hanging down on the left side of the mule, their stiffened legs sticking out awkwardly from the other side, bobbing up and down as the mule walked."[34]

Americans had to lead the mules because the Italian mule-skinners would not walk alongside the dead men. Officers had to lift them off because the soldiers were reluctant to do so. Later in the column, he talks about Waskow: "Then a soldier came into the cowshed and said there were some more bodies outside. We went out into the road. Four mules stood there, in the moonlight, in the road where the trail came down off the mountain. The soldiers who led them stood there waiting. 'This one is Captain Waskow,' one of them said quietly."[35]

Waskow's body was removed from the mule and was laid down with four others, lying alongside the road. Pyle said, "You don't cover up dead men in the combat zone. They just lie there in the shadows until somebody else comes after them."[36] He continued:

> One soldier came and looked down, and he said out loud, "God damn it."
> That's all he said, and then he walked away. Another one came. He said,

"God damn it to hell anyway." He looked down for a few last moments, and then he turned and left.

Another man came; I think he was an officer. It was hard to tell officers from men in the half light, for all were bearded and grimy and dirty. The man looked down into the dead captain's face, and then he spoke directly to him, as though he were alive. He said: "I'm sorry, old man."

Then a soldier came and stood beside the officer, and bent over, and he too spoke to his dead captain, not in a whisper but awfully tenderly, and he said:

"I sure am sorry, sir."

Then the first man squatted down, and he reached down and took the dead hand, and he sat there for a full five minutes, holding the dead hand in his own and looked intently into the dead face, and he never uttered a sound all the time he sat there.

And then finally he put the hand down, and then reached up and gently straightened the points of the captain's shirt collar, and then he sort of rearranged the tattered edges of his uniform around the wound. And then he got up and walked away down the road in the moonlight, all alone.

After that the rest of us went back into the cowshed, leaving the five dead men lying in line, end to end, in the shadow of the low stone wall. We lay down on the straw in the cowshed, and pretty soon we were all asleep.[37]

Pyle went on to the battle at the Anzio beachhead where he almost lost his life. He and other correspondents were staying in a house that was blasted by 500-pound German bombs, some pieces of which fell as close as thirty feet from the house. In a column describing this incident, he reported that he had not felt nervous, but then he realized that afterward he had taken his handkerchief from his pocket and was trying to comb his hair with it. He wrote, "Me nervous? I should say not." He later told a friend, "I was tremendously lucky to come out of that alive."[38]

After Italy, Pyle returned to England where he had hoped to rest, except that his celebrity had preceded him and he was besieged by requests of all sorts. He was so busy that he was able to write only three columns in three weeks because of the demands on his time. Fortunately, he had built a backlog of columns while still in Italy that kept him from missing deadlines.

While in London, Pyle was notified of his winning the Pulitzer Prize for 1943 for his war columns.[39] Six years earlier, Lee Miller had been snubbed by the Pulitzer committee at Columbia University when he submitted some of Pyle's columns for consideration. Then, Pyle had been ignored since the Pulitzer was usually considered only for "serious" work, and his columns were informal and folksy. Now, however, Carl Acherman, secretary to the board, had approached him suggesting that Pyle's columns might be a good entry for a Pulitzer. He was taken aback since no one knew of another instance where the committee had solicited an entry. Pyle had assumed that he would not get a hearing again, but Miller was more enthusiastic. In fact, they made a bet of $100; Pyle later said that there was no bet he was more pleased to lose.

Pyle worried that other correspondents might be jealous or spiteful because he won a prestigious prize. To his relief he did not find any resentment. He was well liked by almost everyone he encountered, soldier and correspondent alike.[40] Chalmers Roberts, who knew Pyle in Europe, said, "He was a hard guy to be jealous of. He wasn't a blowhard or a show-off or a name-dropper. . . . He was such a sweet guy. Everybody liked Ernie."[41]

Pyle had returned to England in preparation for the invasion of Normandy, an event everyone expected, but its date was shrouded in secrecy. General Eisenhower had been in England for months preparing the largest amphibious invasion ever attempted in world history. When the cross-Channel drive to France began, Ernie waited one day and then walked on the beach to see the carnage. He was at Saint-Lô when the army mistakenly fired on American troops—"friendly fire." On Omaha Beach, for example, he wrote of the destruction and the role of the ground troops, but he seldom described injuries. His account of the scene on the second day is moving:

> Submerged tanks and overturned boats and burned trucks and shell-shattered jeeps and sad little personal belongings were strewn all over these bitter sands. That plus the bodies of soldiers lying in rows covered with blankets, the toes of their shoes sticking up in a line as though on drill. And other bodies, uncollected, still sprawling grotesquely in the sand or half hidden by the high grass beyond the beach. That plus an intense, grim determination of work-weary men to get this chaotic beach organized and get all the vital supplies and the reinforcements moving more rapidly over it from the stacked-up ships standing in droves out to sea.[42]

Ernie accompanied French troops across France and was with them when they entered Paris in triumph. He wrote about the coming of the end of the war in Europe and what would be required in rebuilding. But he also reminded his readers that the war in the Pacific was not over, and it could still be a long, bloody struggle. He had already decided to go there himself. Before embarking for the Pacific, he spent another brief time at home.[43]

In mid-September 1944, Pyle returned to the United States, where he was besieged with requests to speak and write special pieces. The honorary degree of doctor of humane letters came from Indiana University, his alma mater, although he had not completed his senior year.

Since Albuquerque was his adopted home, the University of New Mexico bestowed upon him a honorary doctorate of laws. He did not speak at either ceremony.[44] The movie based on his life was being filmed at the time. The visit was marred again by his wife's emotional instability. She made another unsuccessful attempt at suicide, apparently because Pyle had promised her earlier that his second trip abroad would be his last. Yet, by this time, he had already decided to go to the Pacific theater of war.[45]

Pyle left the United States in January 1945, but he stopped off in Hawaii first. He was such a celebrity that he was overwhelmed by the crowds that greeted him in Honolulu, but he was really surprised by the size of the crowds in Guam. He moved on to Saipan where he encountered Jack Bales, his aunt's grandson by marriage. They spent some time together before Pyle boarded a light aircraft carrier for the cruise to the battle zone. His columns during this period emphasized the comfort enjoyed by the men and women in Saipan and on board ship. In a letter to his wife, he wrote, "It was such a contrast to what I'd known for so long in Europe that I felt almost ashamed. . . . They're . . . safe and living like kings and don't know it."[46]

Some readers in the States, as well as military personnel in the Pacific, were disappointed in Pyle's columns after he reached the Pacific theater. When staffers at Scripps-Howard wondered about the lack of excitement in his columns, Pyle replied that little of interest occurred on board ship. From that vantage point there was little he could say about the average soldier's life—the "worm's-eye view" for which he was famous. In fact, Pyle was criticized by some people for forgetting the combat soldier and spending too much time with officers. This observation caught Pyle by surprise and bothered him a great deal.[47]

As the invasion of Okinawa approached, Pyle understood that it was one of the penultimate steps to the Japanese home islands. Although he was advised against it, Pyle decided to go ashore in Okinawa with an invasion of Marines. He did not go with the first wave, but he was in the second. As it turned out, the invasion was hardly contested because the Japanese had pulled their troops back and concentrated them in the interior of the island. The fight to dislodge the Japanese from their entrenched position would be bloody and costly.[48]

As Pyle prepared to go toward the front lines in the Pacific, he had told people that he had a premonition that he would not survive this tour. He had made similar remarks before, but he seemed more serious this time.[49] On April 17, 1945, Pyle went ashore on the island of Ie

Shima and spent the night on the beach. The next morning, he hitched a ride in a jeep with Col. Joseph Coolidge. Most of the drive across the island was uneventful, but about 10 A.M. a Japanese machine gun could be heard. The men abandoned the jeep and took refuge in a ditch. In a minute or two, Pyle raised his head to look around; "the machine gunner fired again hitting Ernie in the temple just below the line of his helmet," killing him.[50] Pyle was buried first on the island of Ie Shima, but his remains several years later were moved to the National Memorial Cemetery of the Pacific in Hawaii. Pyle's wife, Jerry, died in November of that year of complications from influenza. They never had children.[51]

Ernie Pyle was an average American no different from millions of other men of the time. Yet, like so many others, he found himself caught up in the turmoil and excitement of World War II. During this experience, Pyle rose above the masses to achieve a status that he never dreamed of. If one subscribes to Thomas Carlyle's "great man" theory of history, Pyle probably was not great. His actions during the war did not alter its course. In fact, he became famous because of the war, an event that he did not predict and could not have controlled. Without the war, Pyle probably would have been merely one among many newspaper correspondents trying to get by in the world. But with the war, Pyle is still considered one of the best, if not the best, war correspondent that the United States has ever produced. One of the few journalists to die on the battlefield, his life was short. But he left behind a body of work that still fascinates those interested in journalism—and in the history of World War II from a "worm's-eye view."

Notes

1. Victor Bondi, ed., *American Decades, 1940–1949* (Detroit, MI, 1995), 386.
2. *Encyclopedia of World Biography* 12 (Platine, IL, 1987–88), 494.
3. Bondi, *American Decades*, 386.
4. *Contemporary Authors* (Detroit, 1998), 315.
5. *Dictionary of Literary Biography* 29 (Detroit, 1984), 299.
6. Donald Paneth, *The Encyclopedia of American Journalism* (New York, 1983), 415.
7. James Tobin, *Ernie Pyle's War: America's Eyewitness to World War II* (New York, 1977), 5–9, the best and most recent biography of Pyle based upon correspondence and other original sources. This essay draws heavily from this source and the Miller biography listed below.
8. Ibid., 9.
9. *Encyclopedia of World Biography*, 493.

10. Lee G. Miller, *The Story of Ernie Pyle* (New York, 1950), 13–14. Written by Pyle's friend and business associate, this biography omits some personal data that is revealing and possibly unflattering.

11. As quoted in Tobin, *Ernie Pyle's War*, 11.

12. *Dictionary of Literary Biography*, 292; Tobin, *Ernie Pyle's War*, 17.

13. *Encyclopedia of World Biography*, 493.

14. *Dictionary of Literary Biography*, 293–94.

15. Miller, *Story of Ernie Pyle*, 135–40.

16. *Dictionary of Literary Biography*, 295.

17. Ibid.

18. *Dictionary of American Biography*, sup. 3 (New York, 1973), 612.

19. Tobin, *Ernie Pyle's War*, 63–65.

20. Ibid., 66.

21. Ibid., 70.

22. Ibid.

23. Miller, *Story of Ernie Pyle*, 191–95, 243–44; Tobin, *Ernie Pyle's War*, 71, 86.

24. *Encyclopedia of World Biography*, 493.

25. Tobin, *Ernie Pyle's War*, 95.

26. Miller, *Story of Ernie Pyle*, 267–71.

27. Tobin, *Ernie Pyle's War*, 106.

28. Miller, *Story of Ernie Pyle*, 270–82.

29. Tobin, *Ernie Pyle's War*, 114. President Roosevelt, in a message to Congress in January 1941, stated that any postwar agreements should include "four freedoms": of speech, of worship, from want, and from fear.

30. *Contemporary Authors*, 317.

31. Tobin, *Ernie Pyle's War*, 127.

32. All quotes from ibid., 127–29.

33. *Dictionary of Literary Biography*, 297.

34. As quoted in Miller, *Story of Ernie Pyle*, 298.

35. Ibid., 299.

36. Ibid.

37. Ibid., 299–300.

38. Ibid.

39. *Dictionary of American Biography*, 613.

40. Miller, *Story of Ernie Pyle*, 313, 320–22; Tobin, *Ernie Pyle's War*, 158–59.

41. Tobin, *Ernie Pyle's War*, 159.

42. As quoted in Miller, *Story of Ernie Pyle*, 265.

43. Ibid., 169–83, 337–58.

44. Ibid., 369–72.

45. Ibid., 365–69.

46. Tobin, *Ernie Pyle's War*, 230.

47. Ibid., 223–31.

48. Ibid., 237–40.

49. Miller, *Story of Ernie Pyle*, 412–18; Tobin, *Ernie Pyle's War*, 234–40.

50. Tobin, *Ernie Pyle's War*, 240.

51. Miller, *Story of Ernie Pyle*, 425–26; Tobin, *Ernie Pyle's War*, 243.

Suggested Readings

Blum, John Morton. *V Was for Victory, Politics, and American Culture during World War II*. New York, 1976.

Miller, Lee G. *An Ernie Pyle Album: Indiana to Ie Shima*. New York, 1946.

_____. *The Story of Ernie Pyle*. New York, 1950.

Nichols, David, ed. *Ernie's War: The Best of Ernie Pyle's World War II Dispatches*. New York, 1986.

Pyle, Ernie, *Here Is Your War*. New York, 1943.

_____. *Brave Men*. New York, 1944.

_____. *Last Chapter*. New York, 1946.

_____. *Home Country*. New York, 1947.

Tobin, James. *Ernie Pyle's War: America's Eyewitness to World War II*. New York, 1977.

Index